Little Nothings

UNEASY HAPPINESS

Little Nothings
Uneasy Happiness
LEWIS TRONDHEIM

ComicsLit

ISBN 978-1-56163-576-4
Library of Congress Control Number: 2009942112
© 2007 Trondheim
Rights arranged through Sylvain Coissard Agency, France.
© 2010 NBM for the English translation
Translation by Joe Johnson
Lettering by Ortho
Printed in China

3   2   1

Comicslit is an imprint
and trademark of

NANTIER · BEALL · MINOUSTCHINE
Publishing inc.
new york

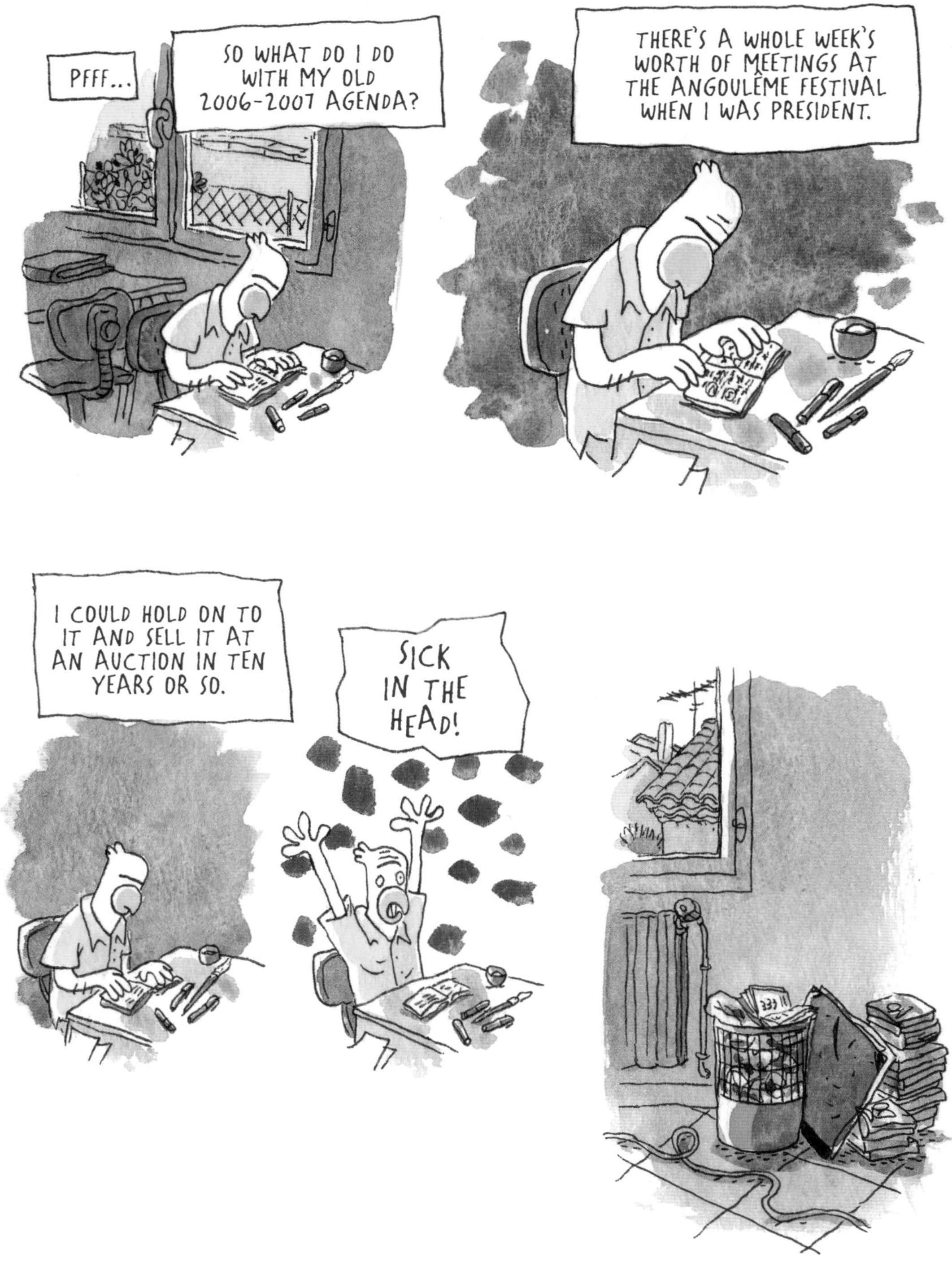
PFFF...
SO WHAT DO I DO WITH MY OLD 2006-2007 AGENDA?
THERE'S A WHOLE WEEK'S WORTH OF MEETINGS AT THE ANGOULÊME FESTIVAL WHEN I WAS PRESIDENT.
I COULD HOLD ON TO IT AND SELL IT AT AN AUCTION IN TEN YEARS OR SO.
SICK IN THE HEAD!

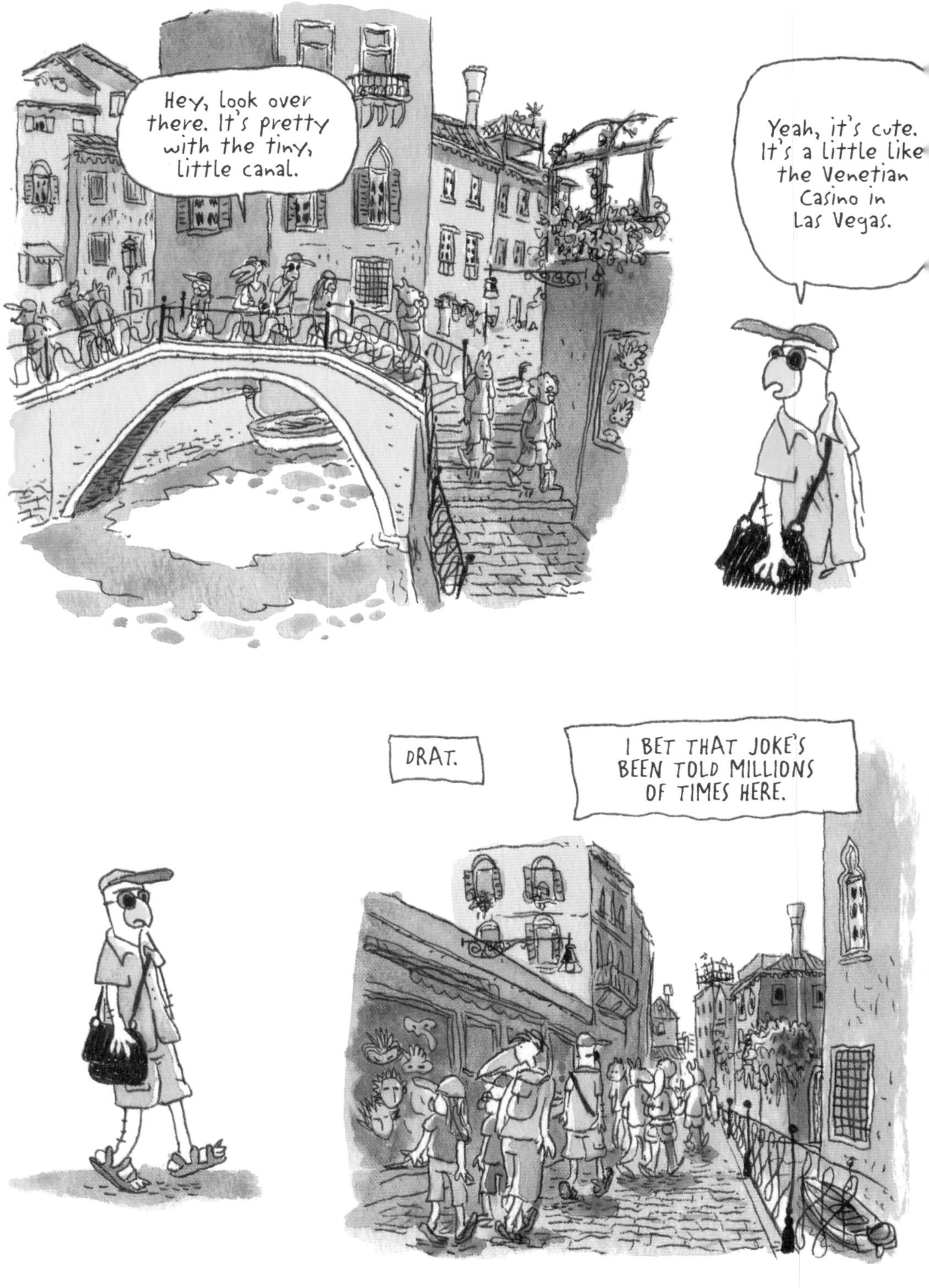
Hey, look over there. It's pretty with the tiny, little canal.
Yeah, it's cute. It's a little like the Venetian Casino in Las Vegas.
DRAT.
I BET THAT JOKE'S BEEN TOLD MILLIONS OF TIMES HERE.

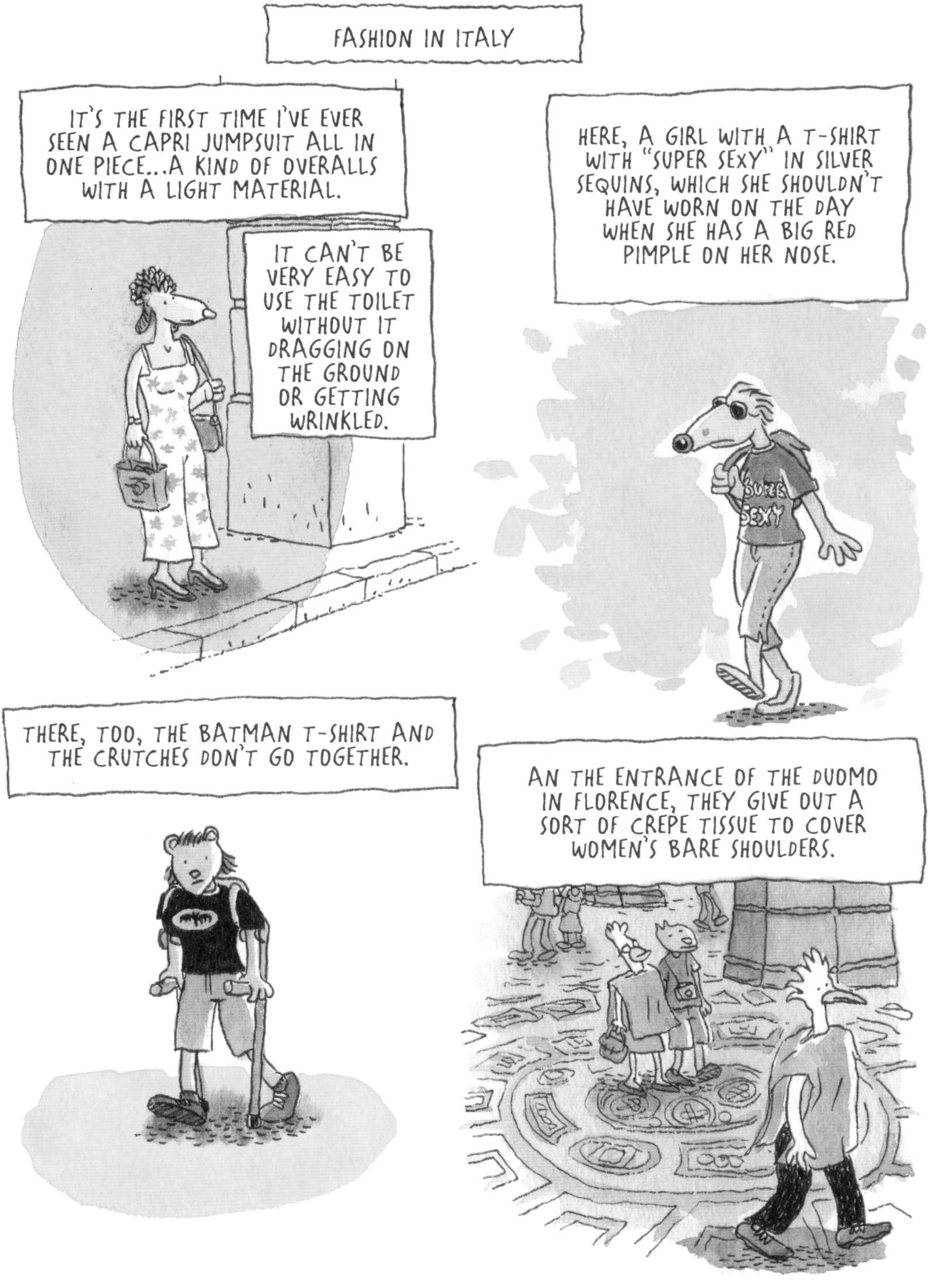
FASHION IN ITALY
IT'S THE FIRST TIME I'VE EVER SEEN A CAPRI JUMPSUIT ALL IN ONE PIECE...A KIND OF OVERALLS WITH A LIGHT MATERIAL.
IT CAN'T BE VERY EASY TO USE THE TOILET WITHOUT IT DRAGGING ON THE GROUND OR GETTING WRINKLED.
HERE, A GIRL WITH A T-SHIRT WITH "SUPER SEXY" IN SILVER SEQUINS, WHICH SHE SHOULDN'T HAVE WORN ON THE DAY WHEN SHE HAS A BIG RED PIMPLE ON HER NOSE.
SUPER SEXY
THERE, TOO, THE BATMAN T-SHIRT AND THE CRUTCHES DON'T GO TOGETHER.
AN THE ENTRANCE OF THE DUOMO IN FLORENCE, THEY GIVE OUT A SORT OF CREPE TISSUE TO COVER WOMEN'S BARE SHOULDERS.

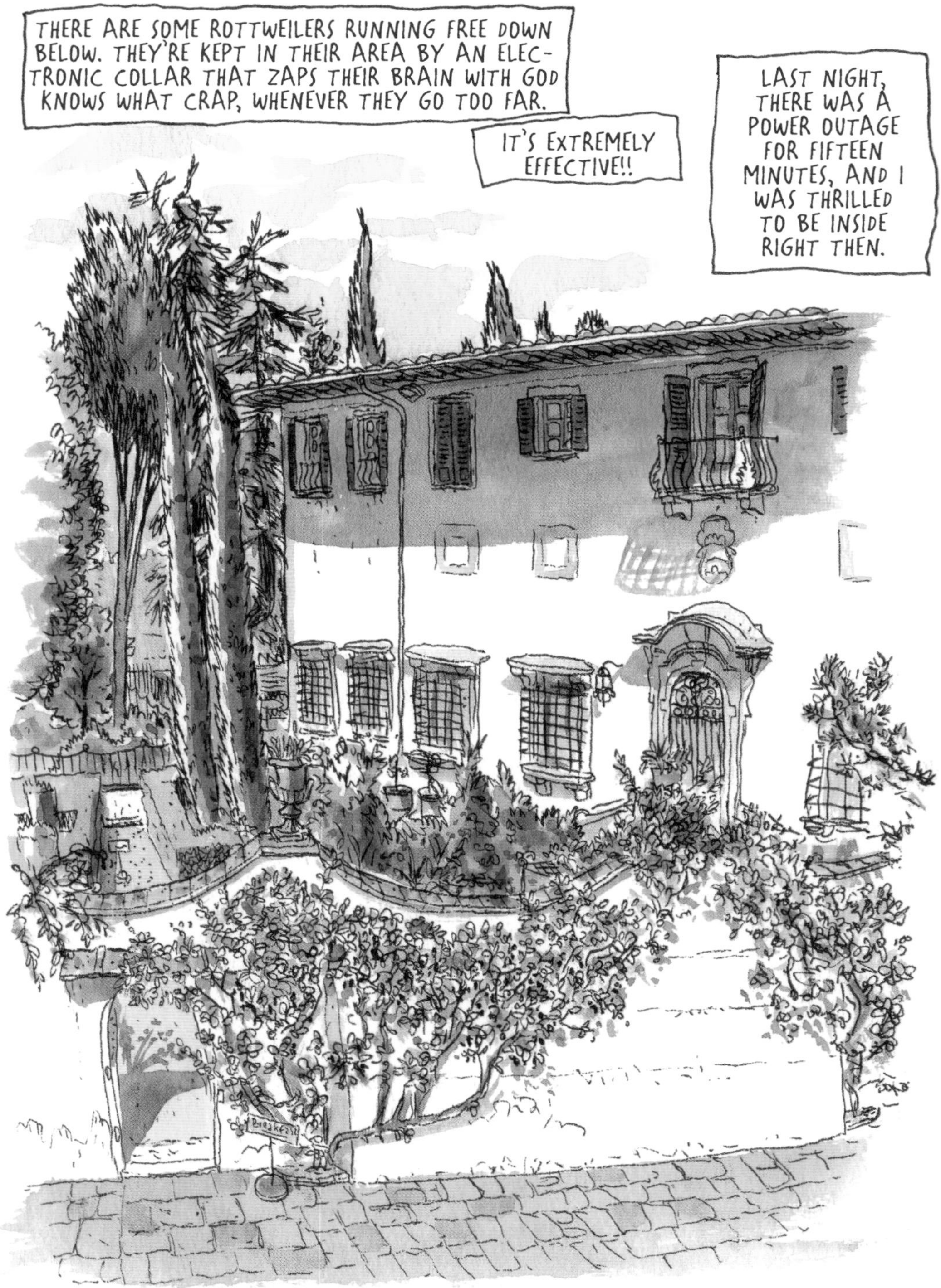
THERE ARE SOME ROTTWEILERS RUNNING FREE DOWN BELOW. THEY'RE KEPT IN THEIR AREA BY AN ELEC-TRONIC COLLAR THAT ZAPS THEIR BRAIN WITH GOD KNOWS WHAT CRAP, WHENEVER THEY GO TOO FAR.
IT'S EXTREMELY EFFECTIVE!!
LAST NIGHT, THERE WAS A POWER OUTAGE FOR FIFTEEN MINUTES, AND I WAS THRILLED TO BE INSIDE RIGHT THEN.

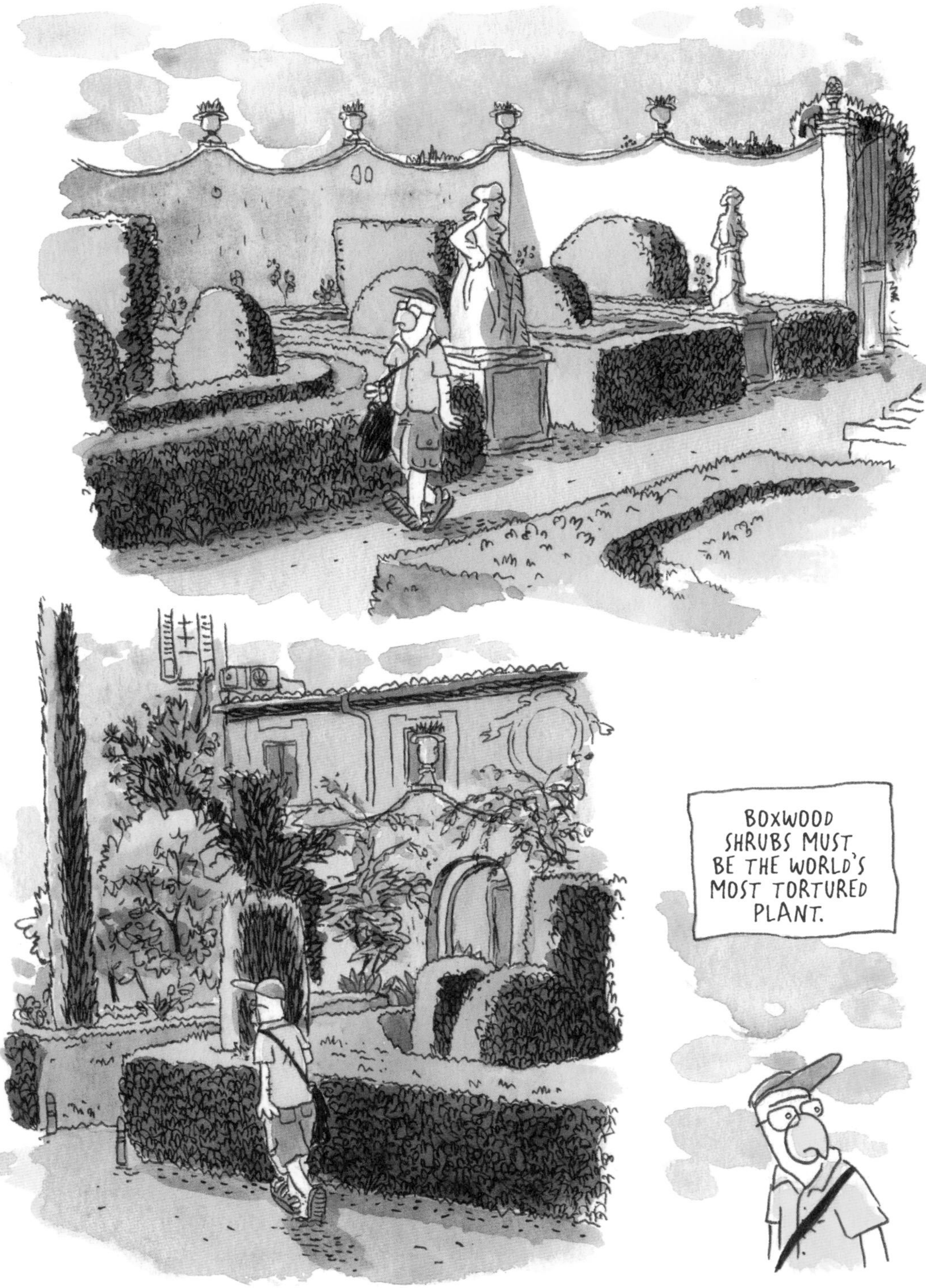
BOXWOOD SHRUBS MUST BE THE WORLD'S MOST TORTURED PLANT.

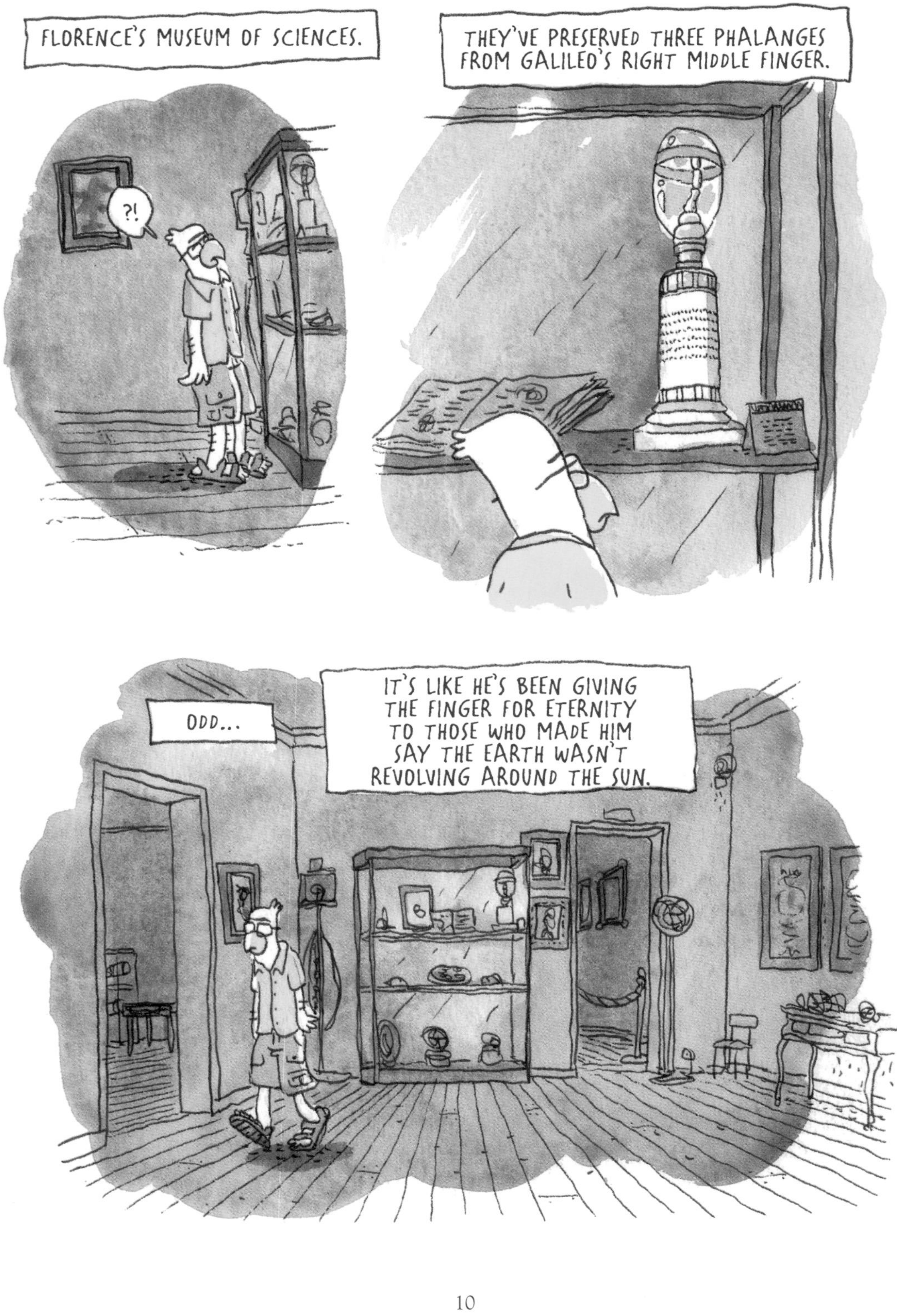
FLORENCE'S MUSEUM OF SCIENCES.
?!
THEY'VE PRESERVED THREE PHALANGES FROM GALILEO'S RIGHT MIDDLE FINGER.
ODD...
IT'S LIKE HE'S BEEN GIVING THE FINGER FOR ETERNITY TO THOSE WHO MADE HIM SAY THE EARTH WASN'T REVOLVING AROUND THE SUN.

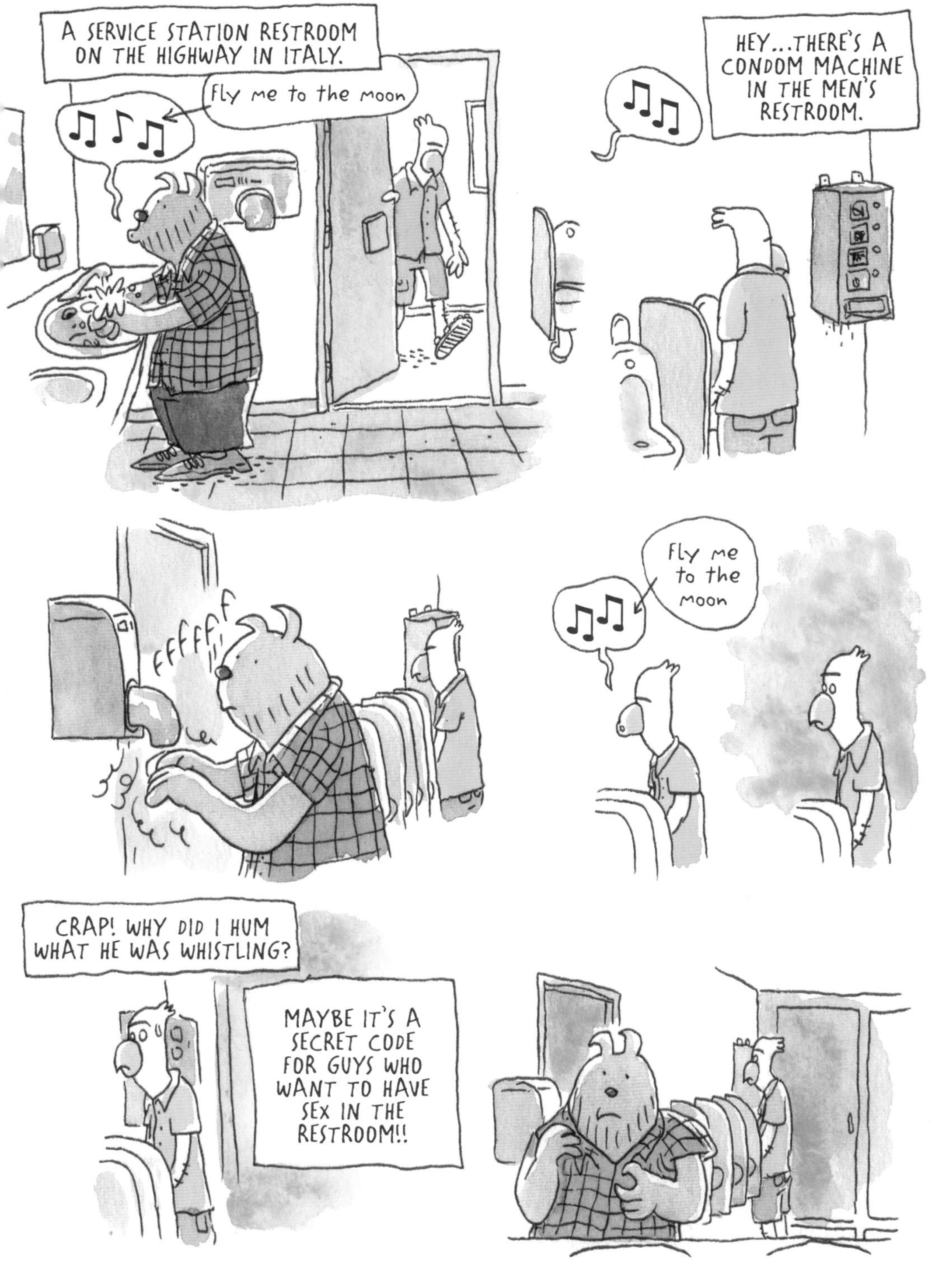
A SERVICE STATION RESTROOM ON THE HIGHWAY IN ITALY.
Fly me to the moon
HEY...THERE'S A CONDOM MACHINE IN THE MEN'S RESTROOM.
FFFFFF
Fly me to the moon
CRAP! WHY DID I HUM WHAT HE WAS WHISTLING?
MAYBE IT'S A SECRET CODE FOR GUYS WHO WANT TO HAVE SEX IN THE RESTROOM!!

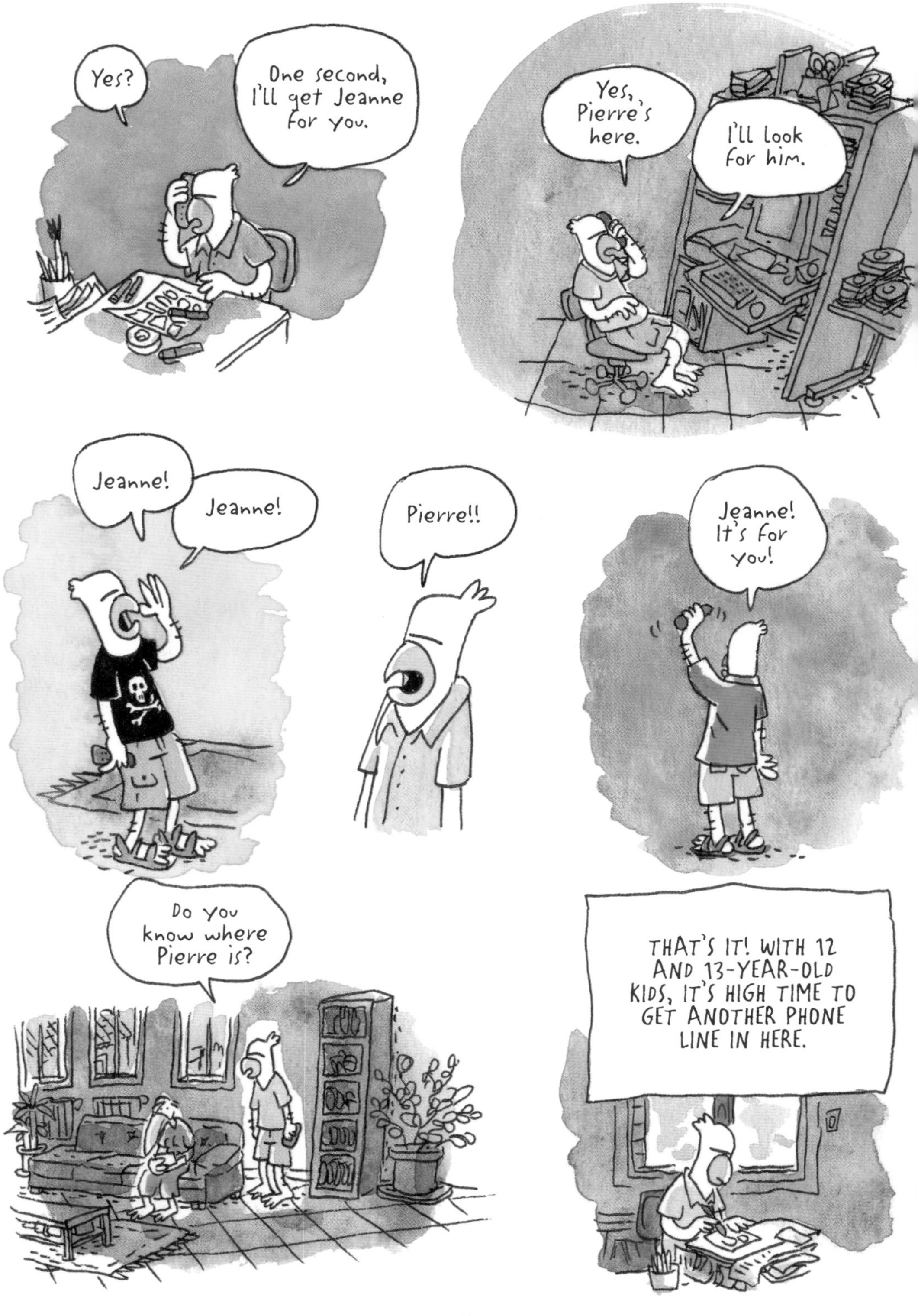
Yes?
One second, I'll get Jeanne for you.
Yes, Pierre's here.
I'll look for him.
Jeanne!
Jeanne!
Pierre!!
Jeanne! It's for you!
Do you know where Pierre is?
THAT'S IT! WITH 12 AND 13-YEAR-OLD KIDS, IT'S HIGH TIME TO GET ANOTHER PHONE LINE IN HERE.

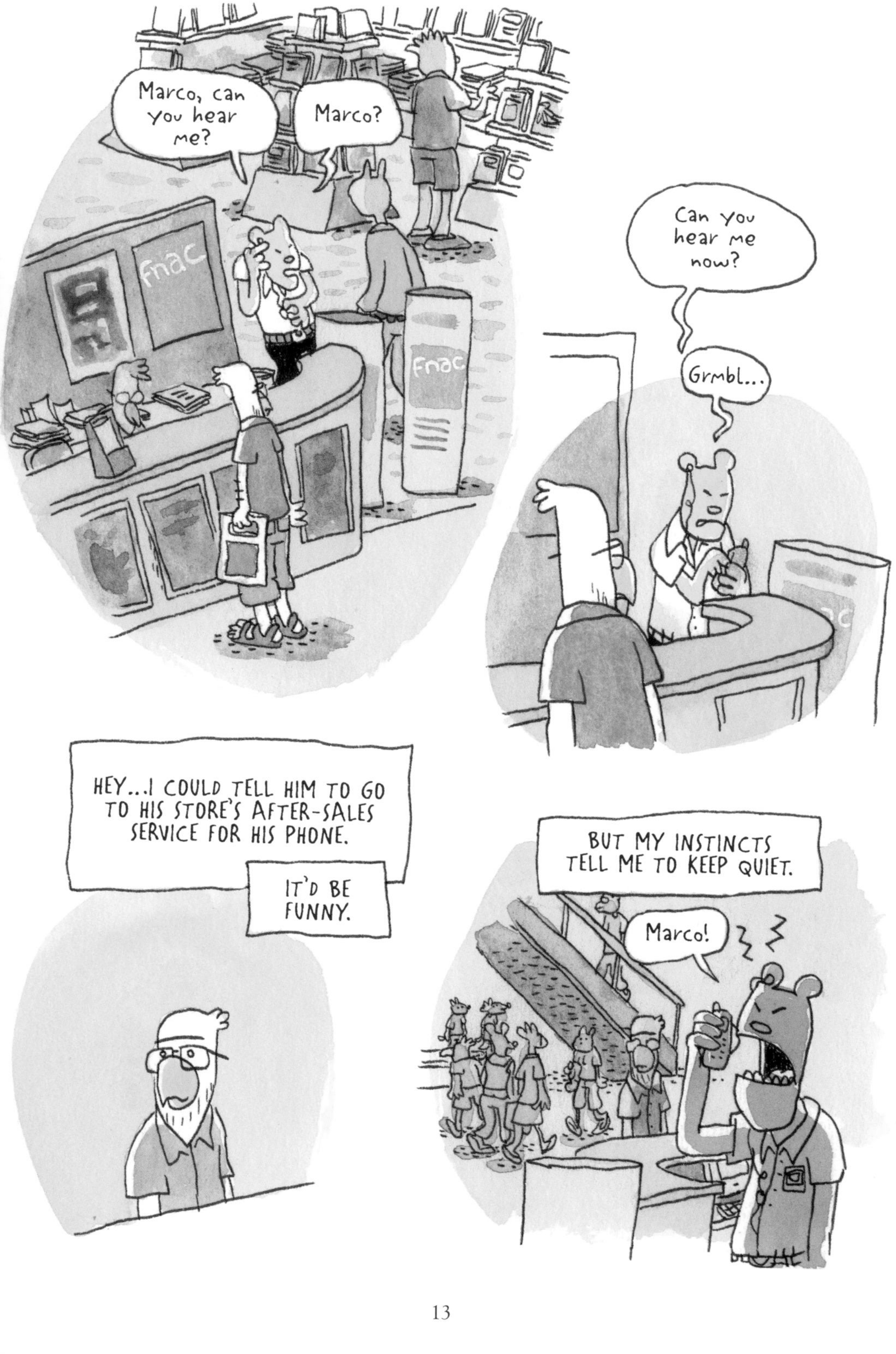
Marco, can you hear me?
Marco?
fnac
Fnac
Can you hear me now?
Grmbl...
HEY...I COULD TELL HIM TO GO TO HIS STORE'S AFTER-SALES SERVICE FOR HIS PHONE.
IT'D BE FUNNY.
BUT MY INSTINCTS TELL ME TO KEEP QUIET.
Marco!

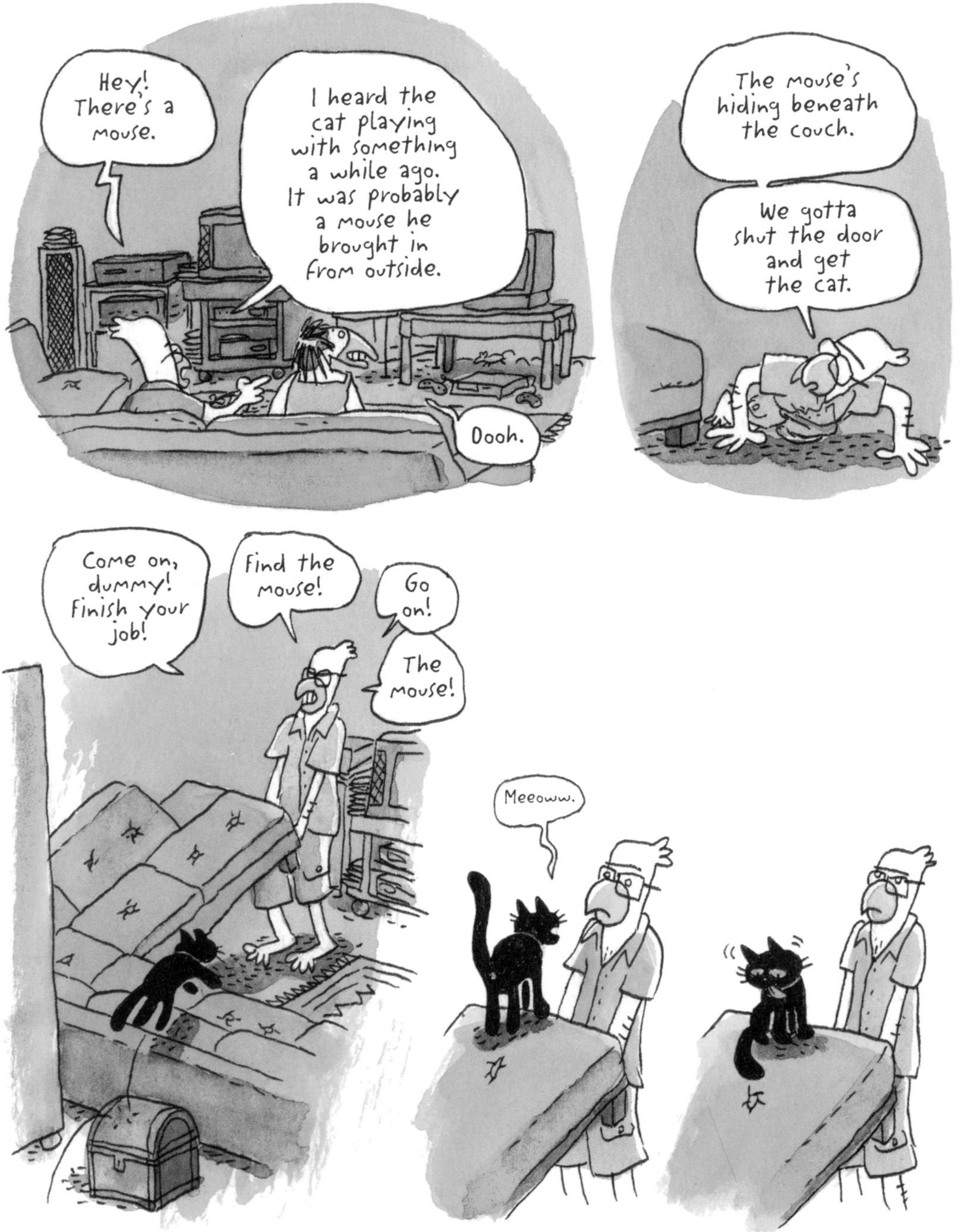

Hey! There's a mouse.
I heard the cat playing with something a while ago. It was probably a mouse he brought in from outside.
Oooh.
The mouse's hiding beneath the couch.
We gotta shut the door and get the cat.
Come on, dummy! Finish your job!
Find the mouse!
Go on!
The mouse!
Meeoww.

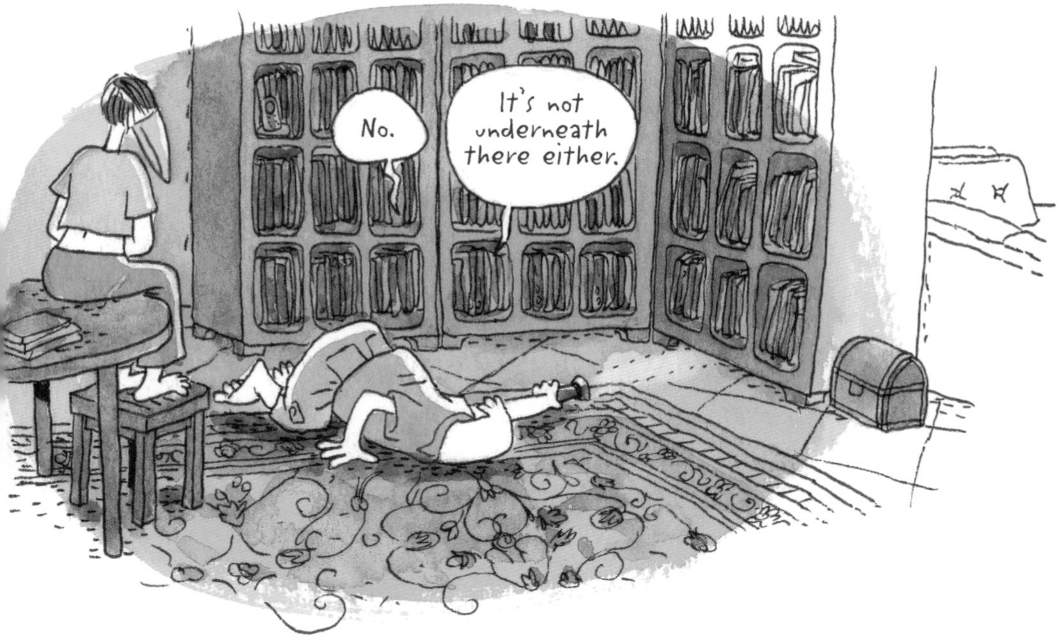
No.
It's not underneath there either.

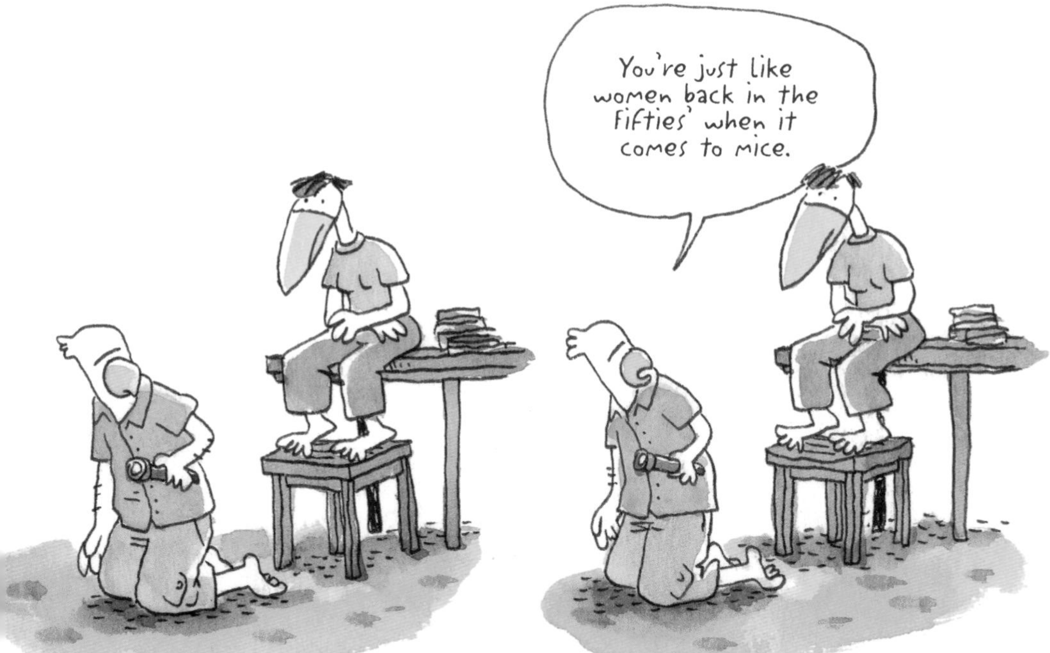
You're just like women back in the Fifties' when it comes to mice.

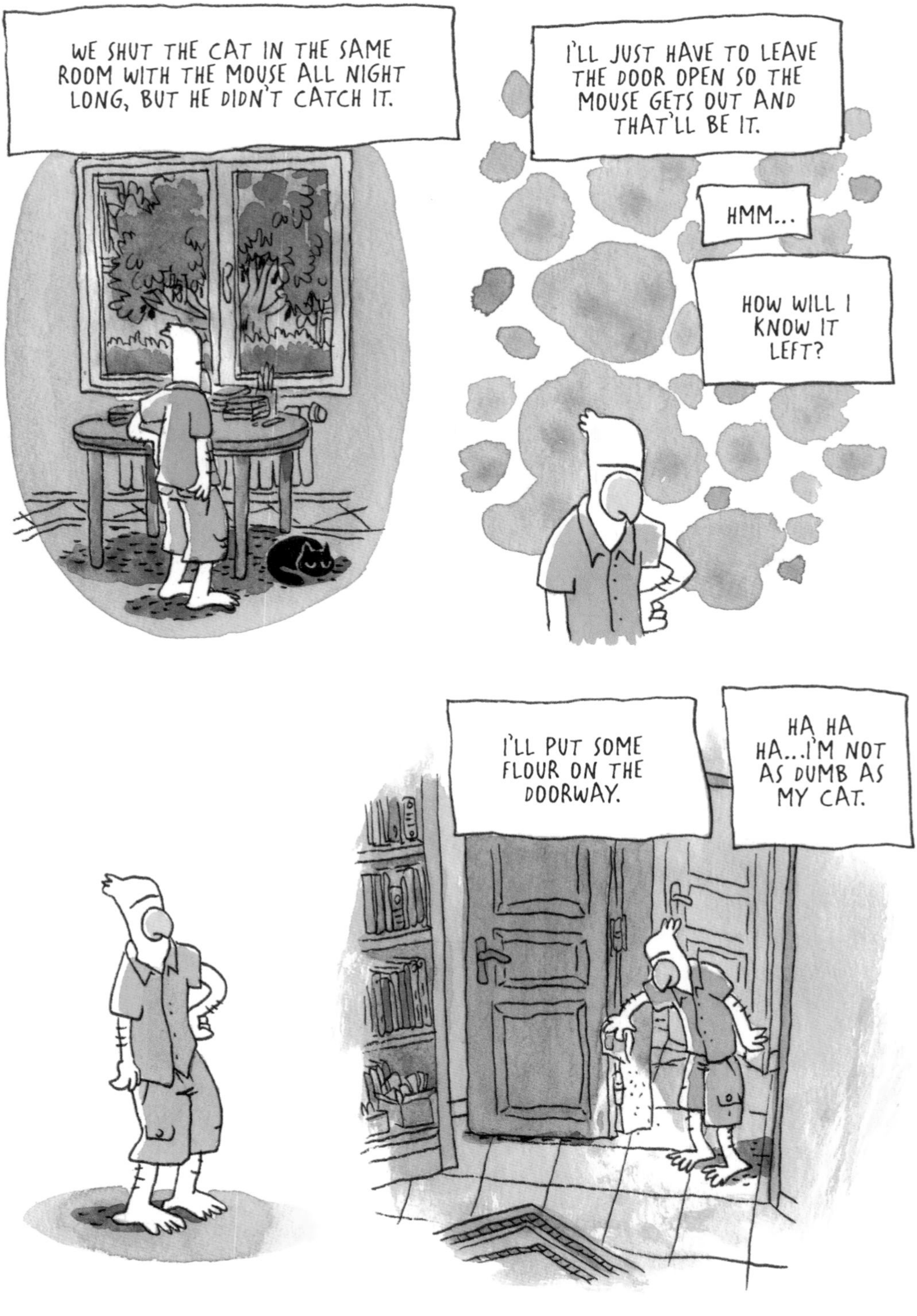
WE SHUT THE CAT IN THE SAME ROOM WITH THE MOUSE ALL NIGHT LONG, BUT HE DIDN'T CATCH IT.
I'LL JUST HAVE TO LEAVE THE DOOR OPEN SO THE MOUSE GETS OUT AND THAT'LL BE IT.
HMM...
HOW WILL I KNOW IT LEFT?
I'LL PUT SOME FLOUR ON THE DOORWAY.
HA HA HA...I'M NOT AS DUMB AS MY CAT.

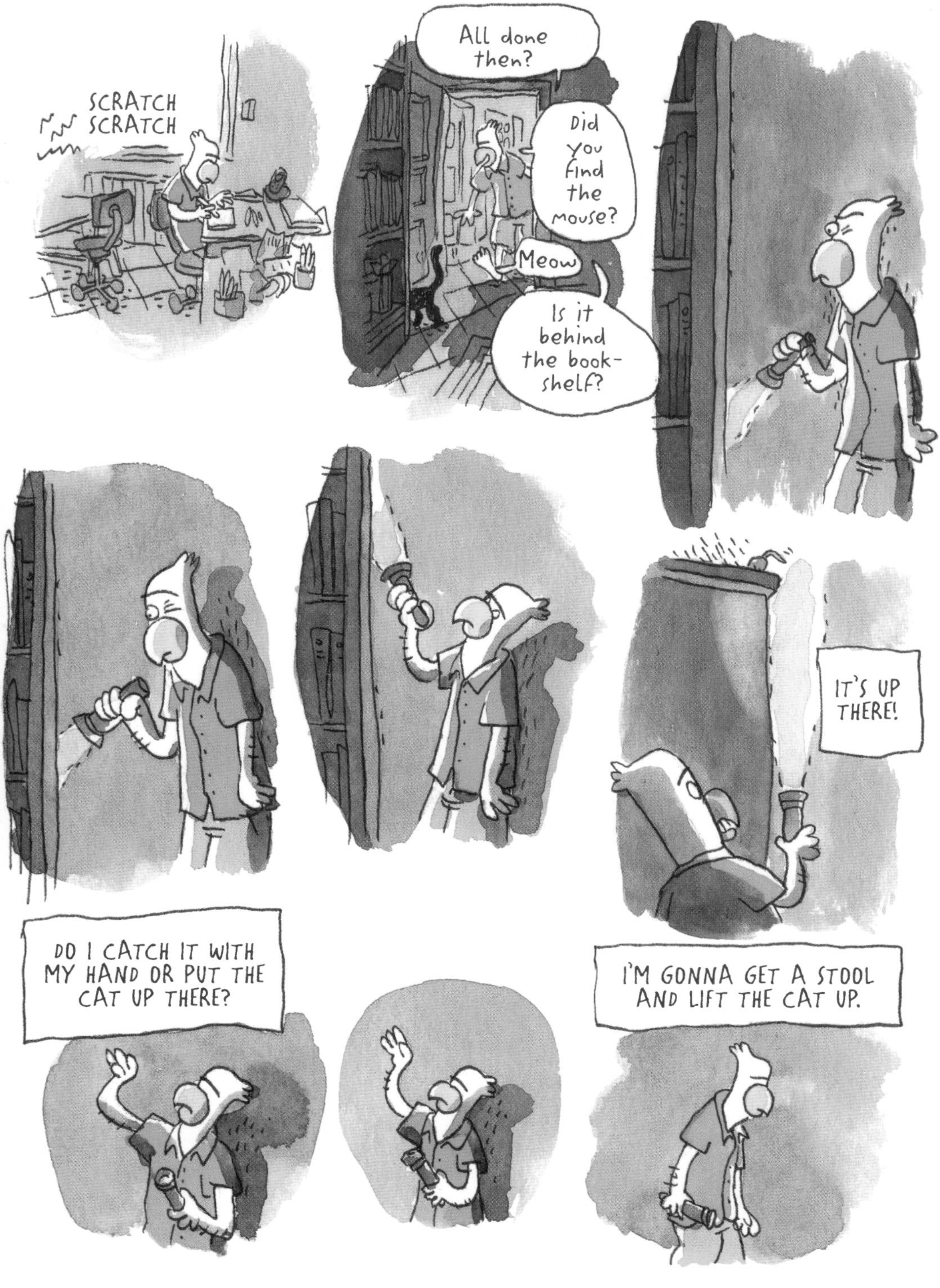
SCRATCH
SCRATCH
All done then?
Did you find the mouse?
Meow
Is it behind the book-shelf?
IT'S UP THERE!
DO I CATCH IT WITH MY HAND OR PUT THE CAT UP THERE?
I'M GONNA GET A STOOL AND LIFT THE CAT UP.

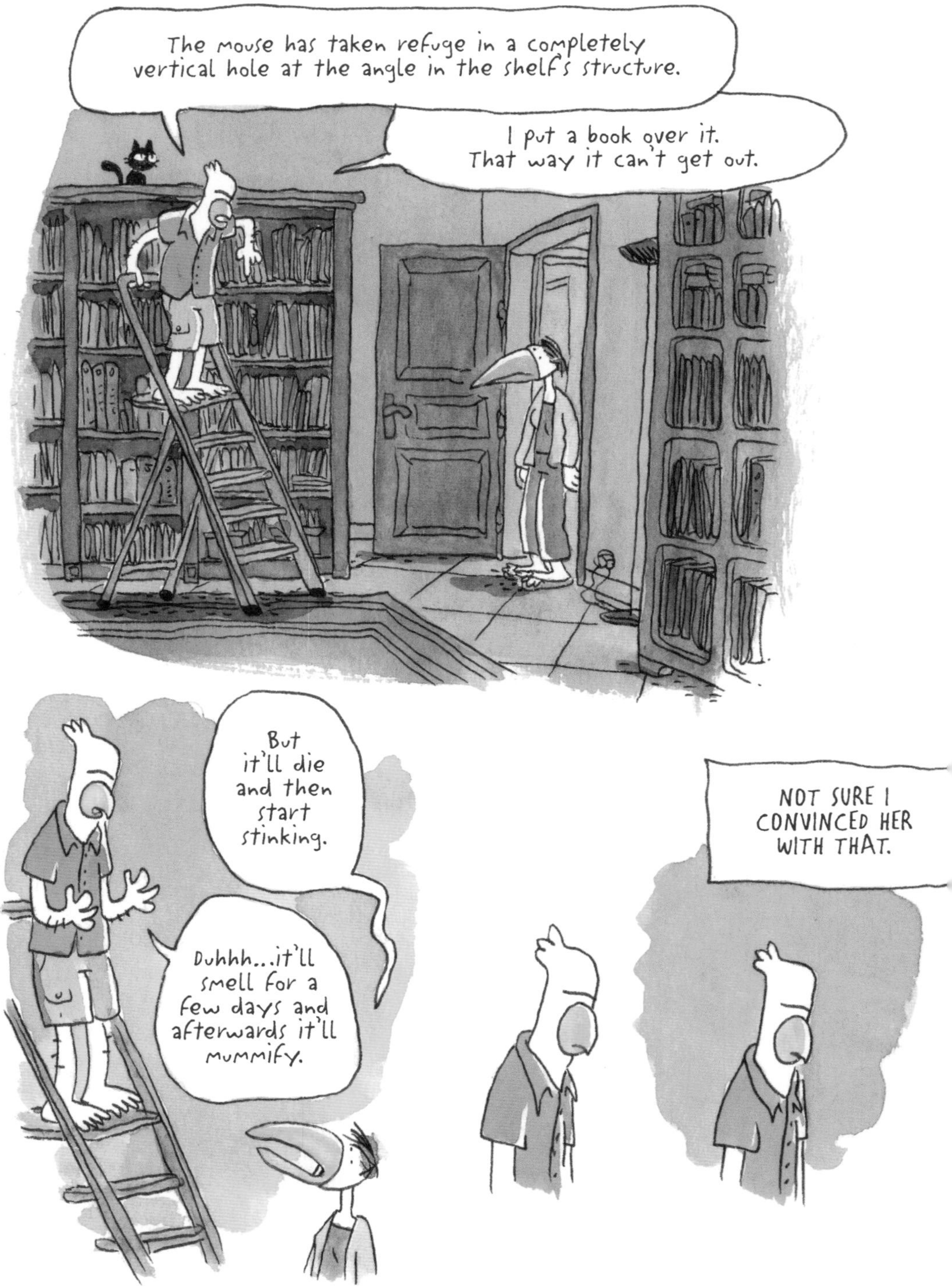

The mouse has taken refuge in a completely vertical hole at the angle in the shelf's structure.
I put a book over it. That way it can't get out.
But it'll die and then start stinking.
Duhhh...it'll smell for a few days and afterwards it'll mummify.
NOT SURE I CONVINCED HER WITH THAT.

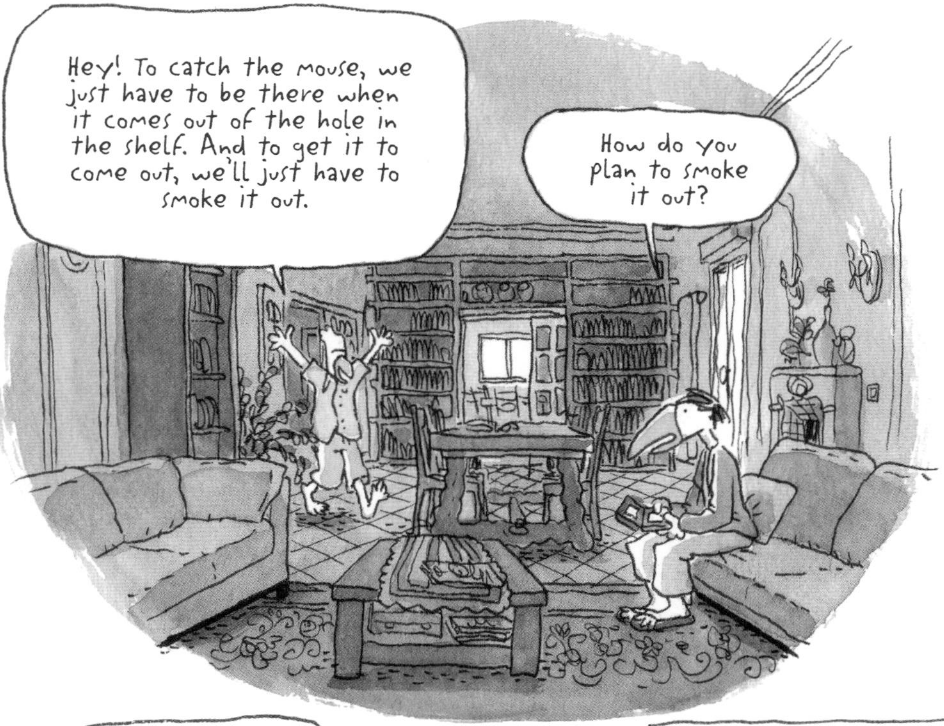
Hey! To catch the mouse, we just have to be there when it comes out of the hole in the shelf. And to get it to come out, we'll just have to smoke it out.
How do you plan to smoke it out?

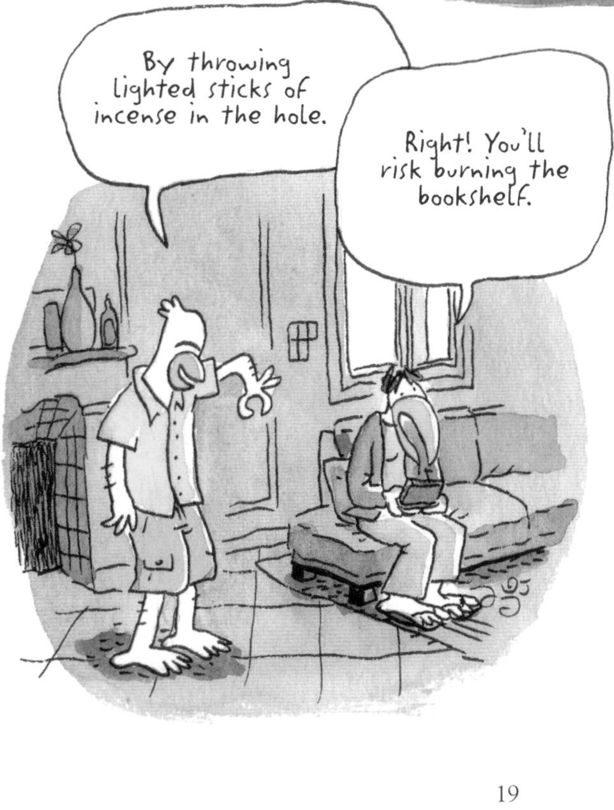
By throwing lighted sticks of incense in the hole.
Right! You'll risk burning the bookshelf.

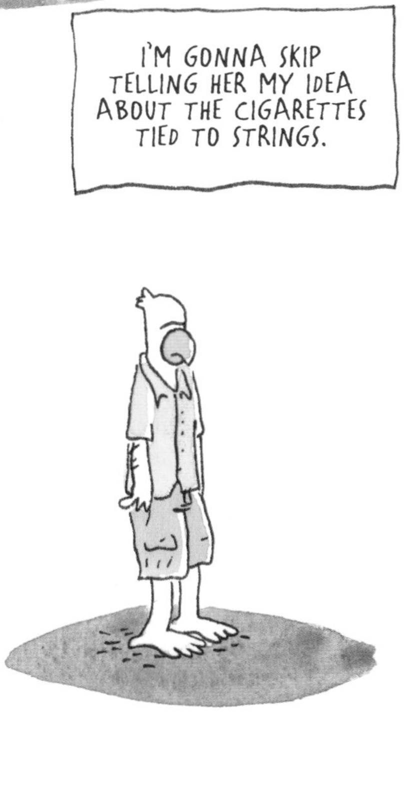
I'M GONNA SKIP TELLING HER MY IDEA ABOUT THE CIGARETTES TIED TO STRINGS.

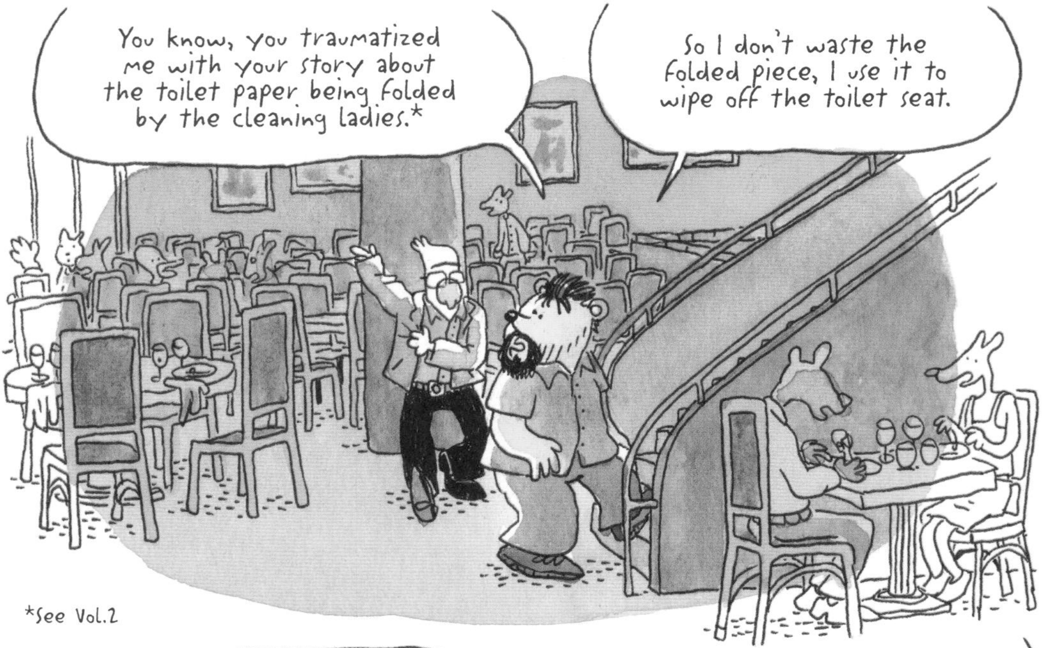
You know, you traumatized me with your story about the toilet paper being folded by the cleaning ladies.*
So I don't waste the folded piece, I use it to wipe off the toilet seat.

*See Vol.2

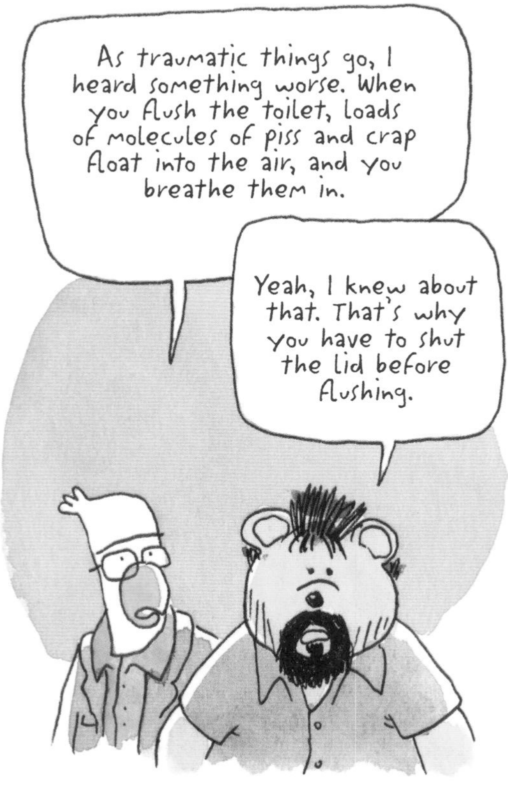
As traumatic things go, I heard something worse. When you flush the toilet, loads of molecules of piss and crap float into the air, and you breathe them in.
Yeah, I knew about that. That's why you have to shut the lid before flushing.

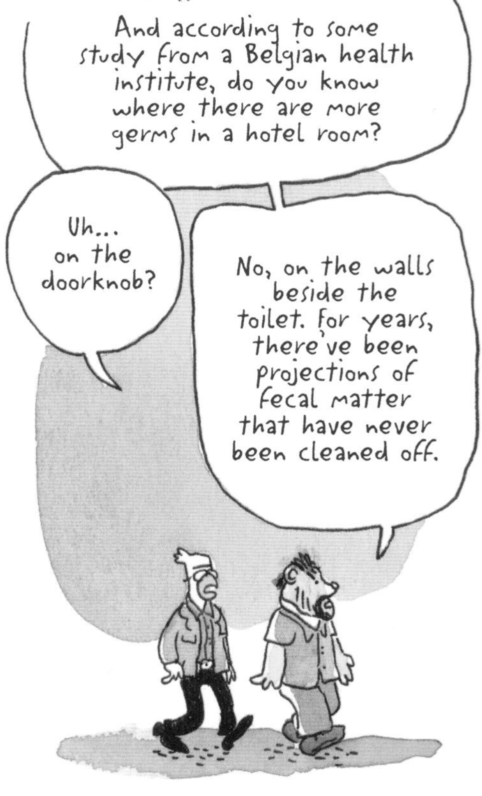
And according to some study from a Belgian health institute, do you know where there are more germs in a hotel room?
Uh... on the doorknob?
No, on the walls beside the toilet. For years, there've been projections of fecal matter that have never been cleaned off.

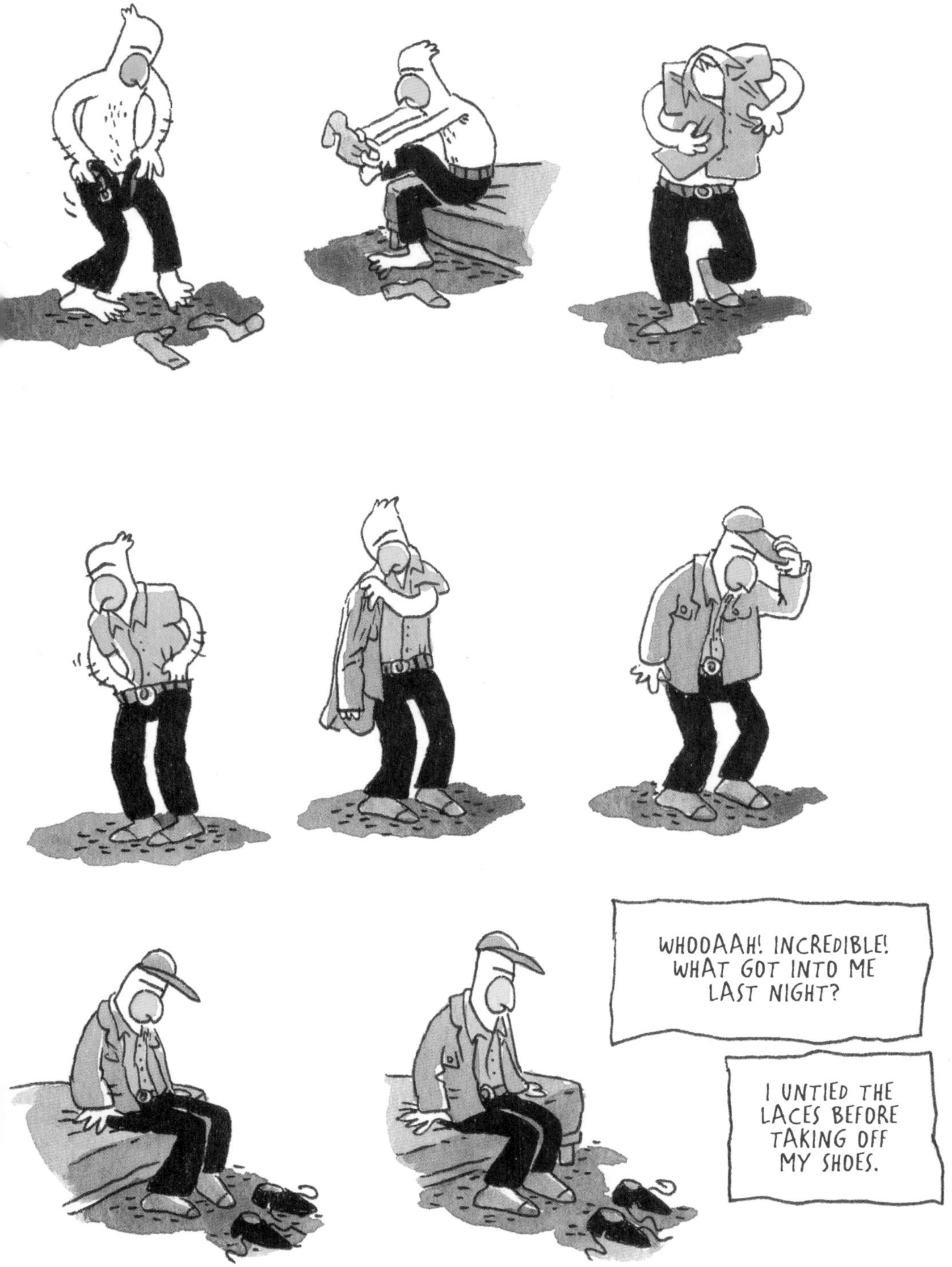
WHOOAAH! INCREDIBLE! WHAT GOT INTO ME LAST NIGHT?
I UNTIED THE LACES BEFORE TAKING OFF MY SHOES.

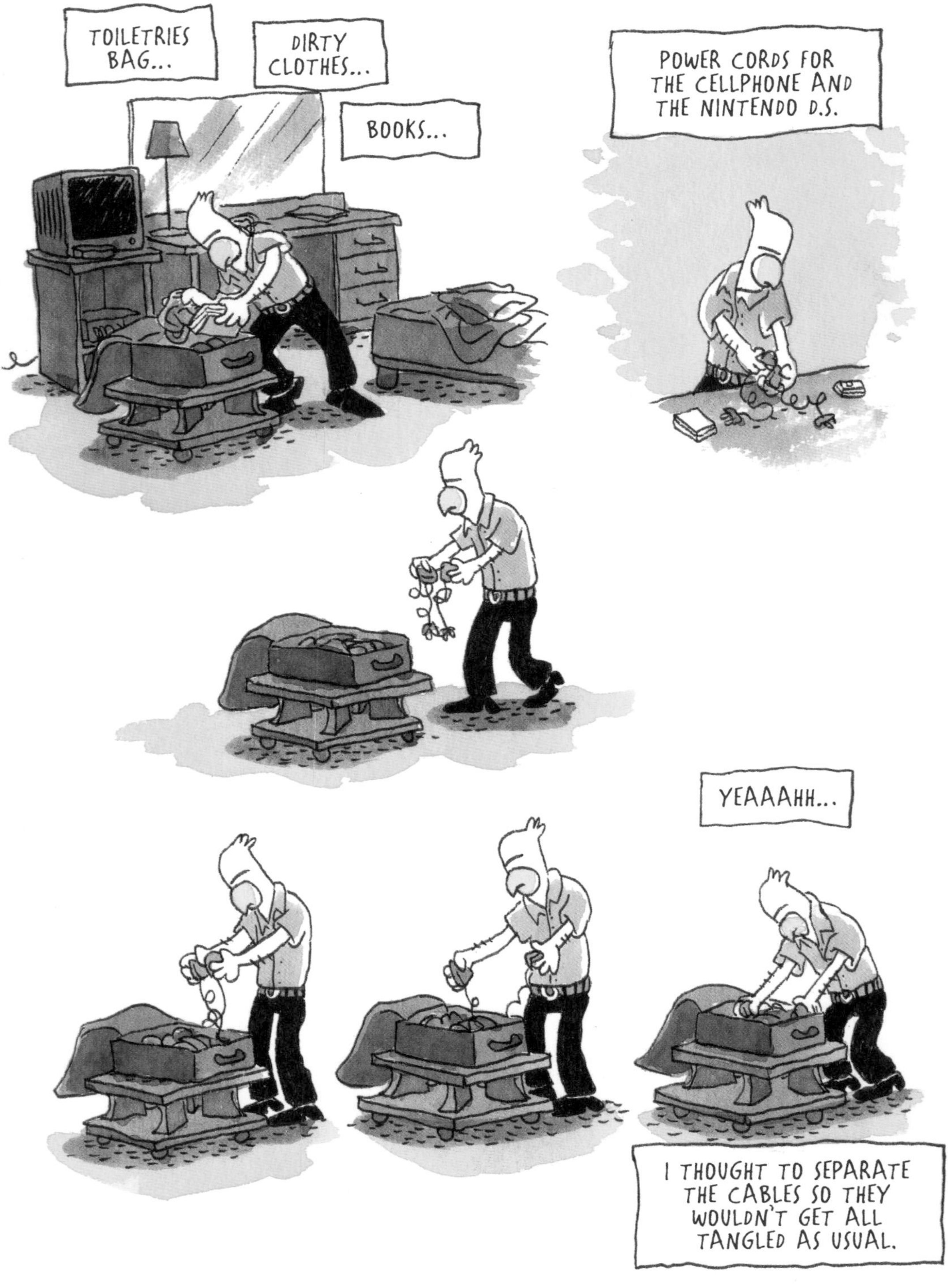
TOILETRIES BAG...
DIRTY CLOTHES...
BOOKS...
POWER CORDS FOR THE CELLPHONE AND THE NINTENDO D.S.
YEAAAHH...
I THOUGHT TO SEPARATE THE CABLES SO THEY WOULDN'T GET ALL TANGLED AS USUAL.

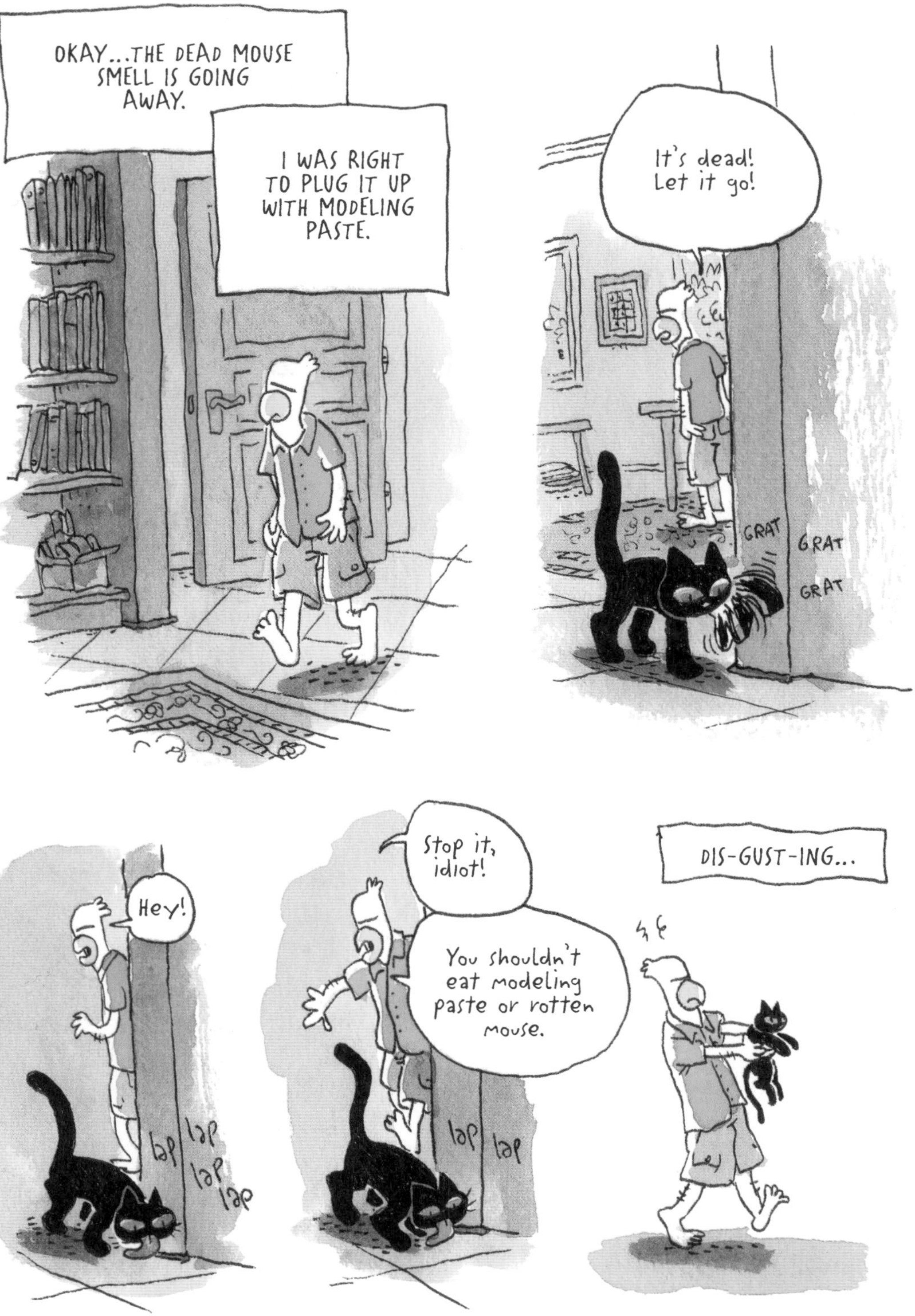
OKAY...THE DEAD MOUSE SMELL IS GOING AWAY.
I WAS RIGHT TO PLUG IT UP WITH MODELING PASTE.
It's dead! Let it go!
GRAT
GRAT
GRAT
Hey!
lap
lap
lap
lap
Stop it, idiot!
You shouldn't eat modeling paste or rotten mouse.
lap
lap
DIS-GUST-ING...

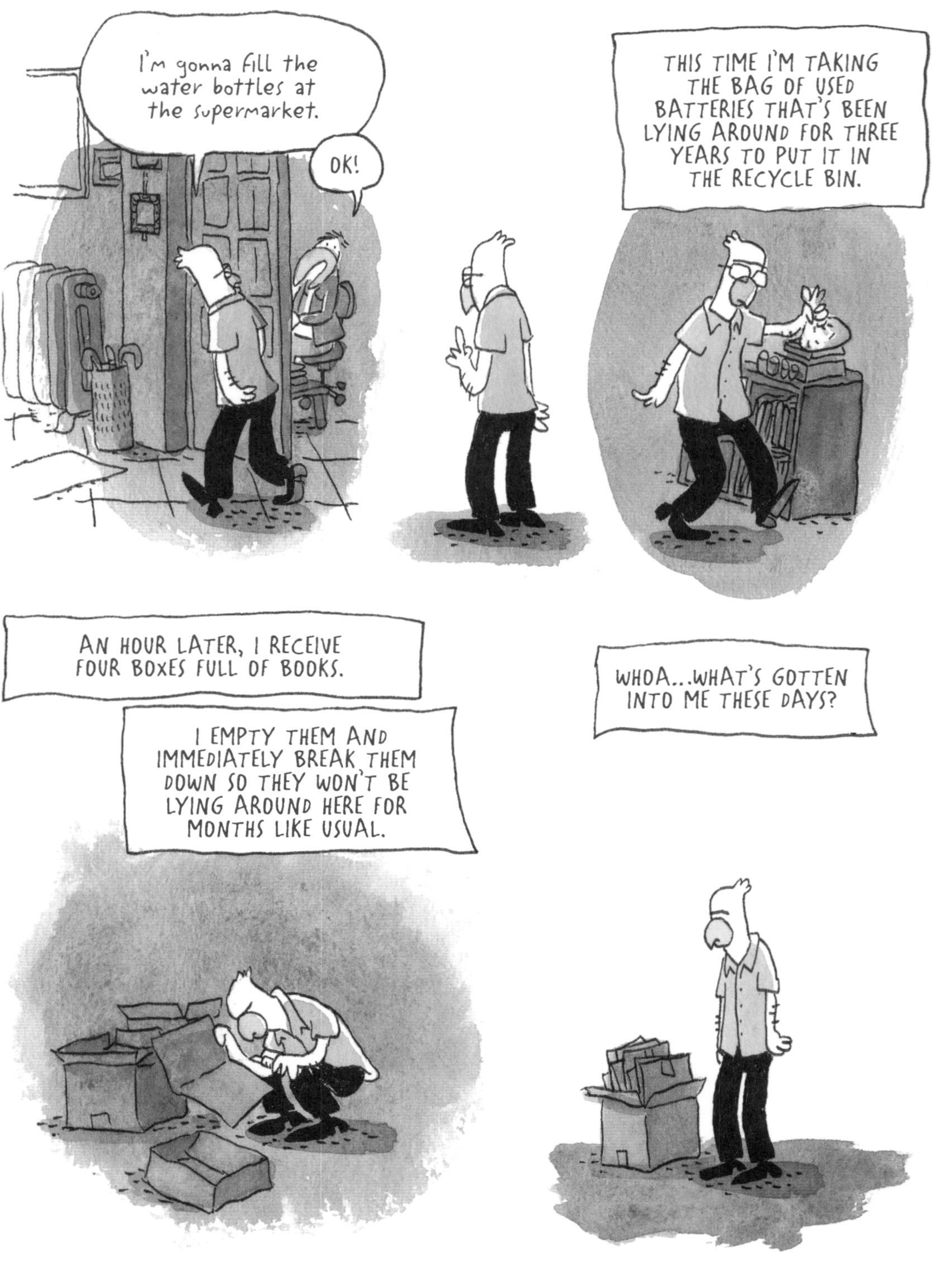
I'm gonna fill the water bottles at the supermarket.
OK!
THIS TIME I'M TAKING THE BAG OF USED BATTERIES THAT'S BEEN LYING AROUND FOR THREE YEARS TO PUT IT IN THE RECYCLE BIN.
AN HOUR LATER, I RECEIVE FOUR BOXES FULL OF BOOKS.
I EMPTY THEM AND IMMEDIATELY BREAK THEM DOWN SO THEY WON'T BE LYING AROUND HERE FOR MONTHS LIKE USUAL.
WHOA...WHAT'S GOTTEN INTO ME THESE DAYS?

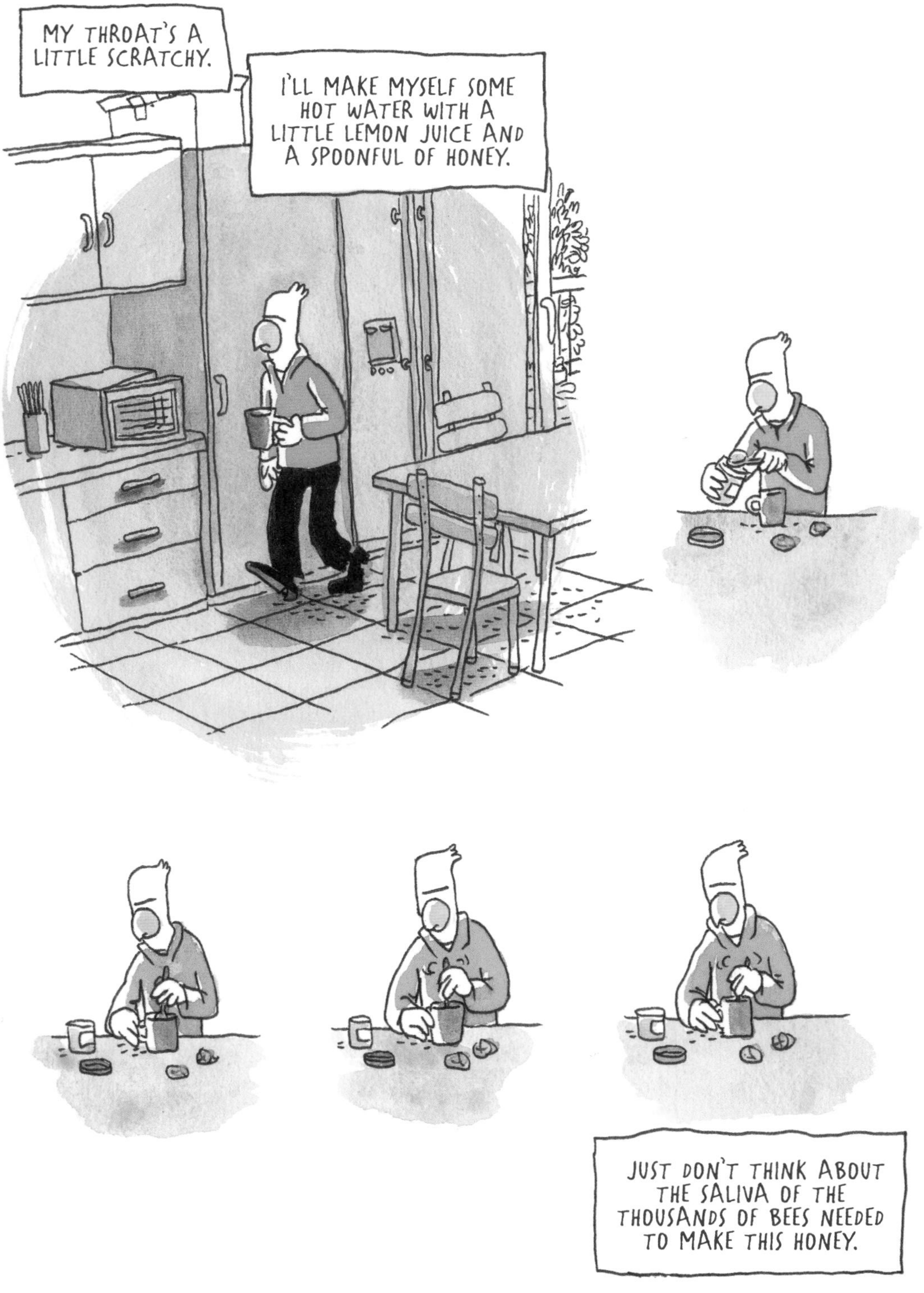
MY THROAT'S A LITTLE SCRATCHY.
I'LL MAKE MYSELF SOME HOT WATER WITH A LITTLE LEMON JUICE AND A SPOONFUL OF HONEY.
JUST DON'T THINK ABOUT THE SALIVA OF THE THOUSANDS OF BEES NEEDED TO MAKE THIS HONEY.

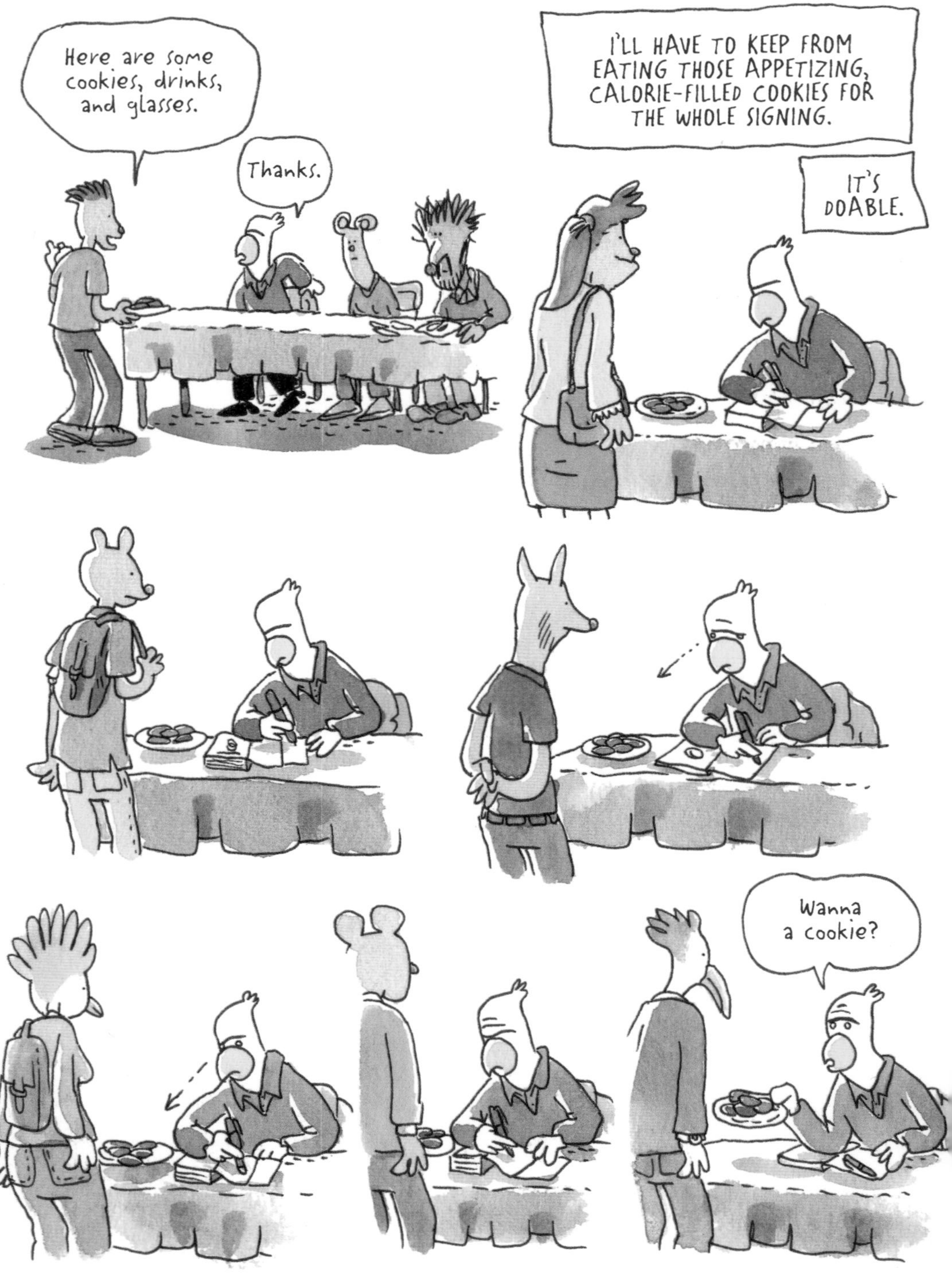
Here are some cookies, drinks, and glasses.
Thanks.
I'LL HAVE TO KEEP FROM EATING THOSE APPETIZING, CALORIE-FILLED COOKIES FOR THE WHOLE SIGNING.
IT'S DOABLE.
Wanna a cookie?

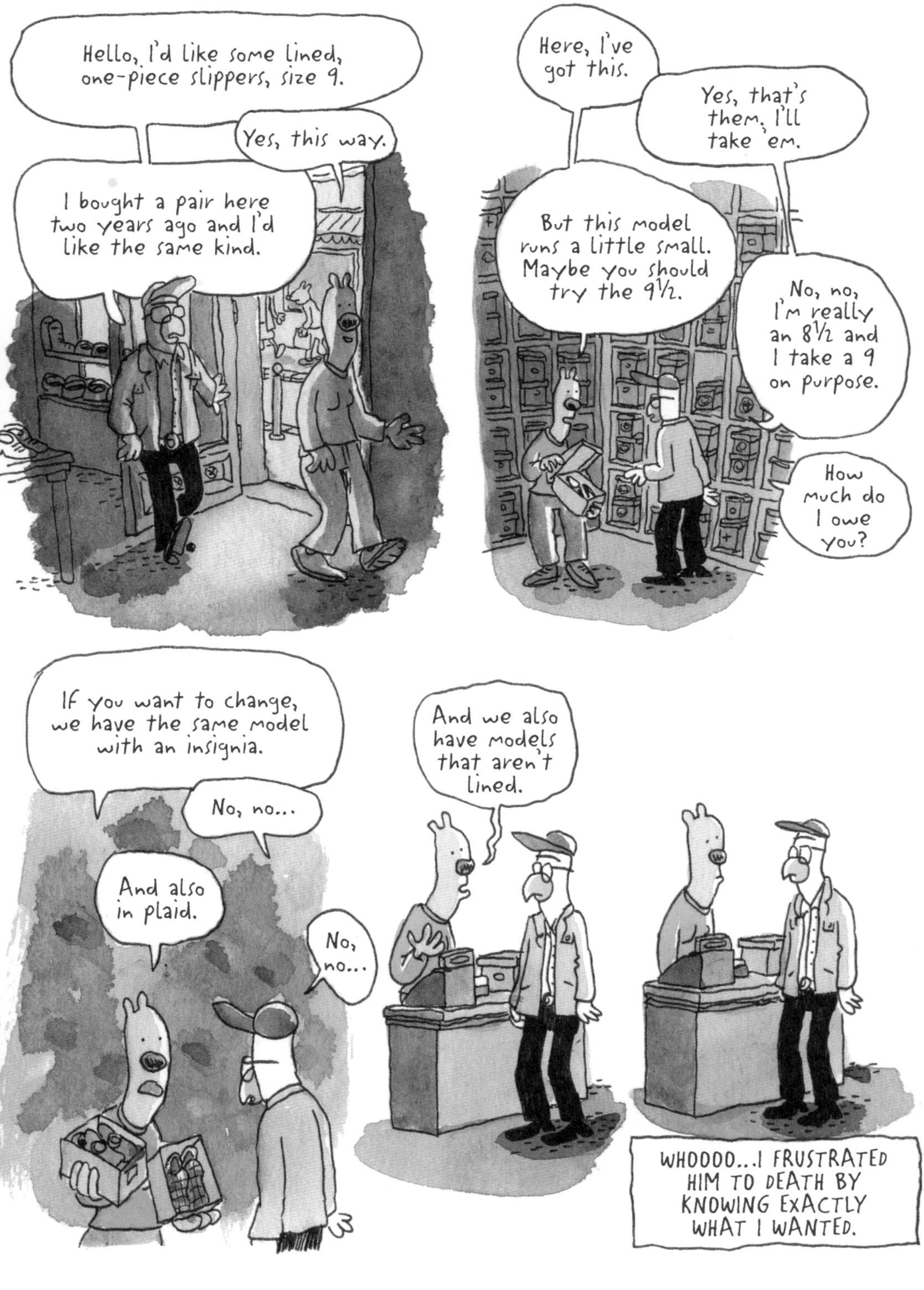
Hello, I'd like some lined, one-piece slippers, size 9.
I bought a pair here two years ago and I'd like the same kind.
Yes, this way.
Here, I've got this.
But this model runs a little small. Maybe you should try the 9½.
Yes, that's them, I'll take 'em.
No, no, I'm really an 8½ and I take a 9 on purpose.
How much do I owe you?
If you want to change, we have the same model with an insignia.
No, no...
And also in plaid.
No, no...
And we also have models that aren't lined.
WHOOOO... I FRUSTRATED HIM TO DEATH BY KNOWING EXACTLY WHAT I WANTED.

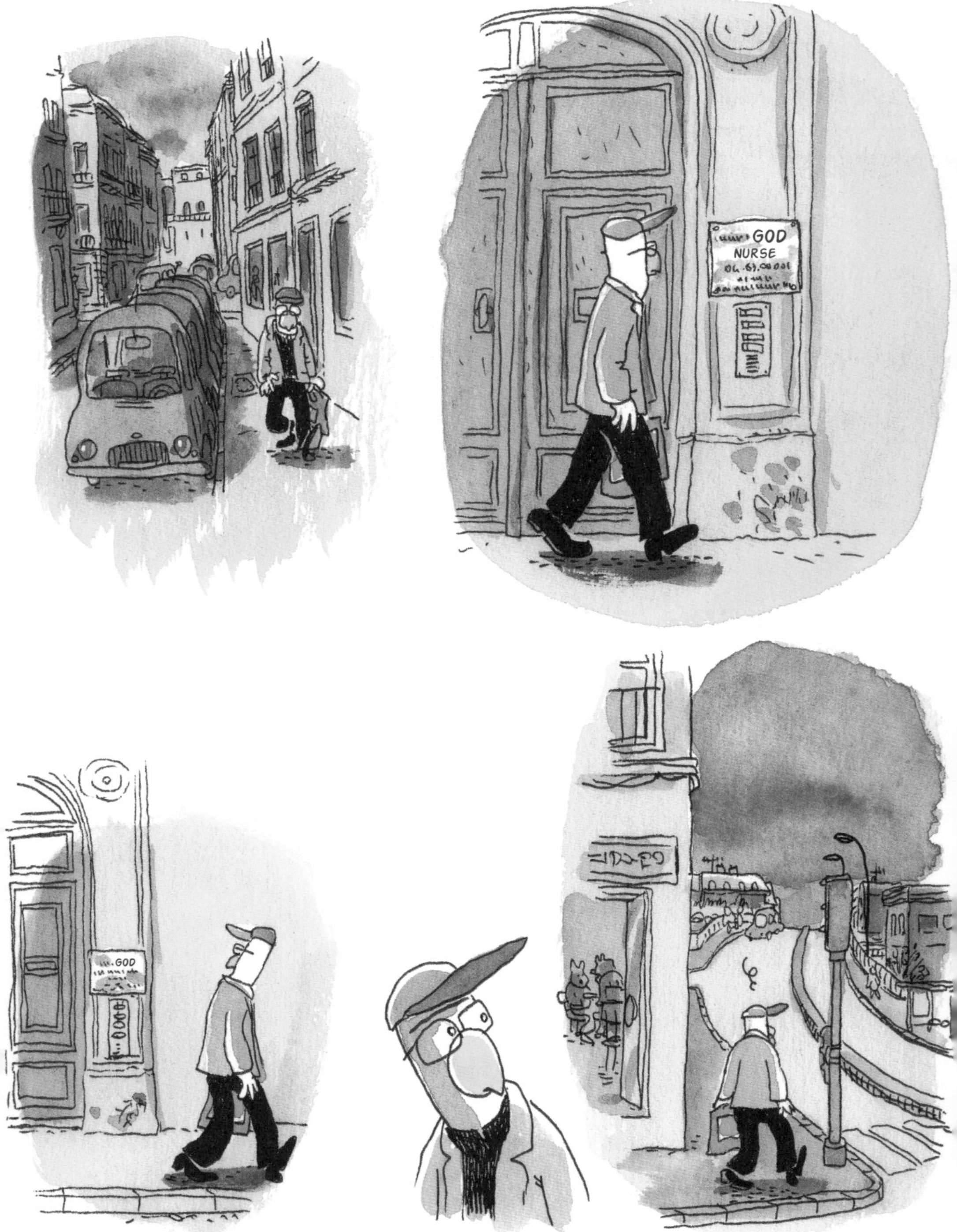
GOD
NURSE

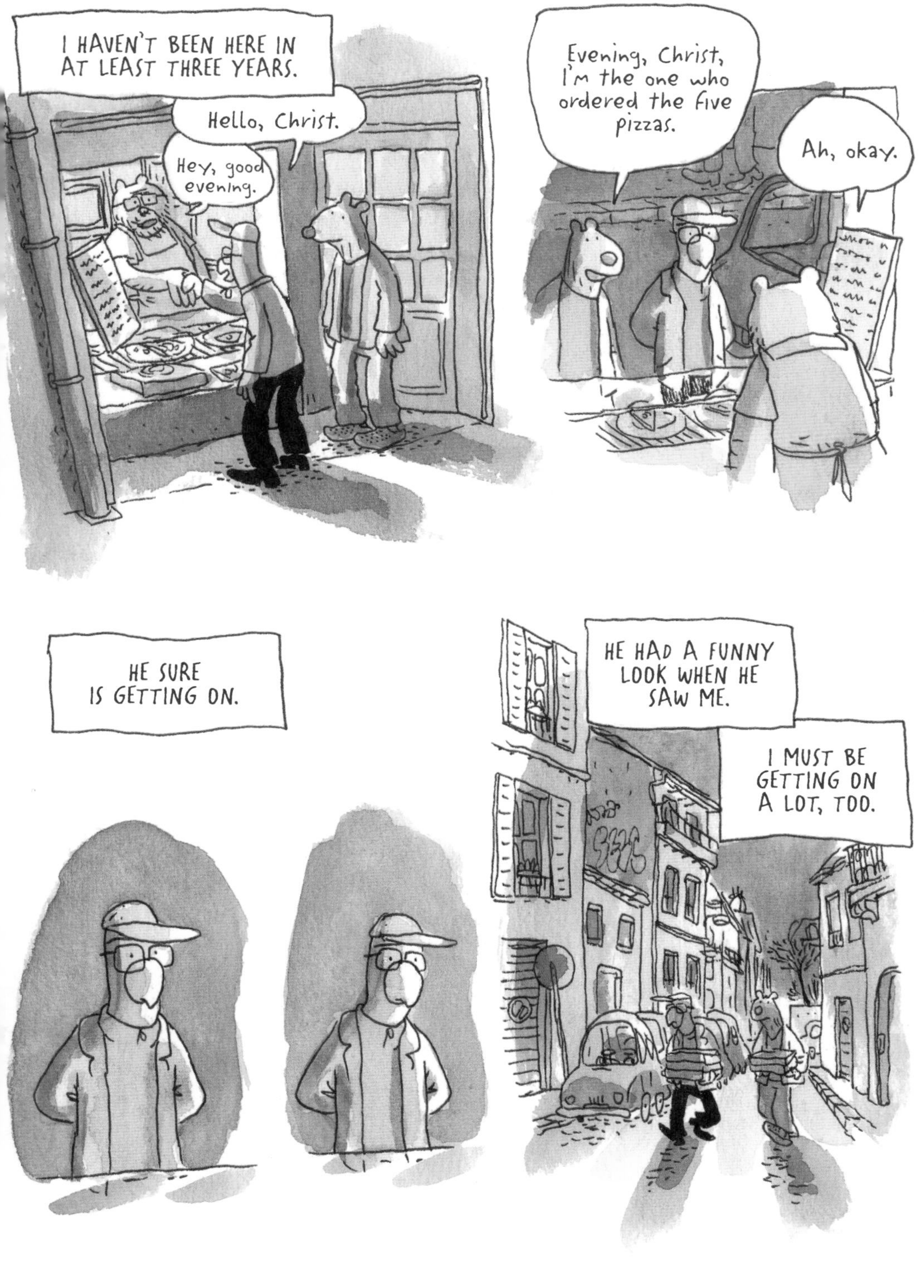
I HAVEN'T BEEN HERE IN AT LEAST THREE YEARS.
Hello, Christ.
Hey, good evening.
Evening, Christ, I'm the one who ordered the five pizzas.
Ah, okay.
HE SURE IS GETTING ON.
HE HAD A FUNNY LOOK WHEN HE SAW ME.
I MUST BE GETTING ON A LOT, TOO.

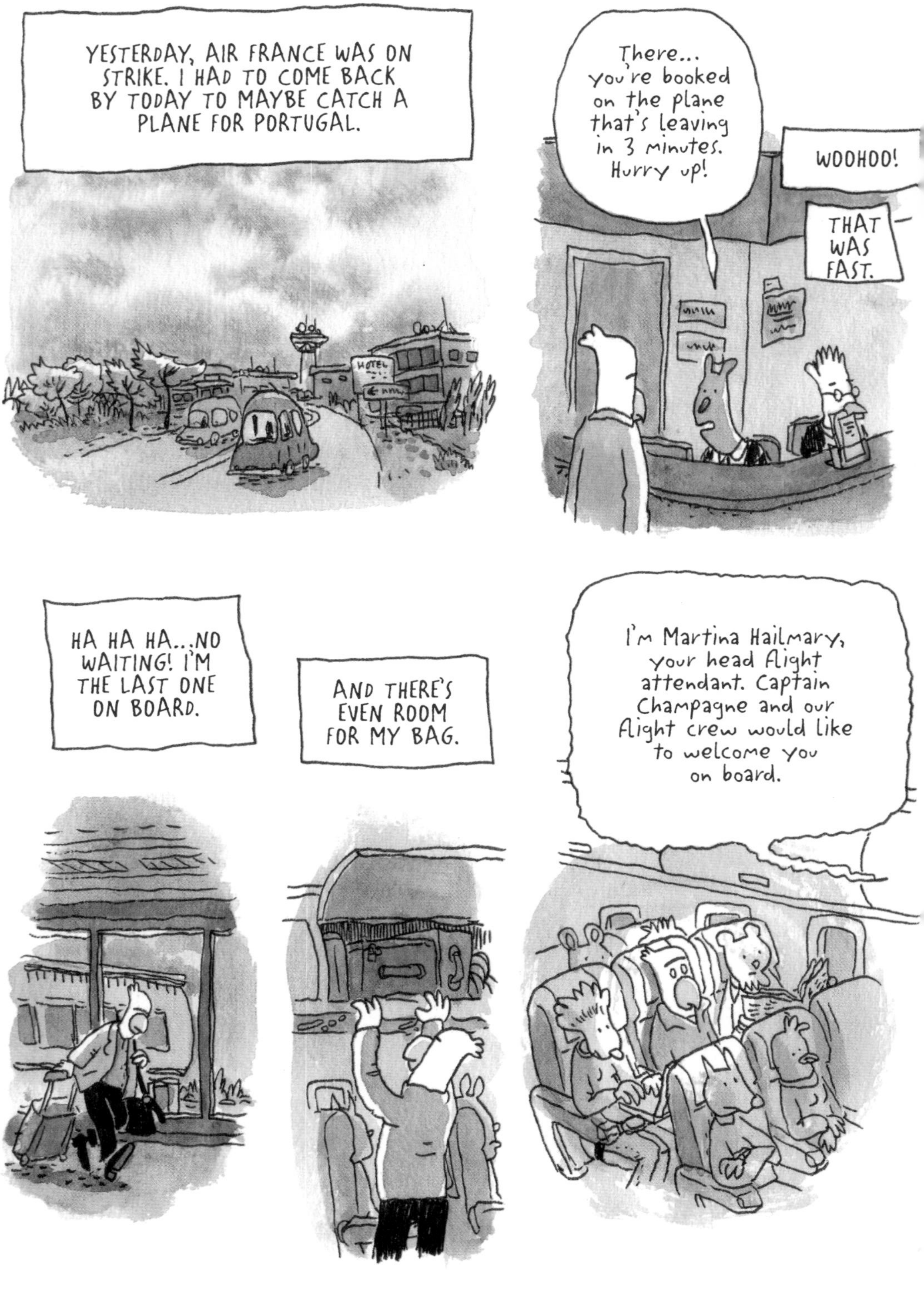
YESTERDAY, AIR FRANCE WAS ON STRIKE. I HAD TO COME BACK BY TODAY TO MAYBE CATCH A PLANE FOR PORTUGAL.
There... you're booked on the plane that's leaving in 3 minutes. Hurry up!
WOOHOO!
THAT WAS FAST.
HA HA HA...NO WAITING! I'M THE LAST ONE ON BOARD.
AND THERE'S EVEN ROOM FOR MY BAG.
I'm Martina Hailmary, your head flight attendant. Captain Champagne and our flight crew would like to welcome you on board.

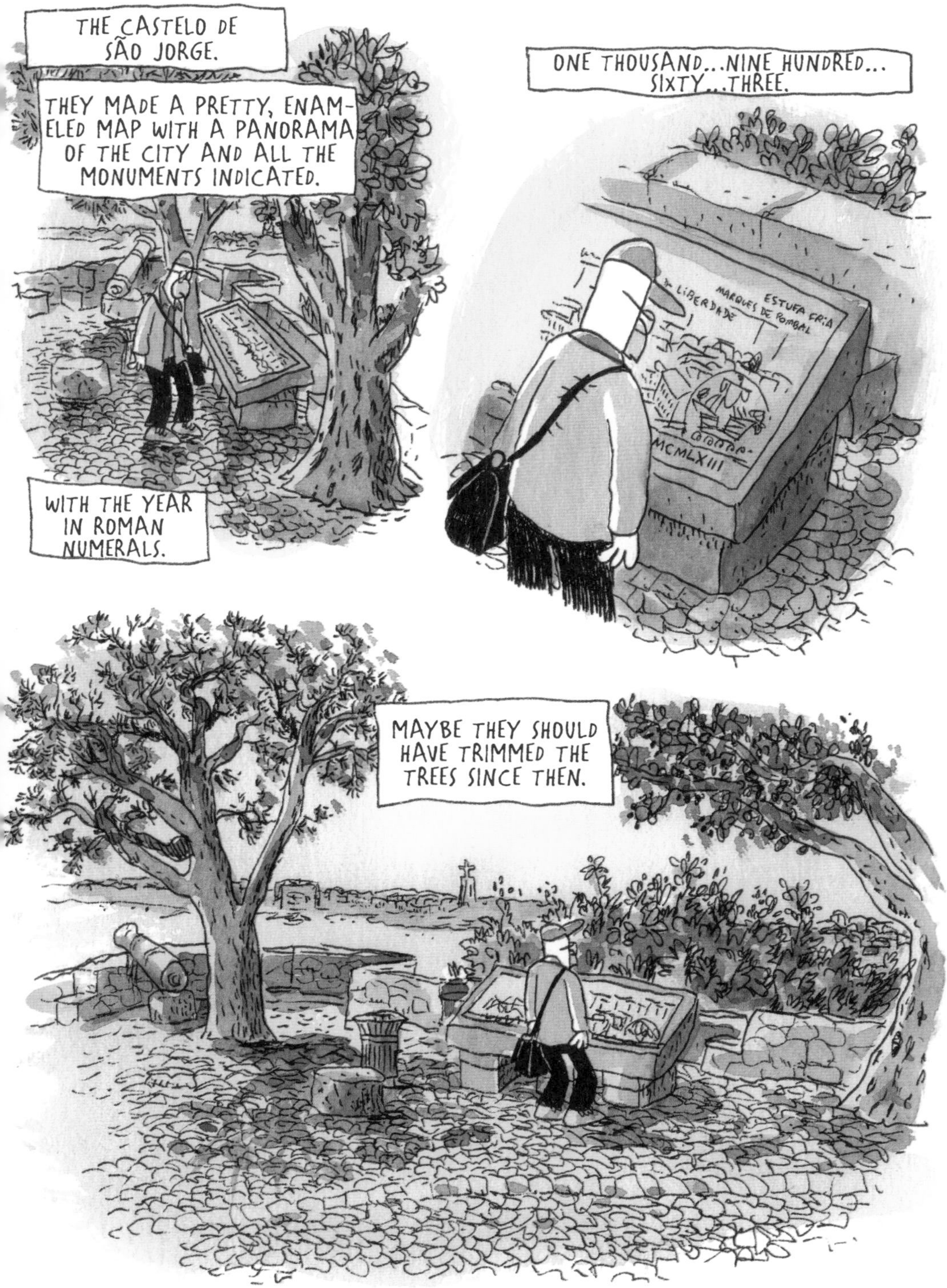
THE CASTELO DE SÃO JORGE.
THEY MADE A PRETTY, ENAMELED MAP WITH A PANORAMA OF THE CITY AND ALL THE MONUMENTS INDICATED.
WITH THE YEAR IN ROMAN NUMERALS.
ONE THOUSAND...NINE HUNDRED... SIXTY...THREE.
LIBERDADE
MARQUES DE POMBAL
ESTUFA FRIA
MCMLXIII
MAYBE THEY SHOULD HAVE TRIMMED THE TREES SINCE THEN.

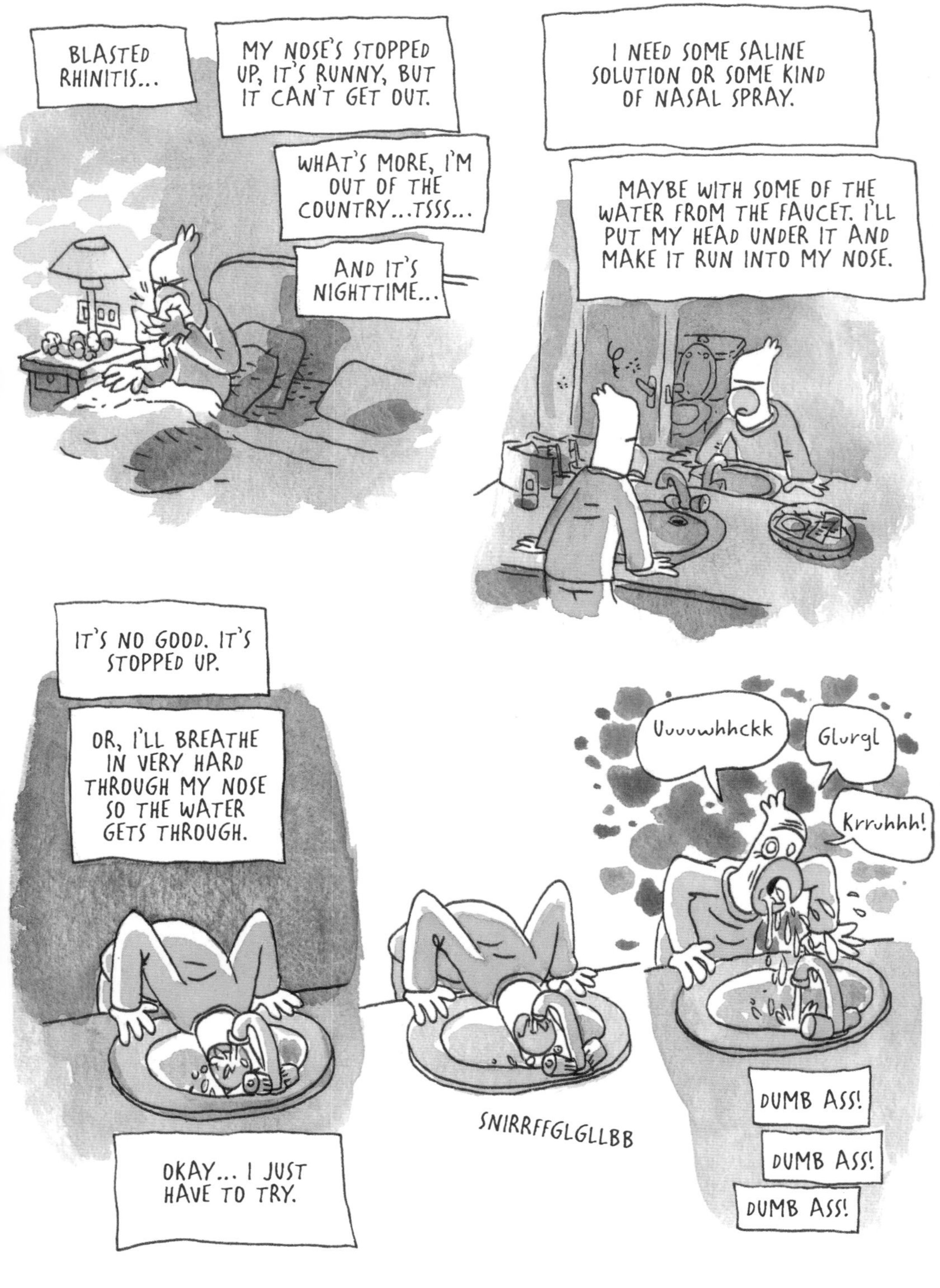

BLASTED RHINITIS...
MY NOSE'S STOPPED UP, IT'S RUNNY, BUT IT CAN'T GET OUT.
WHAT'S MORE, I'M OUT OF THE COUNTRY...TSSS...
AND IT'S NIGHTTIME...
I NEED SOME SALINE SOLUTION OR SOME KIND OF NASAL SPRAY.
MAYBE WITH SOME OF THE WATER FROM THE FAUCET. I'LL PUT MY HEAD UNDER IT AND MAKE IT RUN INTO MY NOSE.
IT'S NO GOOD. IT'S STOPPED UP.
OR, I'LL BREATHE IN VERY HARD THROUGH MY NOSE SO THE WATER GETS THROUGH.
OKAY... I JUST HAVE TO TRY.
SNIRRFFGLGLLBB
Uuuuwhhckk
Glurgl
Krruhhh!
DUMB ASS!
DUMB ASS!
DUMB ASS!

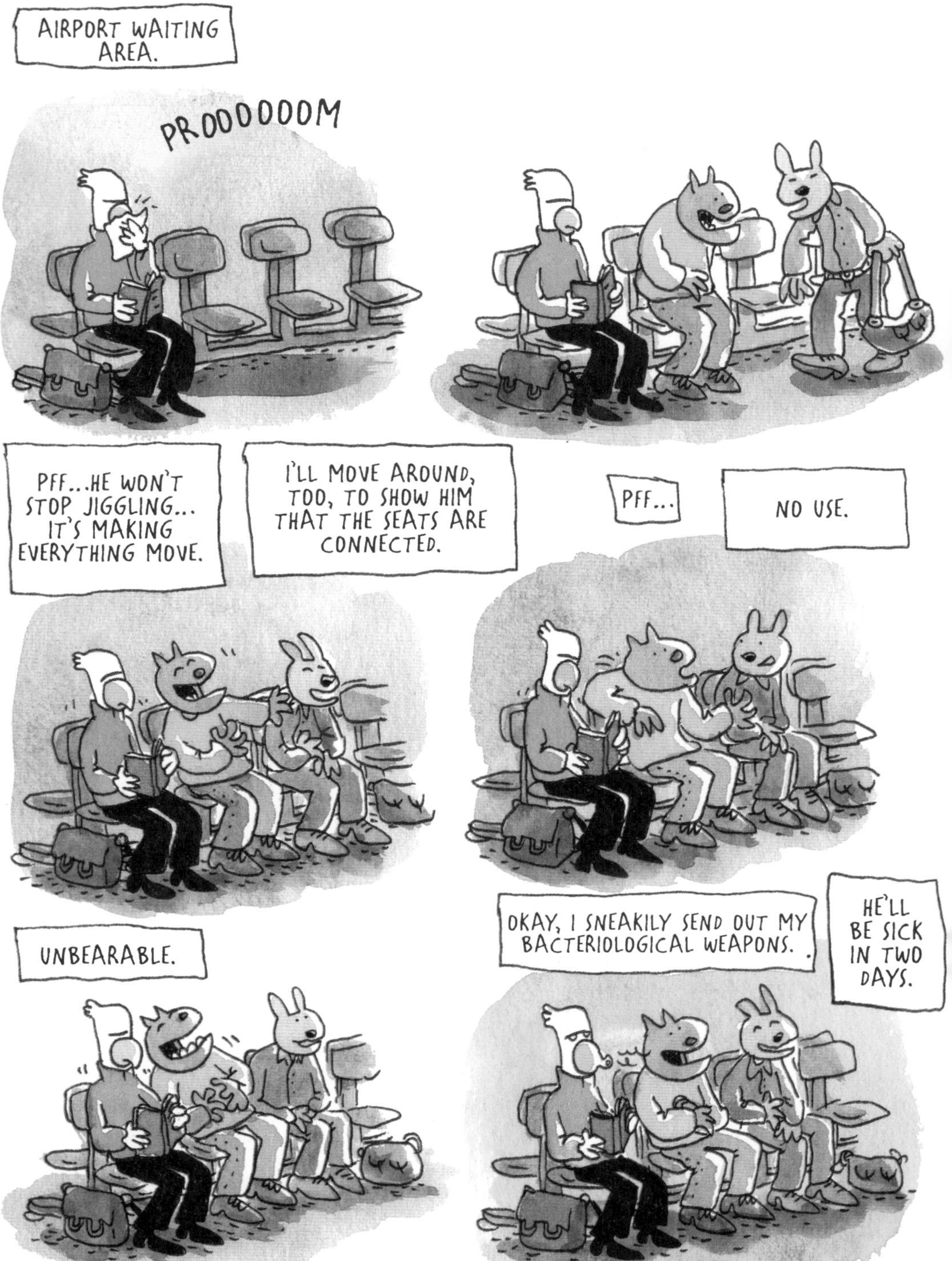
AIRPORT WAITING AREA.
PROOOOOOM
PFF...HE WON'T STOP JIGGLING... IT'S MAKING EVERYTHING MOVE.
I'LL MOVE AROUND, TOO, TO SHOW HIM THAT THE SEATS ARE CONNECTED.
PFF...
NO USE.
UNBEARABLE.
OKAY, I SNEAKILY SEND OUT MY BACTERIOLOGICAL WEAPONS.
HE'LL BE SICK IN TWO DAYS.

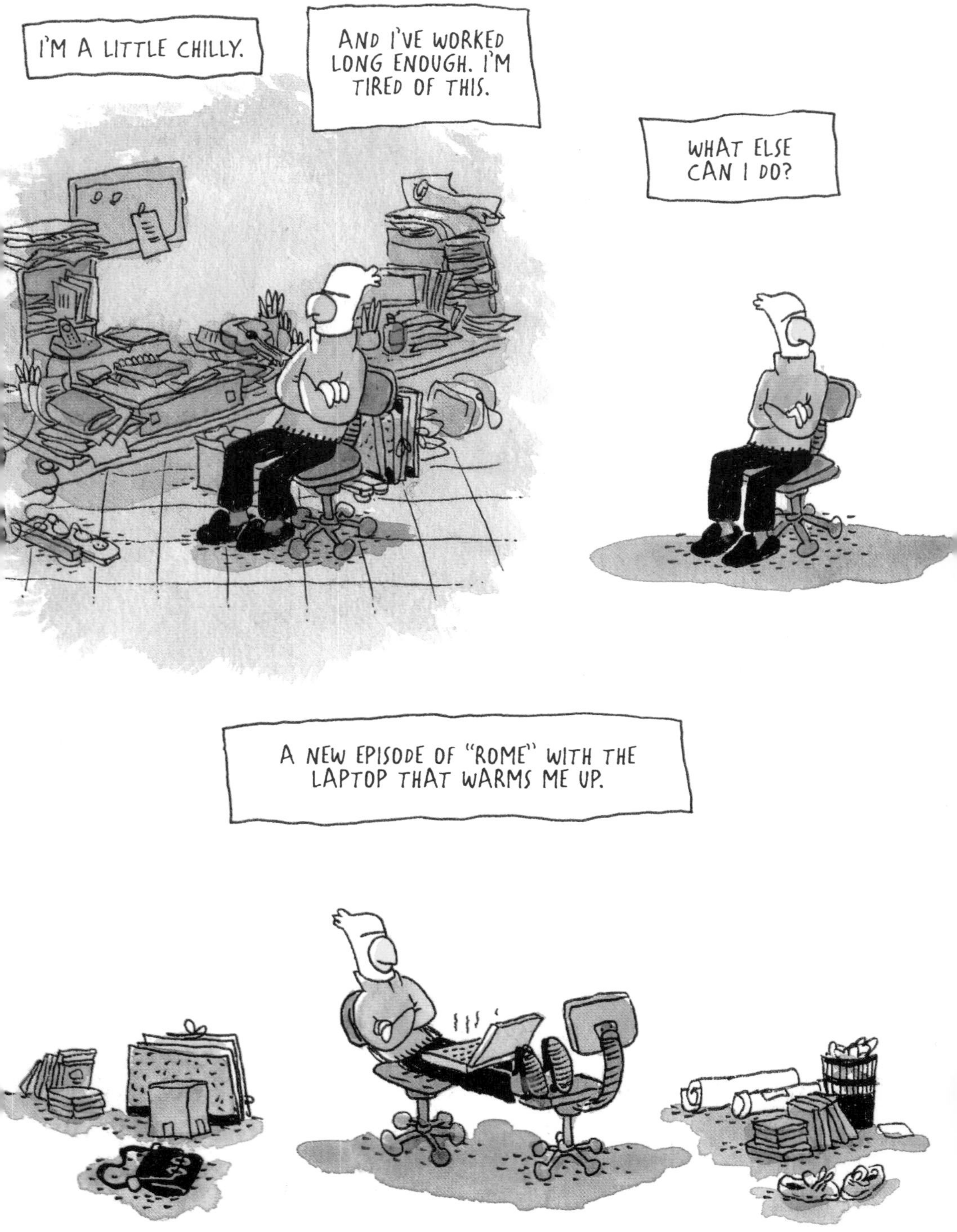
I'M A LITTLE CHILLY.
AND I'VE WORKED LONG ENOUGH. I'M TIRED OF THIS.
WHAT ELSE CAN I DO?
A NEW EPISODE OF "ROME" WITH THE LAPTOP THAT WARMS ME UP.

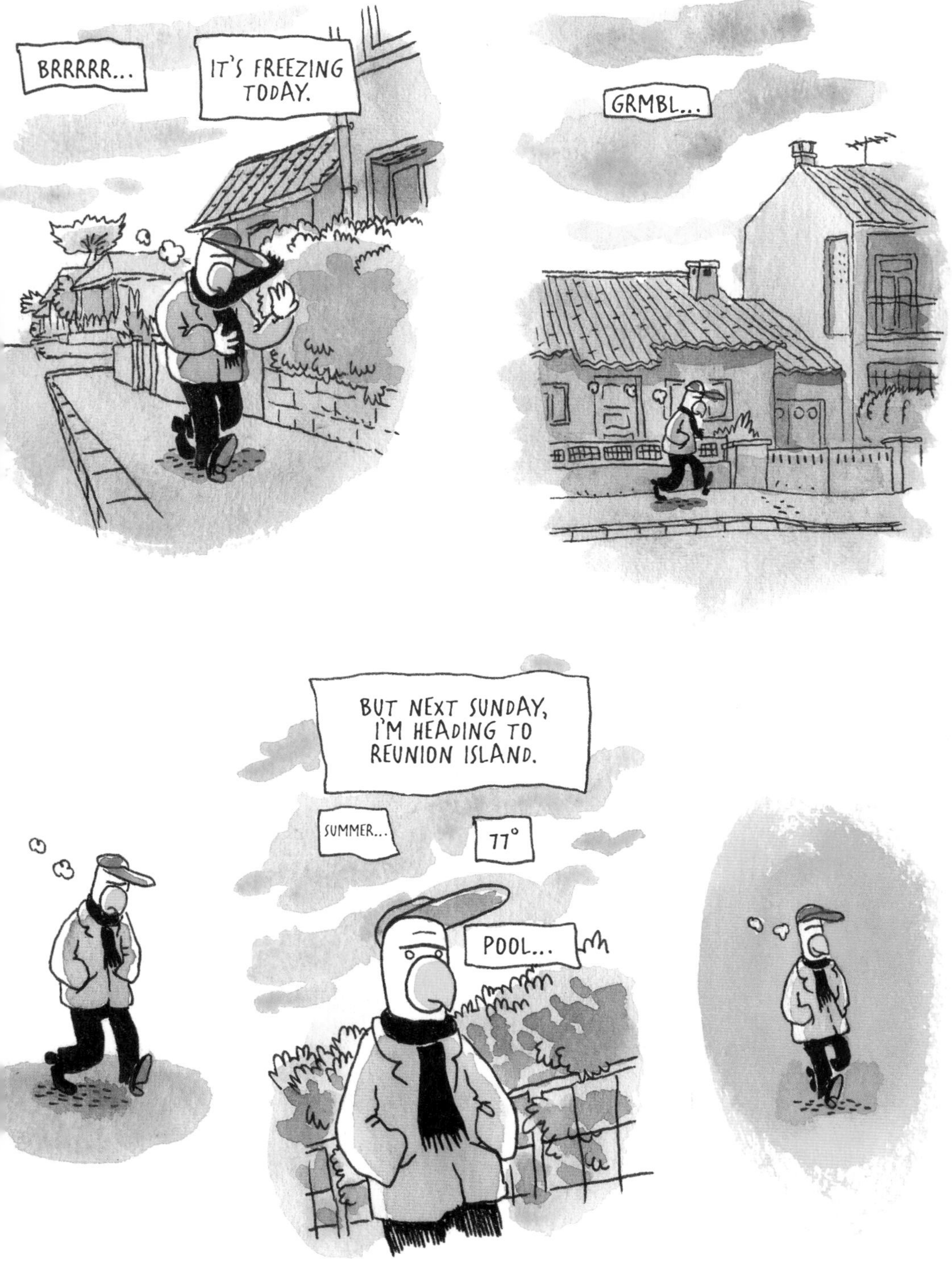
BRRRRR...
IT'S FREEZING TODAY.
GRMBL...
BUT NEXT SUNDAY, I'M HEADING TO REUNION ISLAND.
SUMMER...
77°
POOL...

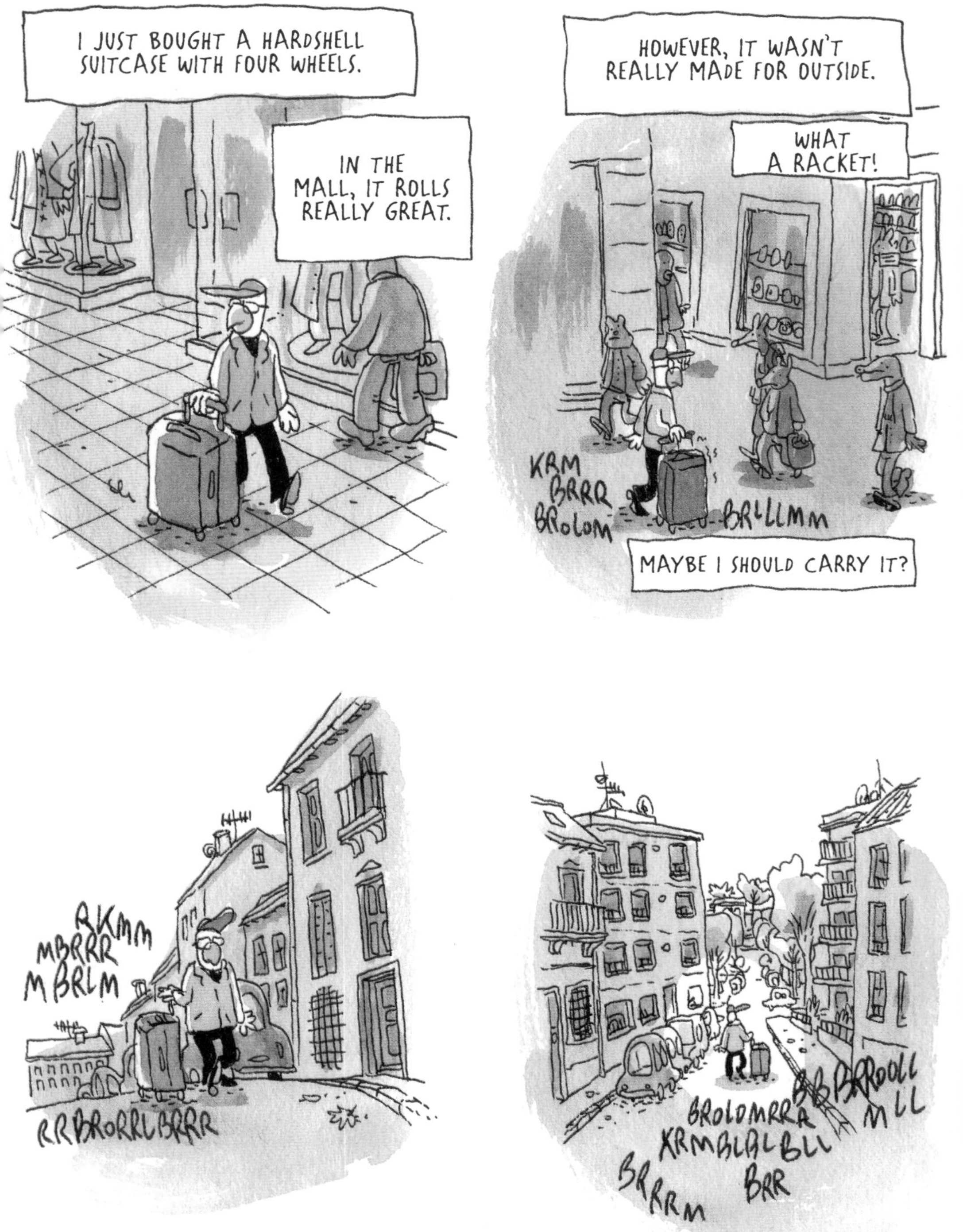
I JUST BOUGHT A HARDSHELL SUITCASE WITH FOUR WHEELS.
IN THE MALL, IT ROLLS REALLY GREAT.
HOWEVER, IT WASN'T REALLY MADE FOR OUTSIDE.
WHAT A RACKET!
KRM BRRR BROLOM
BRLLMM
MAYBE I SHOULD CARRY IT?
AKMM MBRRR MBRLM
RRBRORRLBRRR
BBBRROLL MLL
BROLOMRRA
KRMBLBLBLL
BRRRM
BRR

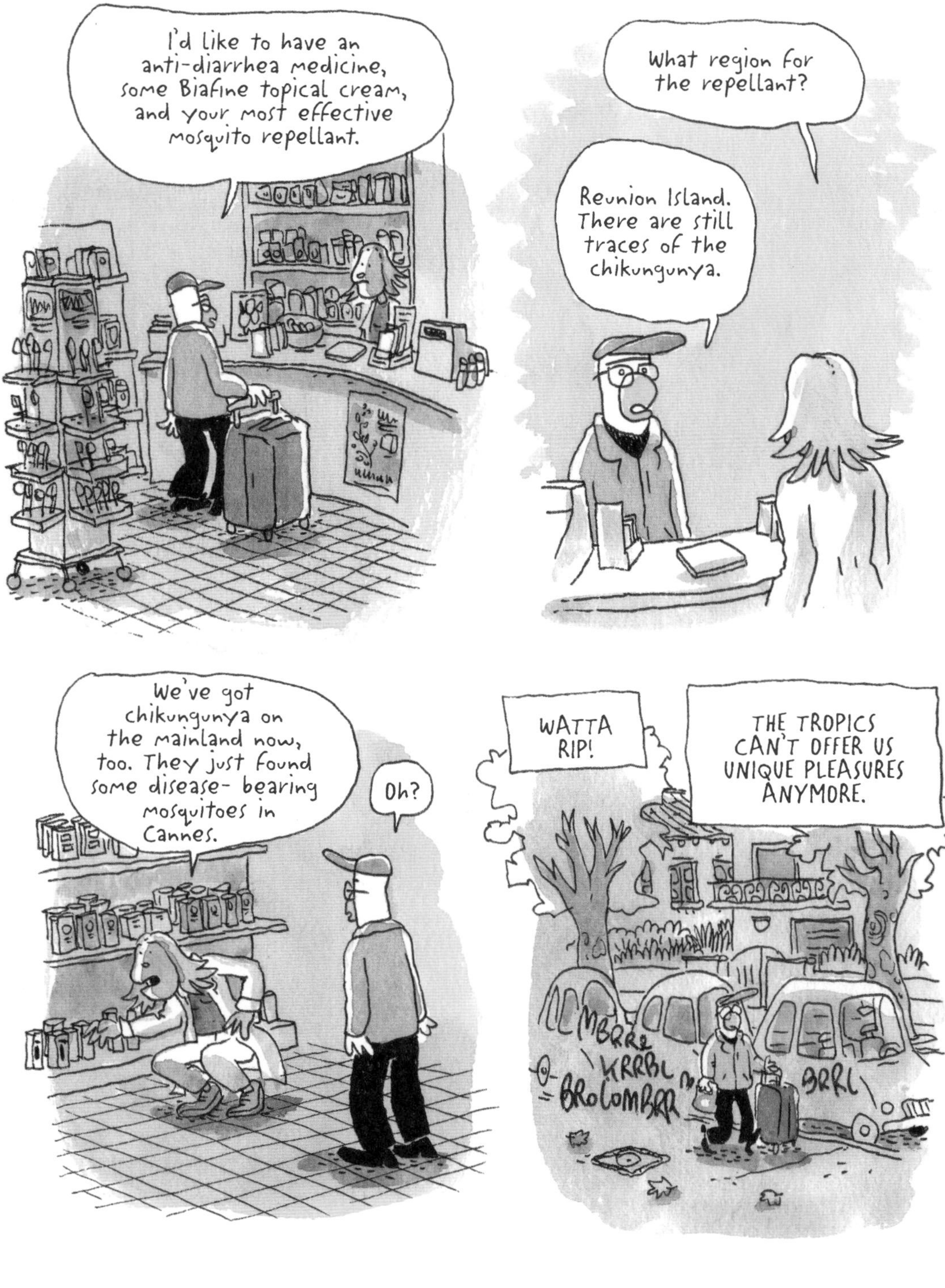
I'd like to have an anti-diarrhea medicine, some Biafine topical cream, and your most effective mosquito repellant.
What region for the repellant?
Reunion Island. There are still traces of the chikungunya.
We've got chikungunya on the mainland now, too. They just found some disease- bearing mosquitoes in Cannes.
Oh?
WATTA RIP!
THE TROPICS CAN'T OFFER US UNIQUE PLEASURES ANYMORE.
MBRRE
KRRBL
BROLOMBRR
BRRL

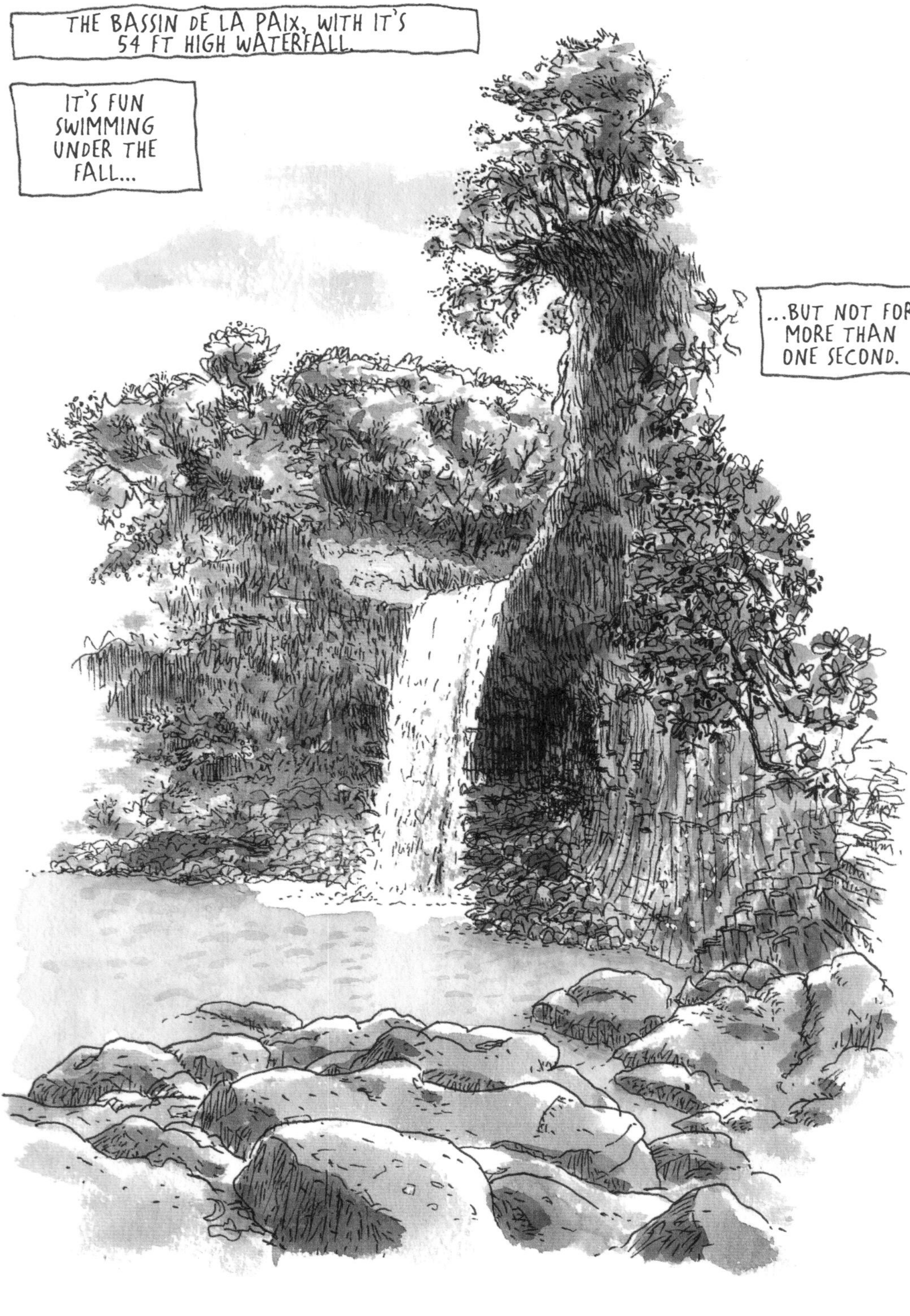
THE BASSIN DE LA PAIX, WITH IT'S 54 FT HIGH WATERFALL.
IT'S FUN SWIMMING UNDER THE FALL...
...BUT NOT FOR MORE THAN ONE SECOND.

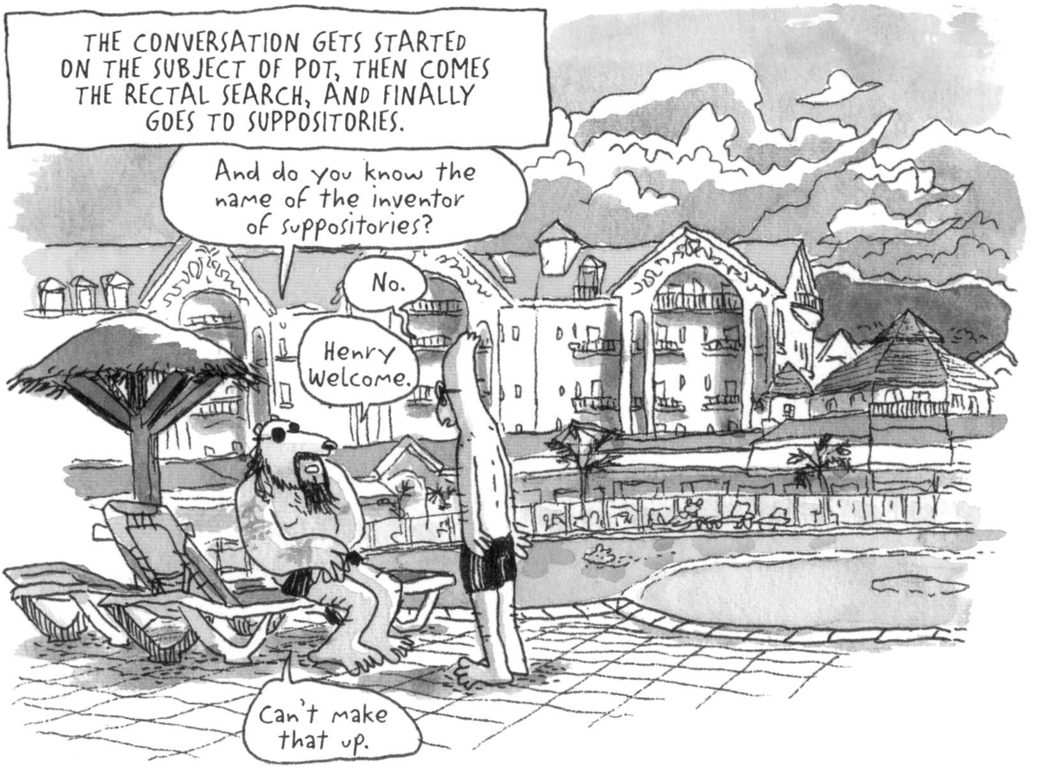
THE CONVERSATION GETS STARTED ON THE SUBJECT OF POT, THEN COMES THE RECTAL SEARCH, AND FINALLY GOES TO SUPPOSITORIES.
And do you know the name of the inventor of suppositories?
No.
Henry Welcome.
Can't make that up.

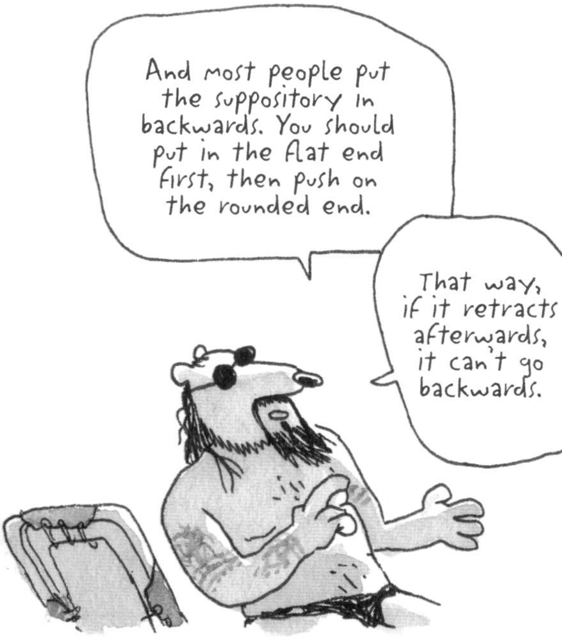
And most people put the suppository in backwards. You should put in the flat end first, then push on the rounded end.
That way, if it retracts afterwards, it can't go backwards.

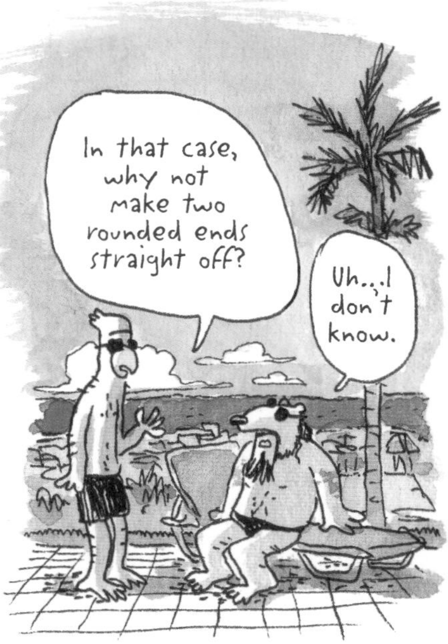
In that case, why not make two rounded ends straight off?
Uh...I don't know.

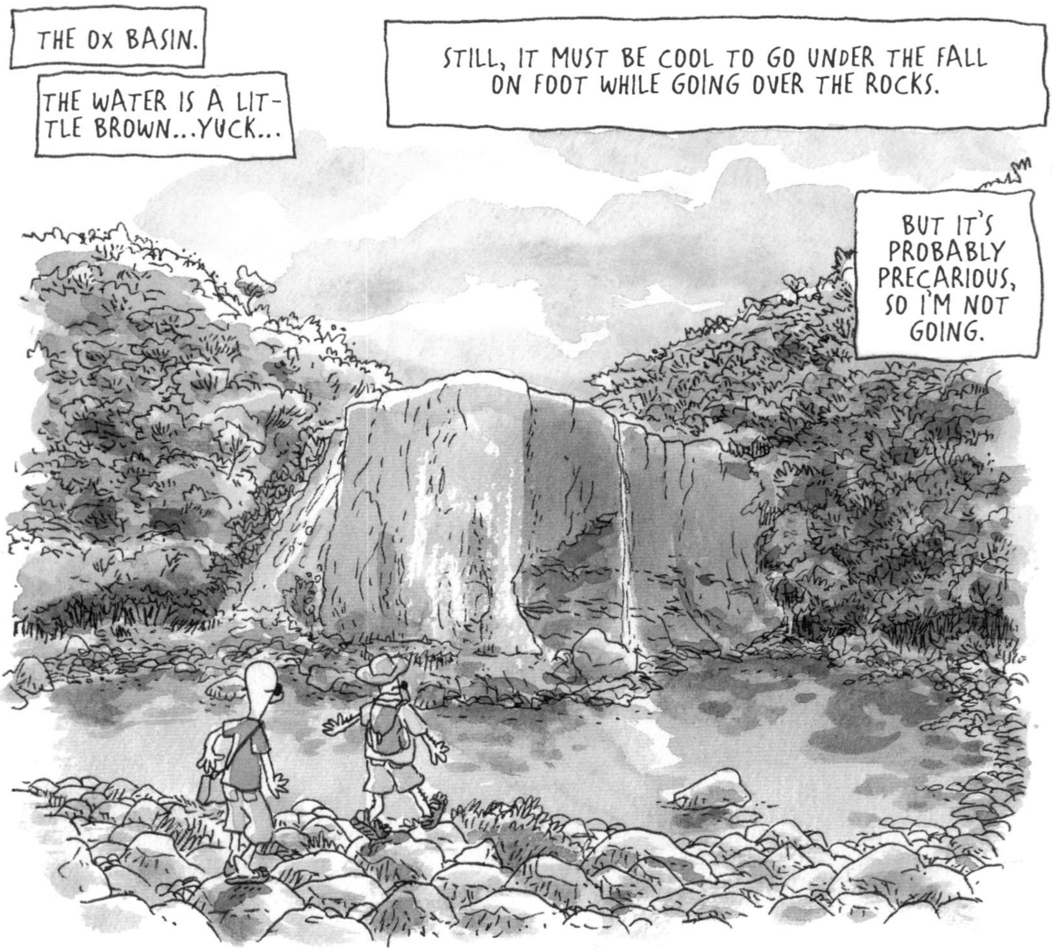
THE OX BASIN.
THE WATER IS A LITTLE BROWN...YUCK...
STILL, IT MUST BE COOL TO GO UNDER THE FALL ON FOOT WHILE GOING OVER THE ROCKS.
BUT IT'S PROBABLY PRECARIOUS, SO I'M NOT GOING.

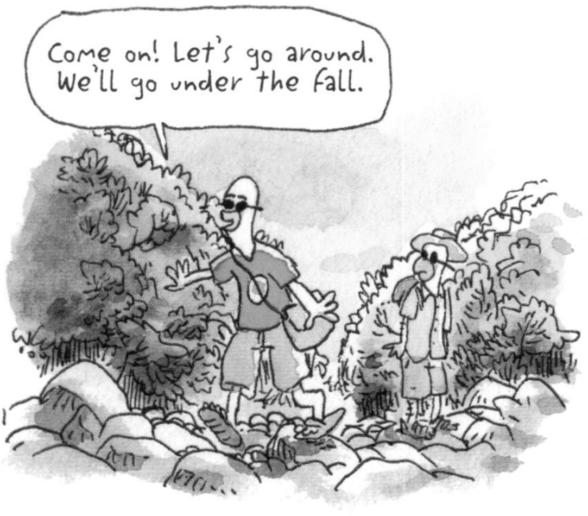
Come on! Let's go around. We'll go under the fall.

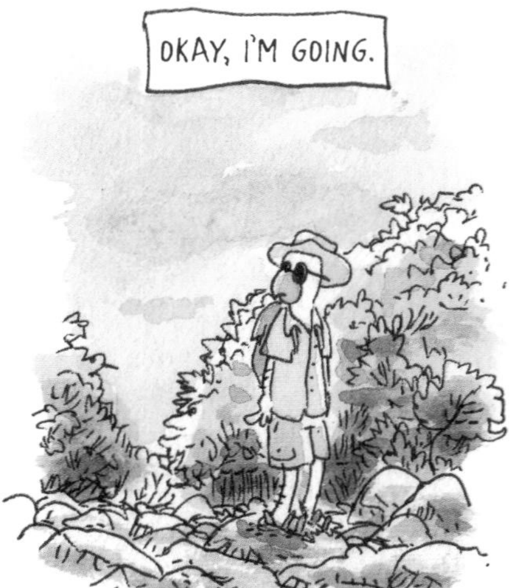
OKAY, I'M GOING.

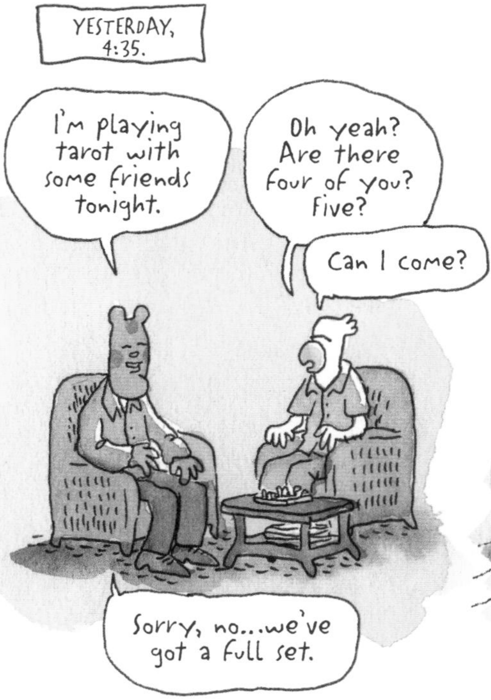
YESTERDAY, 4:35.
I'm playing tarot with some friends tonight.
Oh yeah? Are there four of you? Five?
Can I come?
Sorry, no...we've got a full set.

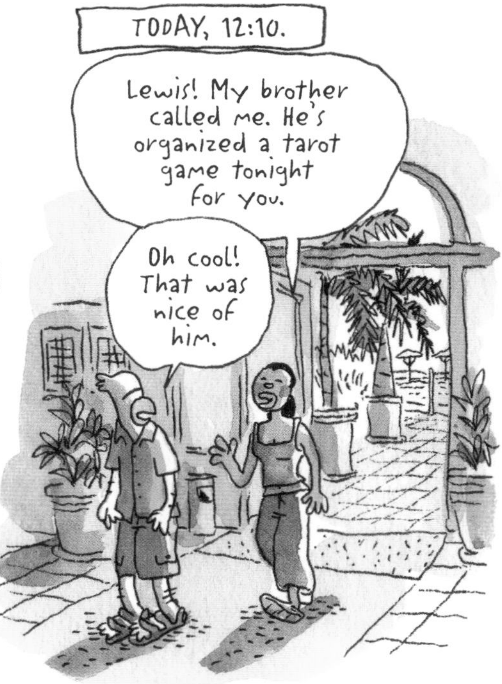
TODAY, 12:10.
Lewis! My brother called me. He's organized a tarot game tonight for you.
Oh cool! That was nice of him.

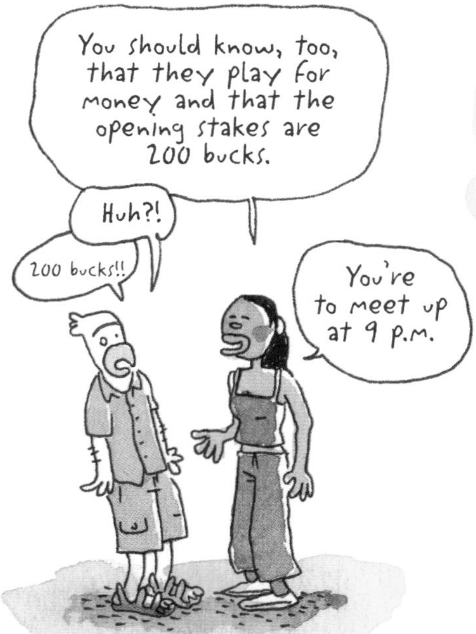
You should know, too, that they play for money and that the opening stakes are 200 bucks.
Huh?!
200 bucks!!
You're to meet up at 9 p.m.

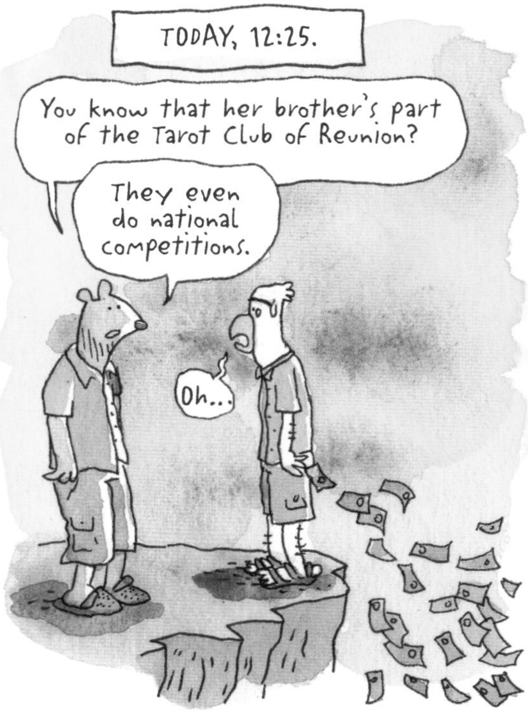
TODAY, 12:25.
You know that her brother's part of the Tarot Club of Reunion?
They even do national competitions.
Oh...

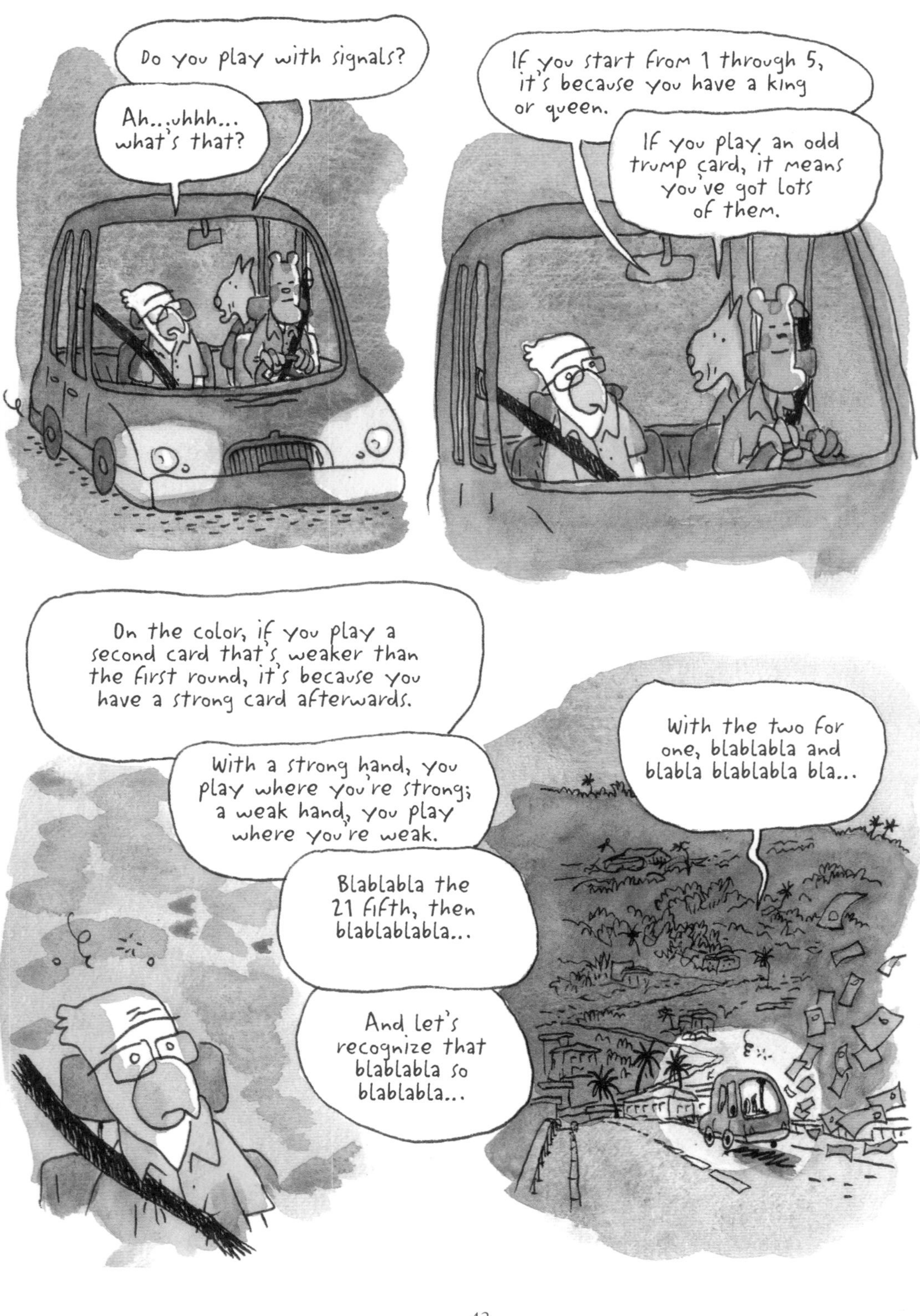
Do you play with signals?
Ah...uhhh... what's that?
If you start from 1 through 5, it's because you have a king or queen.
If you play an odd trump card, it means you've got lots of them.
On the color, if you play a second card that's weaker than the first round, it's because you have a strong card afterwards.
With a strong hand, you play where you're strong; a weak hand, you play where you're weak.
Blablabla the 21 fifth, then blablablabla...
And let's recognize that blablabla so blablabla...
With the two for one, blablabla and blabla blablabla bla...

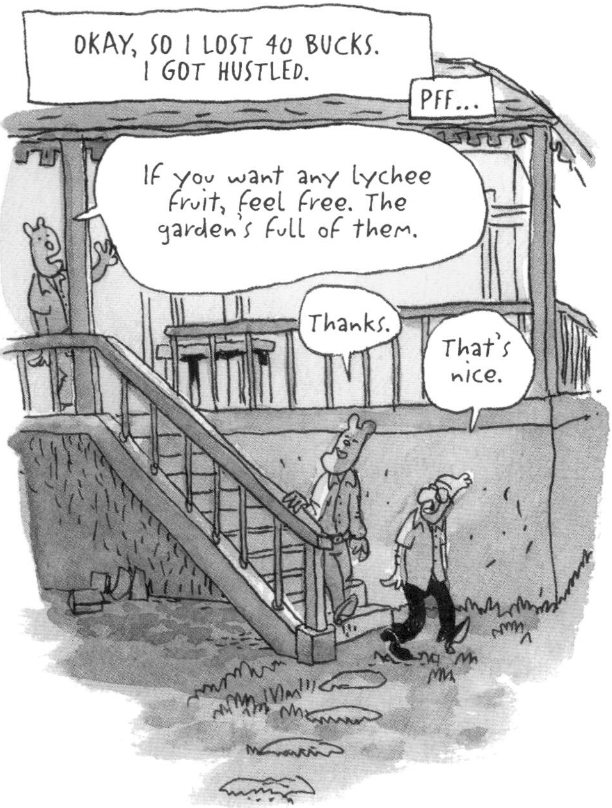
OKAY, SO I LOST 40 BUCKS.
I GOT HUSTLED.
PFF...
If you want any lychee fruit, feel free. The garden's full of them.
Thanks.
That's nice.

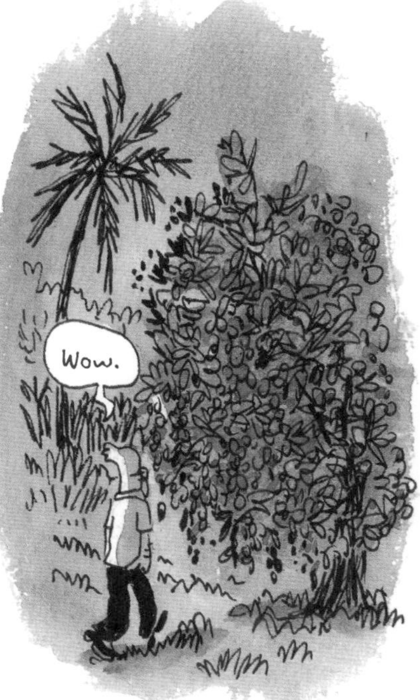
Wow.

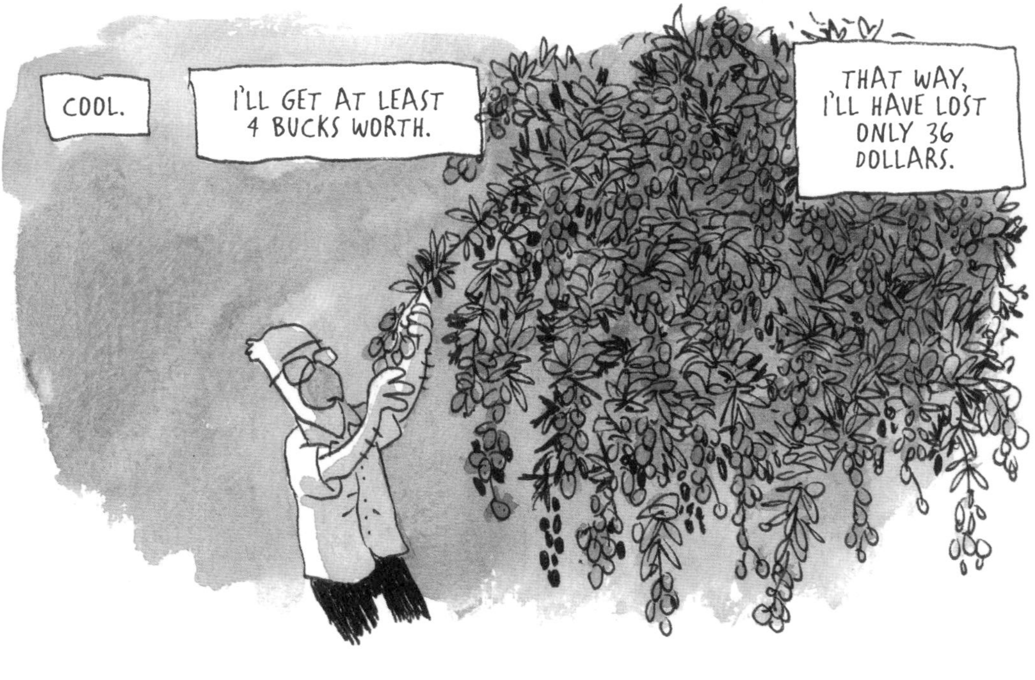
COOL.
I'LL GET AT LEAST 4 BUCKS WORTH.
THAT WAY, I'LL HAVE LOST ONLY 36 DOLLARS.

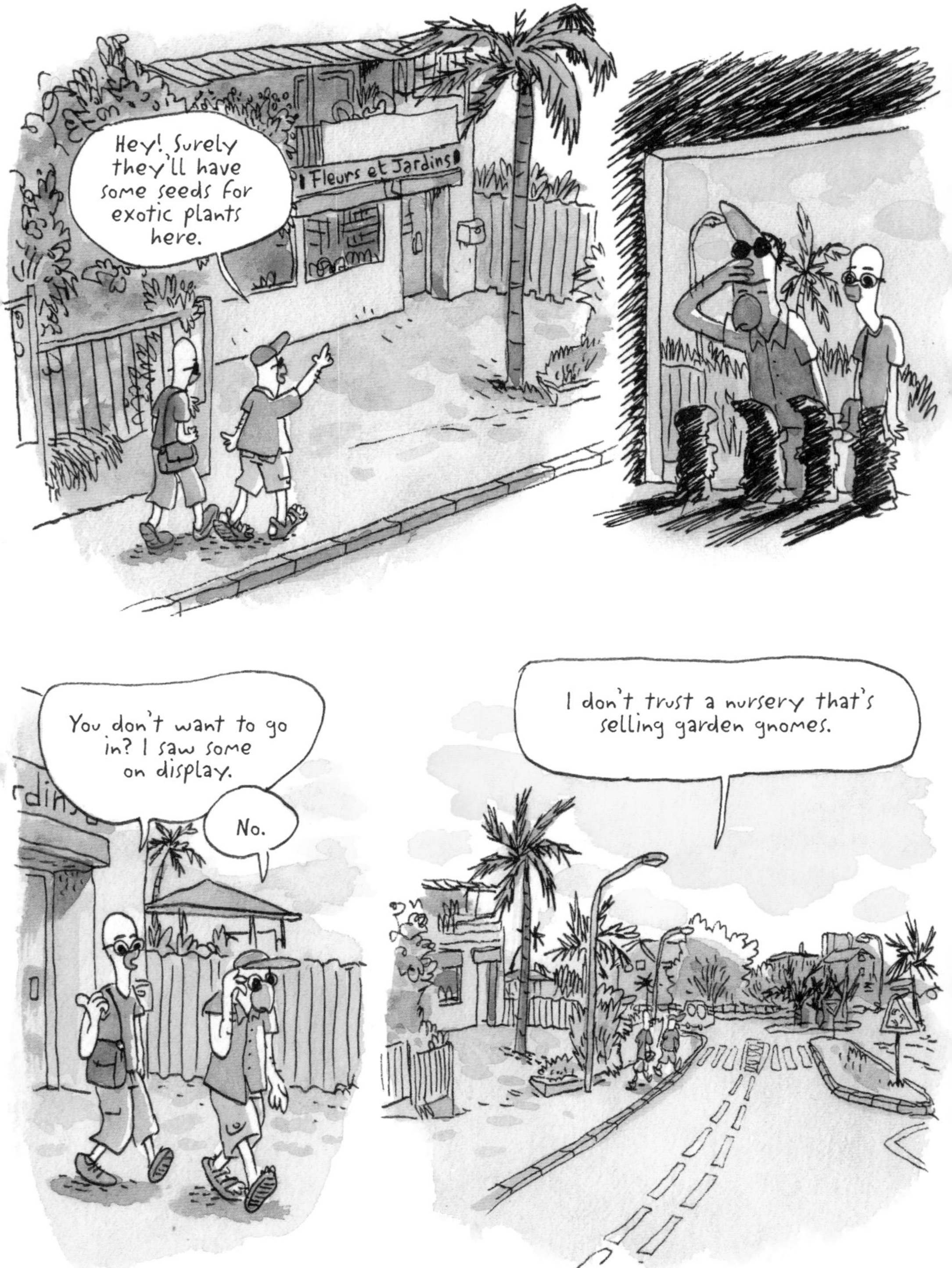
Hey! Surely they'll have some seeds for exotic plants here.
Fleurs et Jardins
You don't want to go in? I saw some on display.
No.
I don't trust a nursery that's selling garden gnomes.

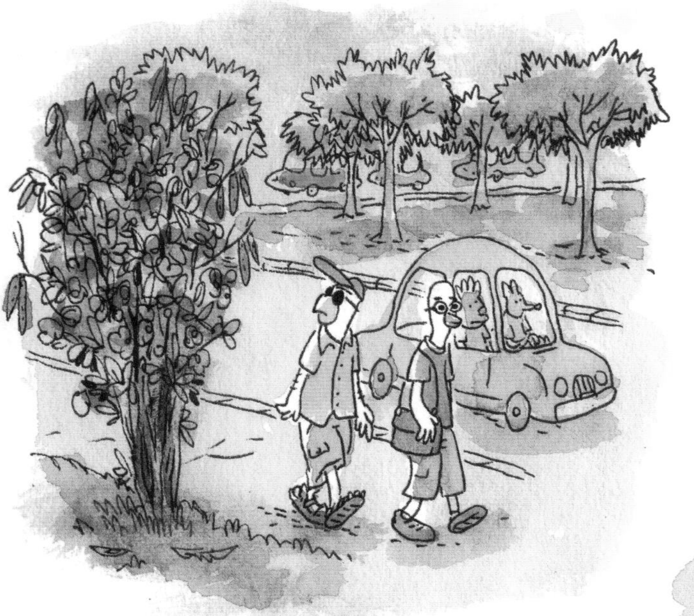

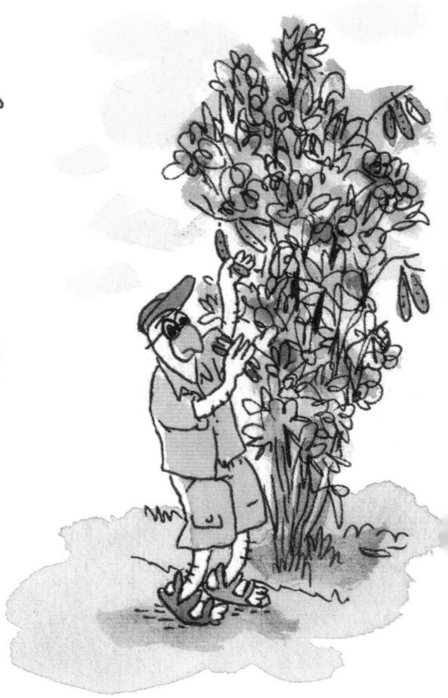

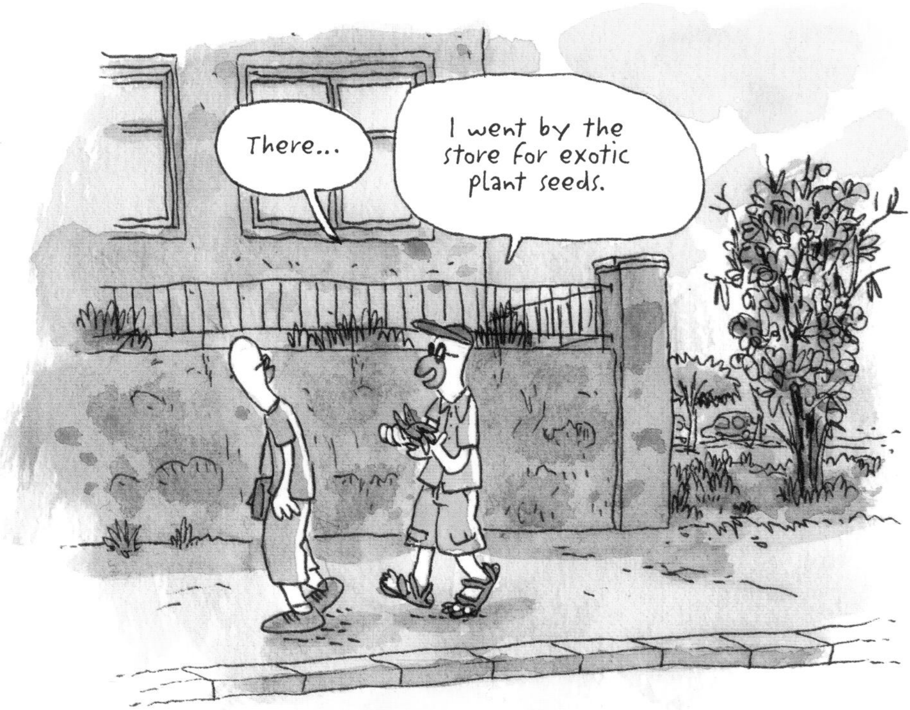
There...
I went by the store for exotic plant seeds.

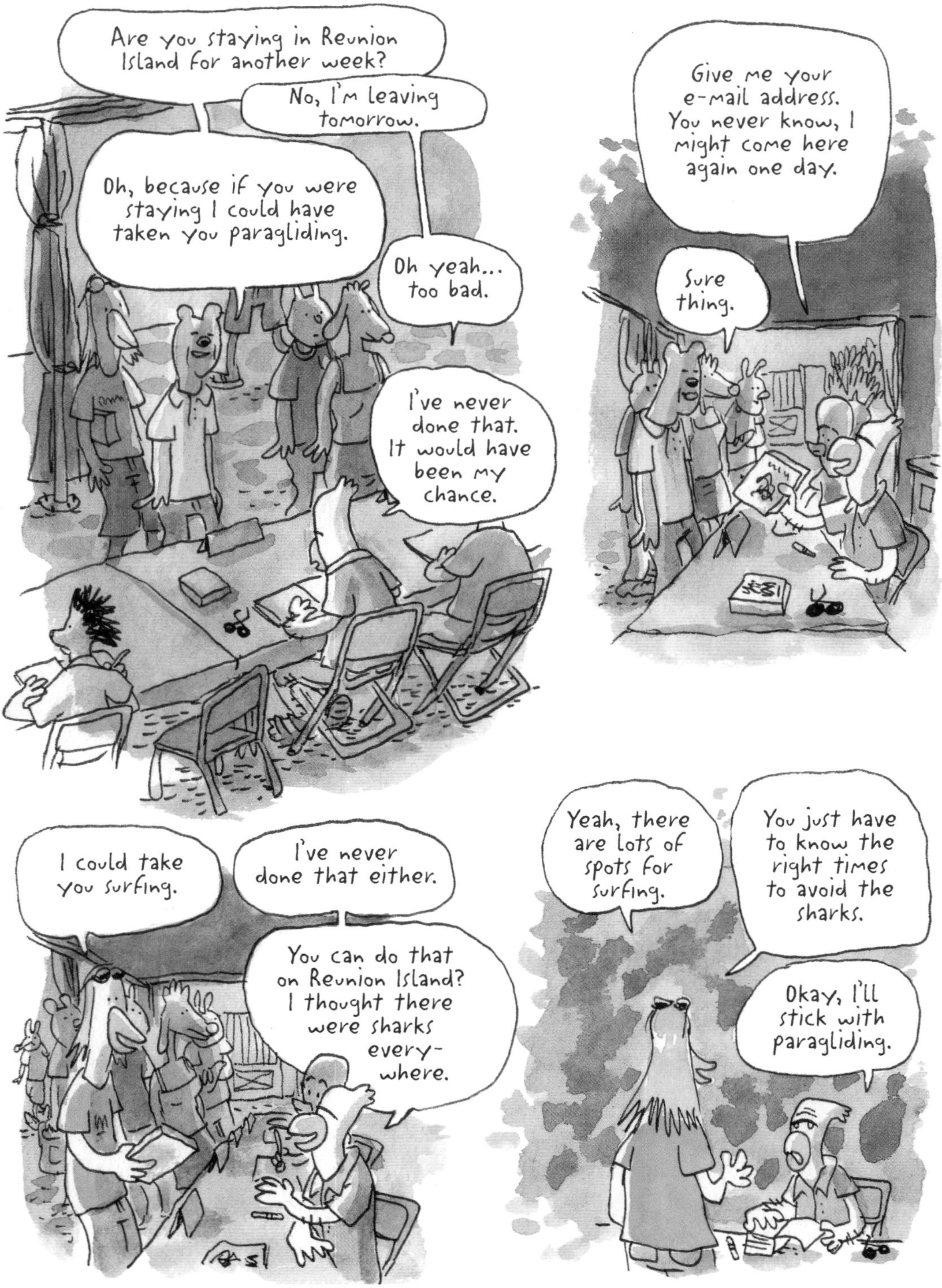
Are you staying in Reunion Island for another week?
No, I'm leaving tomorrow.
Oh, because if you were staying I could have taken you paragliding.
Oh yeah... too bad.
I've never done that. It would have been my chance.
Give me your e-mail address. You never know, I might come here again one day.
Sure thing.
I could take you surfing.
I've never done that either.
You can do that on Reunion Island? I thought there were sharks everywhere.
Yeah, there are lots of spots for surfing.
You just have to know the right times to avoid the sharks.
Okay, I'll stick with paragliding.

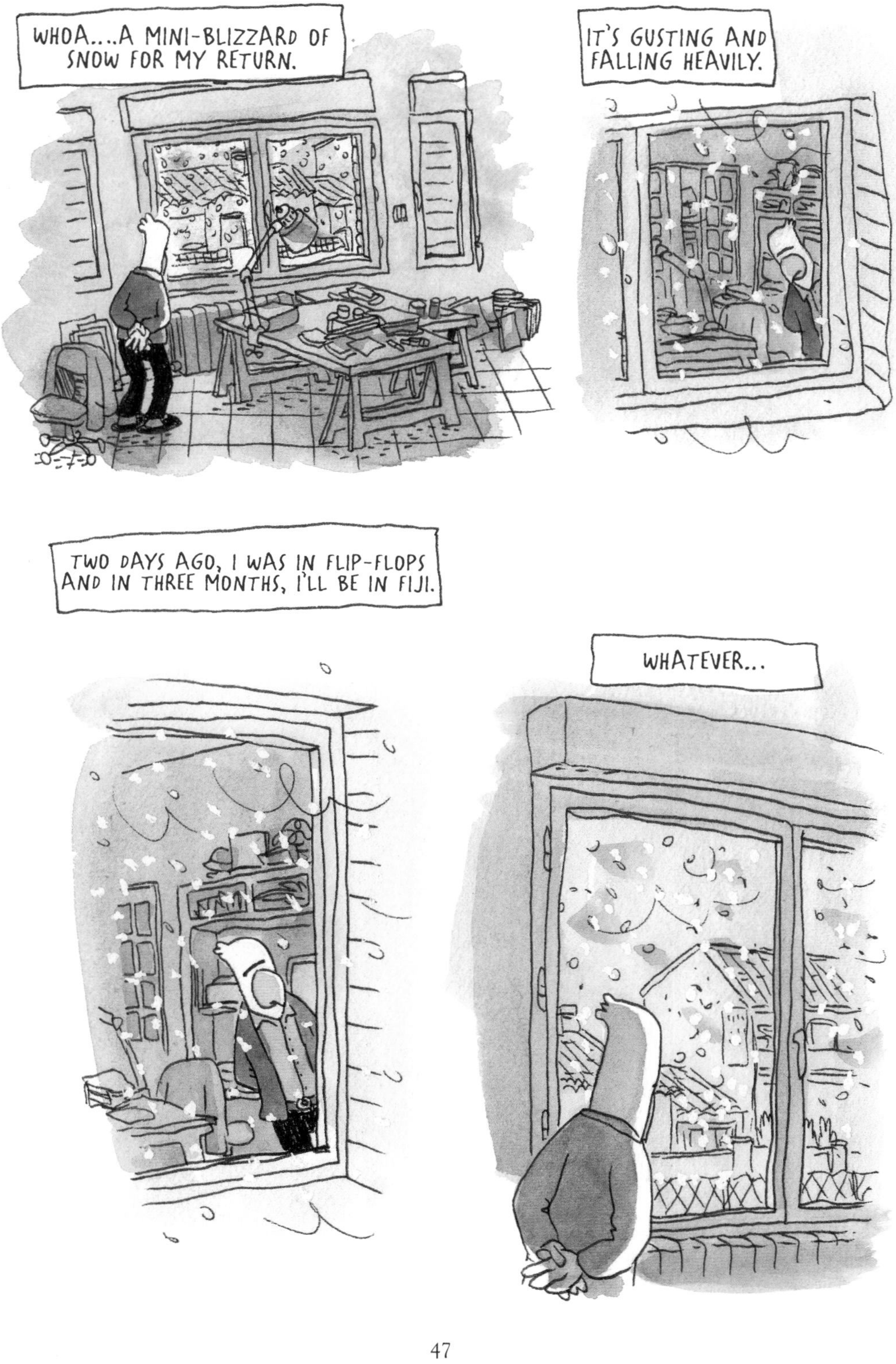
WHOA....A MINI-BLIZZARD OF SNOW FOR MY RETURN.
IT'S GUSTING AND FALLING HEAVILY.
TWO DAYS AGO, I WAS IN FLIP-FLOPS AND IN THREE MONTHS, I'LL BE IN FIJI.
WHATEVER...

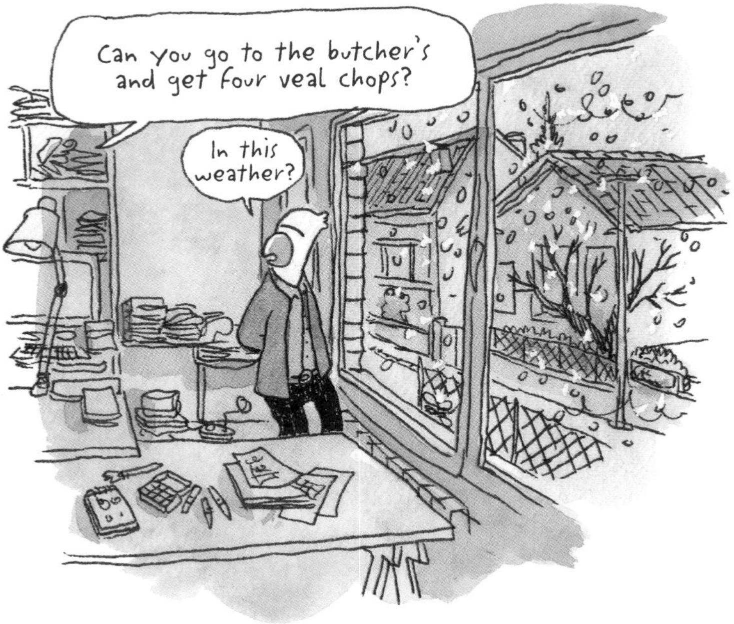
Can you go to the butcher's and get four veal chops?
In this weather?

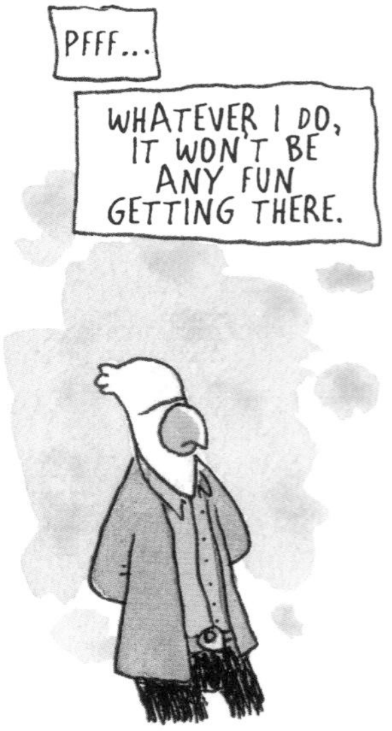
PFFF...
WHATEVER I DO, IT WON'T BE ANY FUN GETTING THERE.

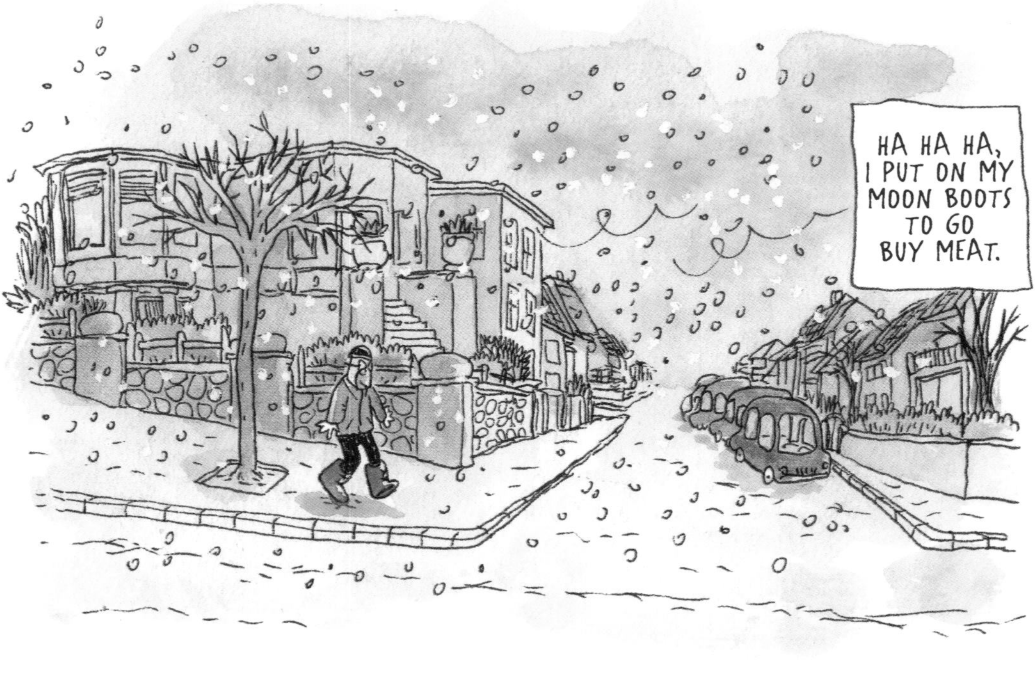
HA HA HA, I PUT ON MY MOON BOOTS TO GO BUY MEAT.

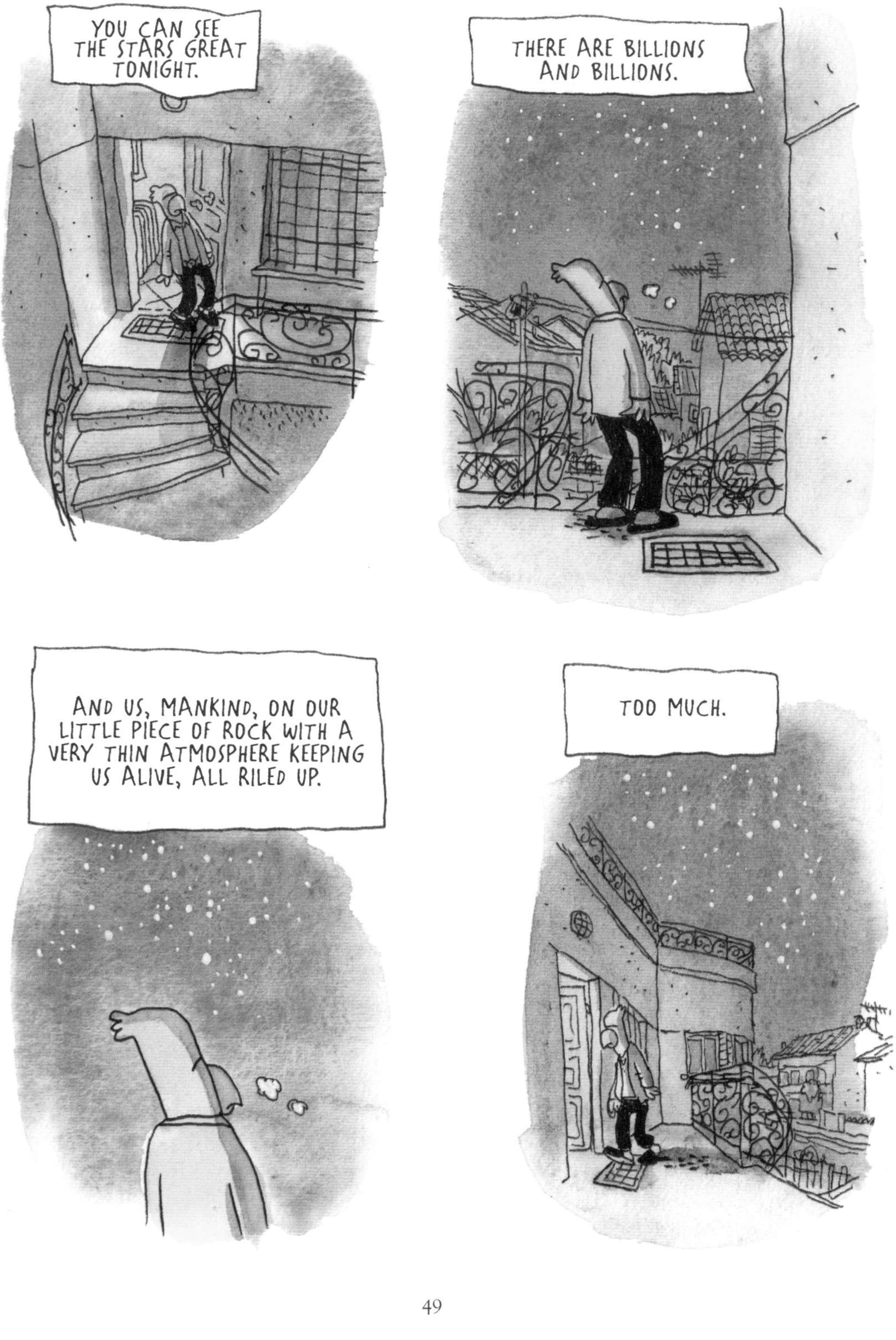
YOU CAN SEE THE STARS GREAT TONIGHT.
THERE ARE BILLIONS AND BILLIONS.
AND US, MANKIND, ON OUR LITTLE PIECE OF ROCK WITH A VERY THIN ATMOSPHERE KEEPING US ALIVE, ALL RILED UP.
TOO MUCH.

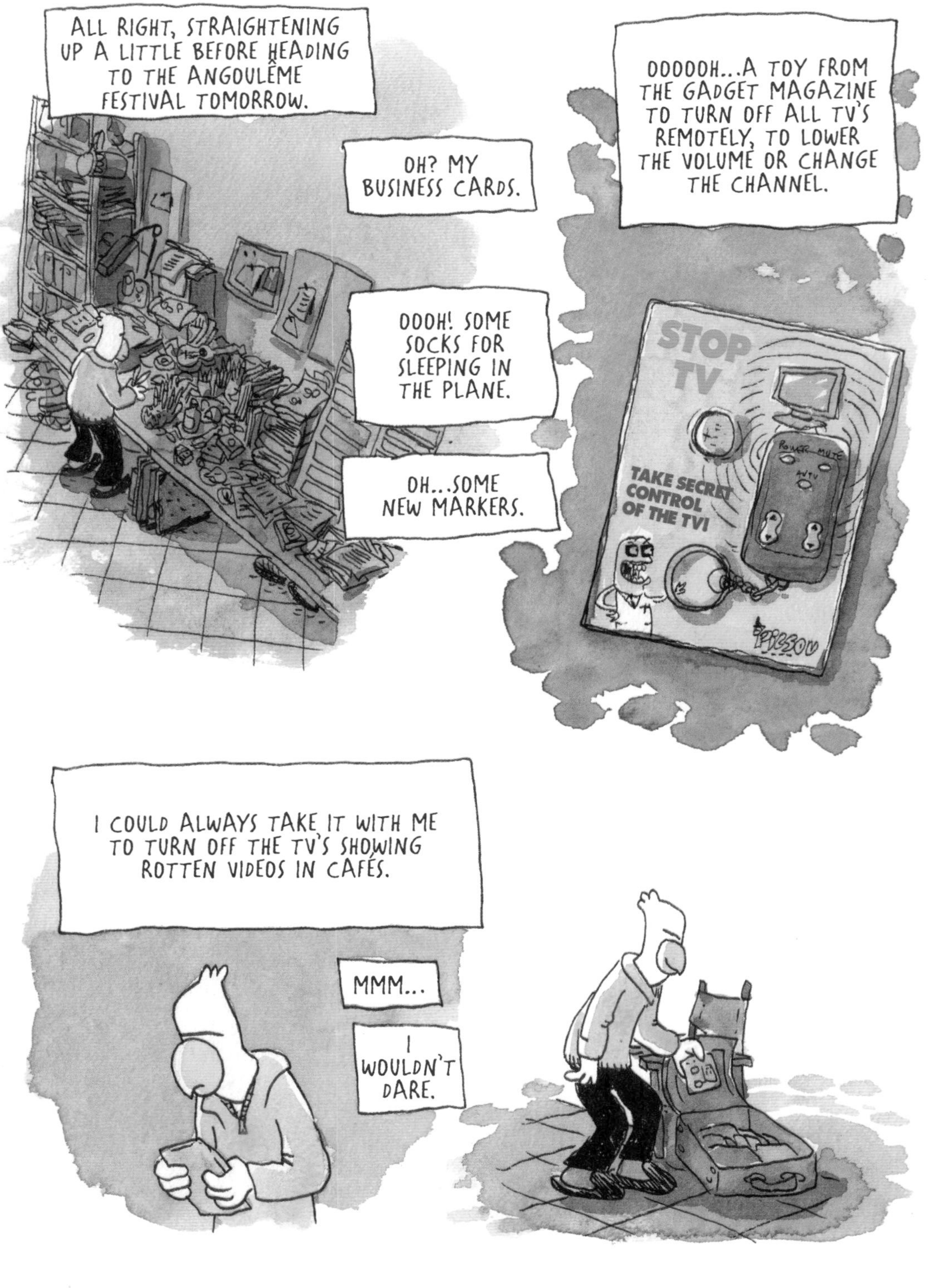
ALL RIGHT, STRAIGHTENING UP A LITTLE BEFORE HEADING TO THE ANGOULÊME FESTIVAL TOMORROW.
OH? MY BUSINESS CARDS.
OOOH! SOME SOCKS FOR SLEEPING IN THE PLANE.
OH...SOME NEW MARKERS.
OOOOOH...A TOY FROM THE GADGET MAGAZINE TO TURN OFF ALL TV'S REMOTELY, TO LOWER THE VOLUME OR CHANGE THE CHANNEL.
STOP TV
TAKE SECRET CONTROL OF THE TV!
I COULD ALWAYS TAKE IT WITH ME TO TURN OFF THE TV'S SHOWING ROTTEN VIDEOS IN CAFÉS.
MMM...
I WOULDN'T DARE.

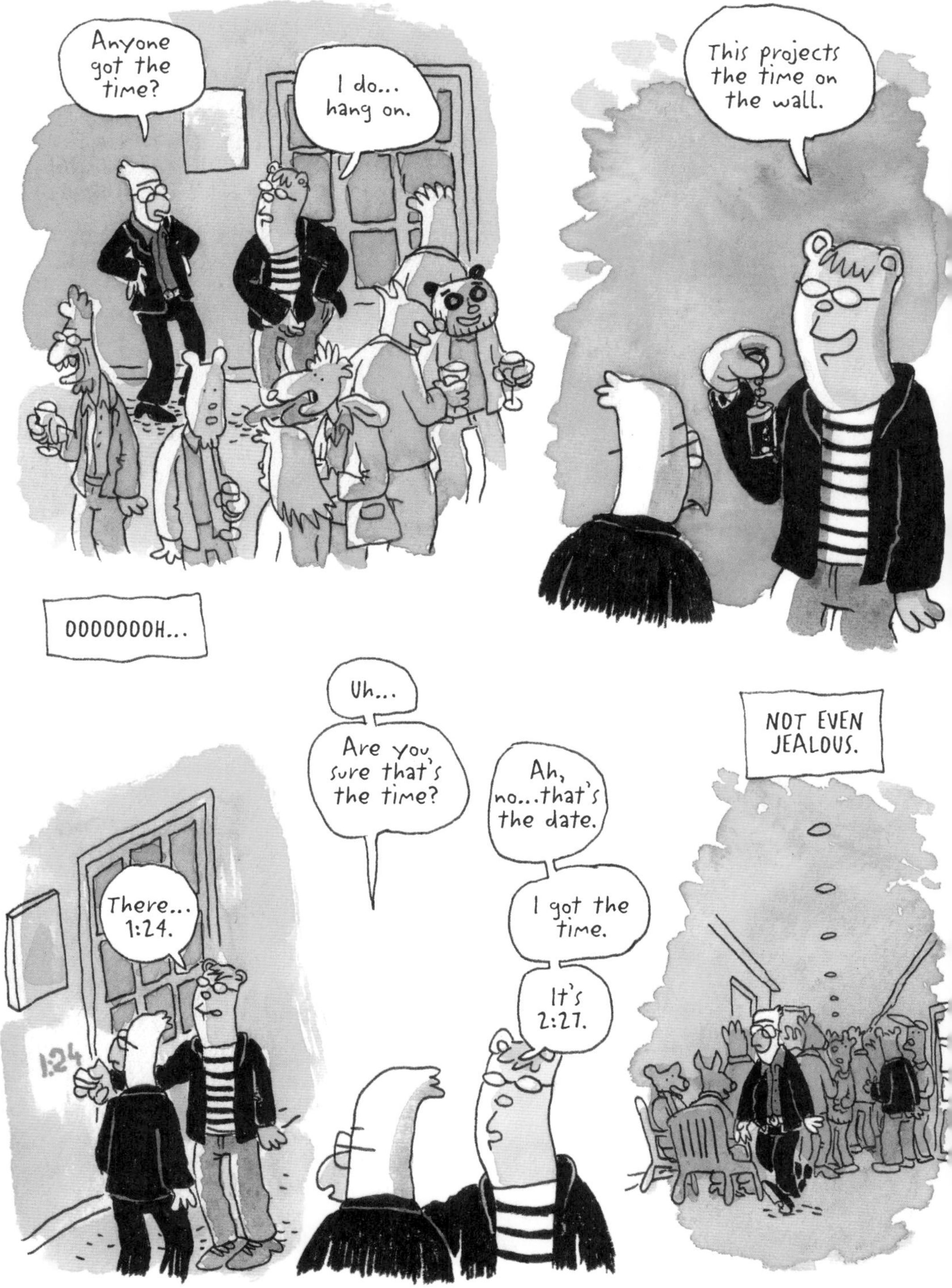
Anyone got the time?
I do... hang on.
This projects the time on the wall.
OOOOOOOH...
There... 1:24.
1:24
Uh...
Are you sure that's the time?
Ah, no...that's the date.
I got the time.
It's 2:27.
NOT EVEN JEALOUS.

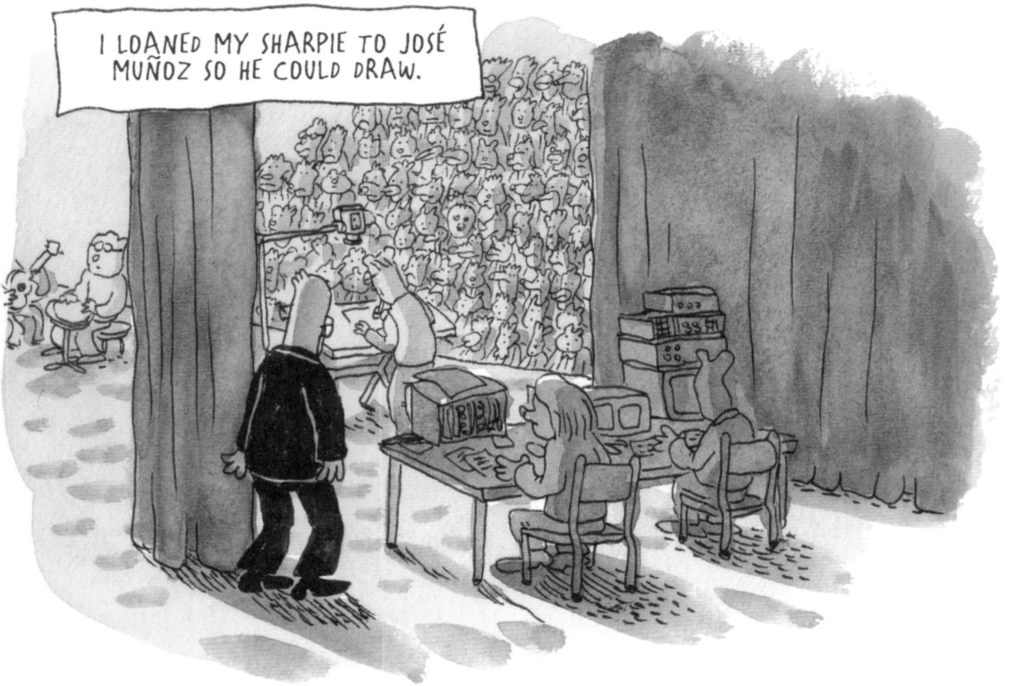
I LOANED MY SHARPIE TO JOSÉ MUÑOZ SO HE COULD DRAW.

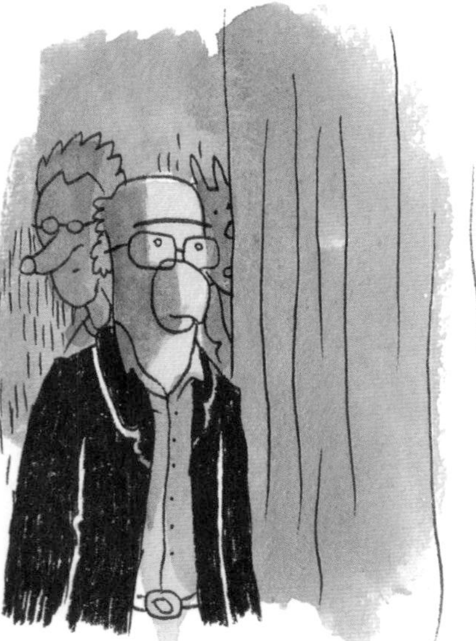

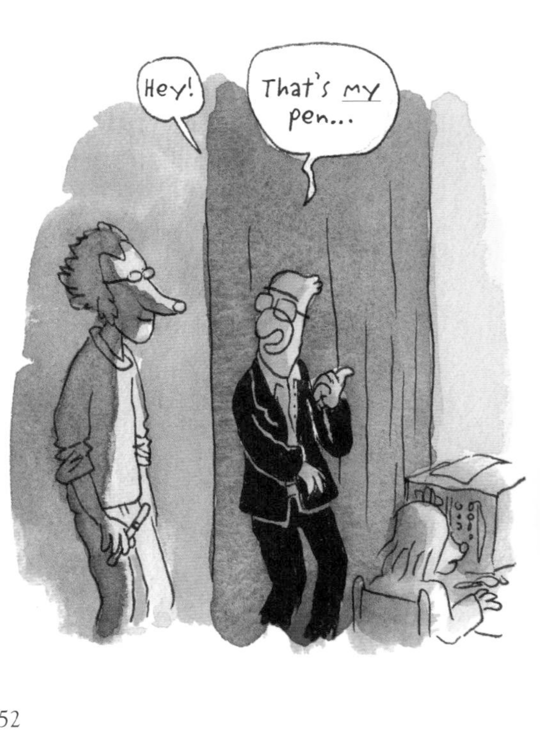
Hey!
That's my pen...

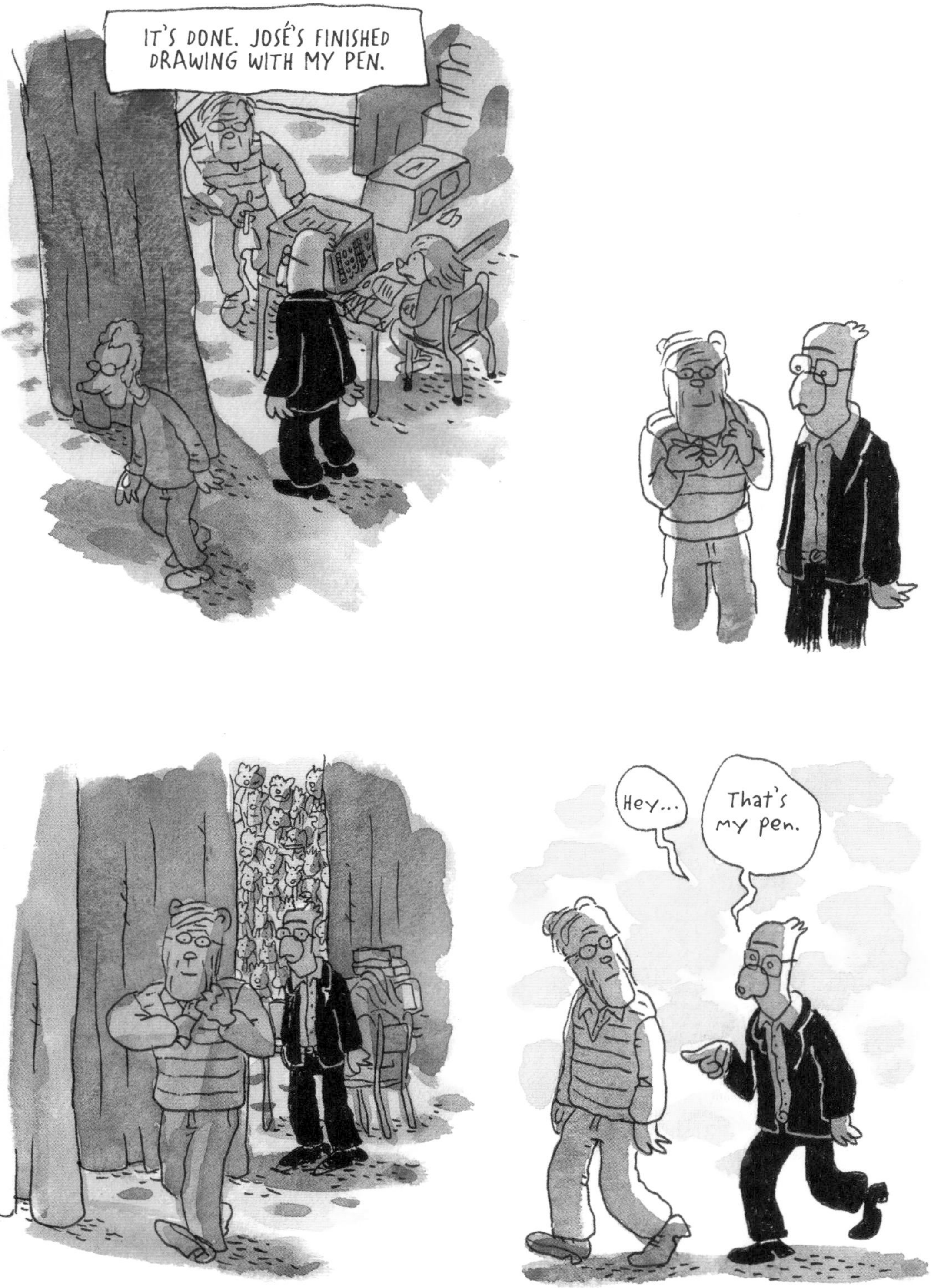
IT'S DONE. JOSÉ'S FINISHED DRAWING WITH MY PEN.
Hey...
That's my pen.

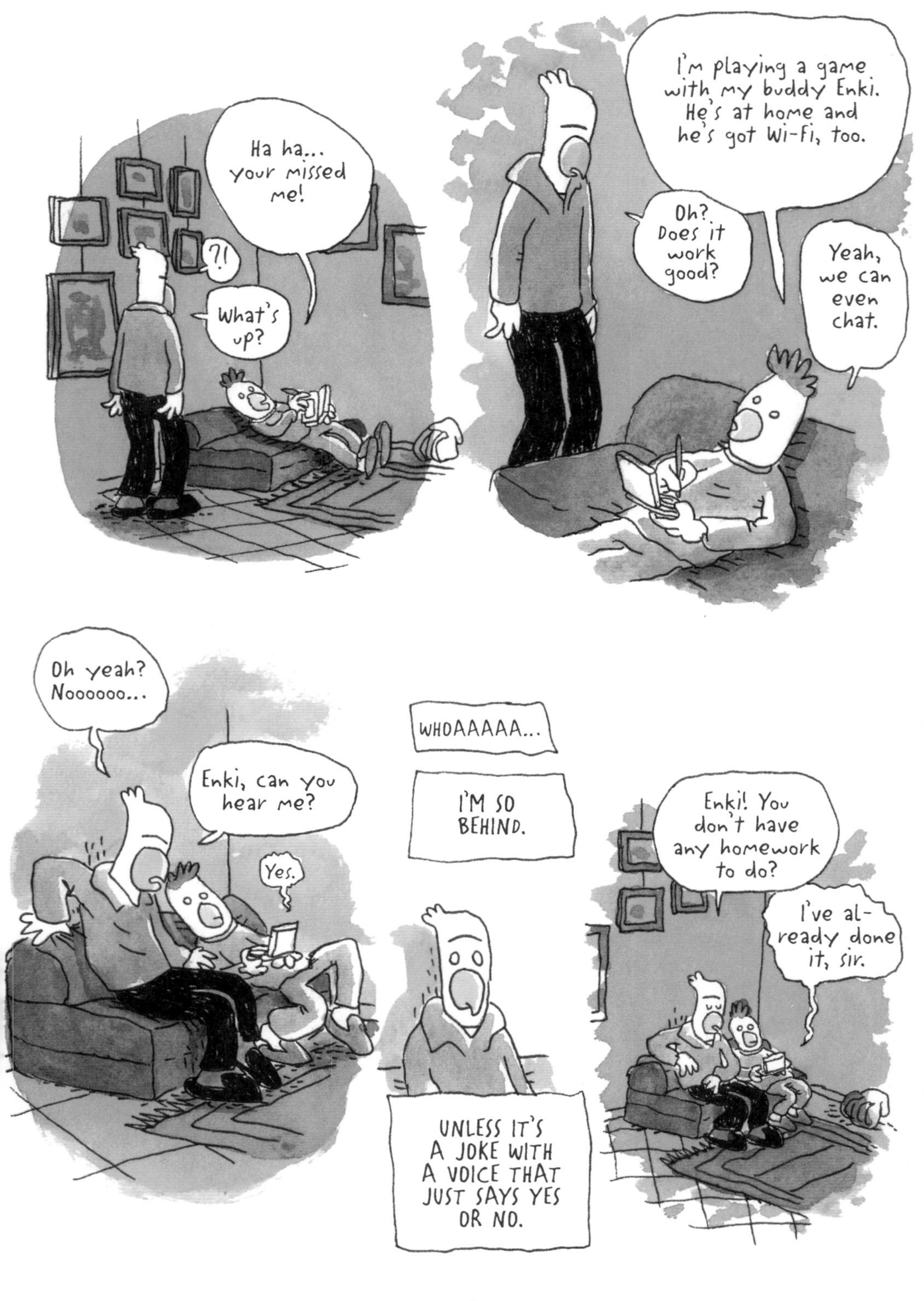
Ha ha... your missed me!
?!
What's up?
I'm playing a game with my buddy Enki. He's at home and he's got Wi-Fi, too.
Oh? Does it work good?
Yeah, we can even chat.
Oh yeah? Noooooo...
Enki, can you hear me?
Yes.
WHOAAAAA...
I'M SO BEHIND.
UNLESS IT'S A JOKE WITH A VOICE THAT JUST SAYS YES OR NO.
Enki! You don't have any homework to do?
I've al-ready done it, sir.

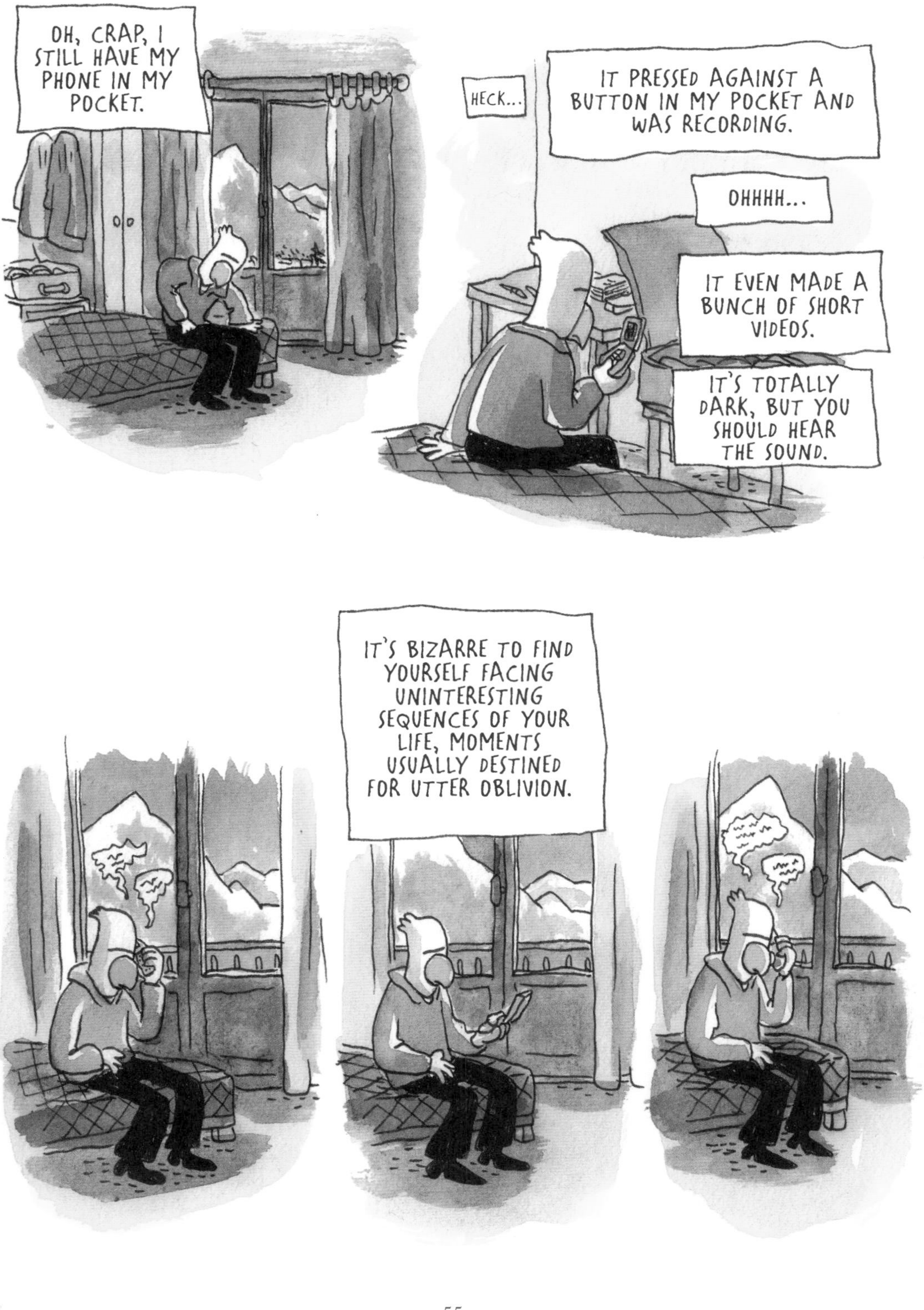
OH, CRAP, I STILL HAVE MY PHONE IN MY POCKET.
HECK...
IT PRESSED AGAINST A BUTTON IN MY POCKET AND WAS RECORDING.
OHHHH...
IT EVEN MADE A BUNCH OF SHORT VIDEOS.
IT'S TOTALLY DARK, BUT YOU SHOULD HEAR THE SOUND.
IT'S BIZARRE TO FIND YOURSELF FACING UNINTERESTING SEQUENCES OF YOUR LIFE, MOMENTS USUALLY DESTINED FOR UTTER OBLIVION.

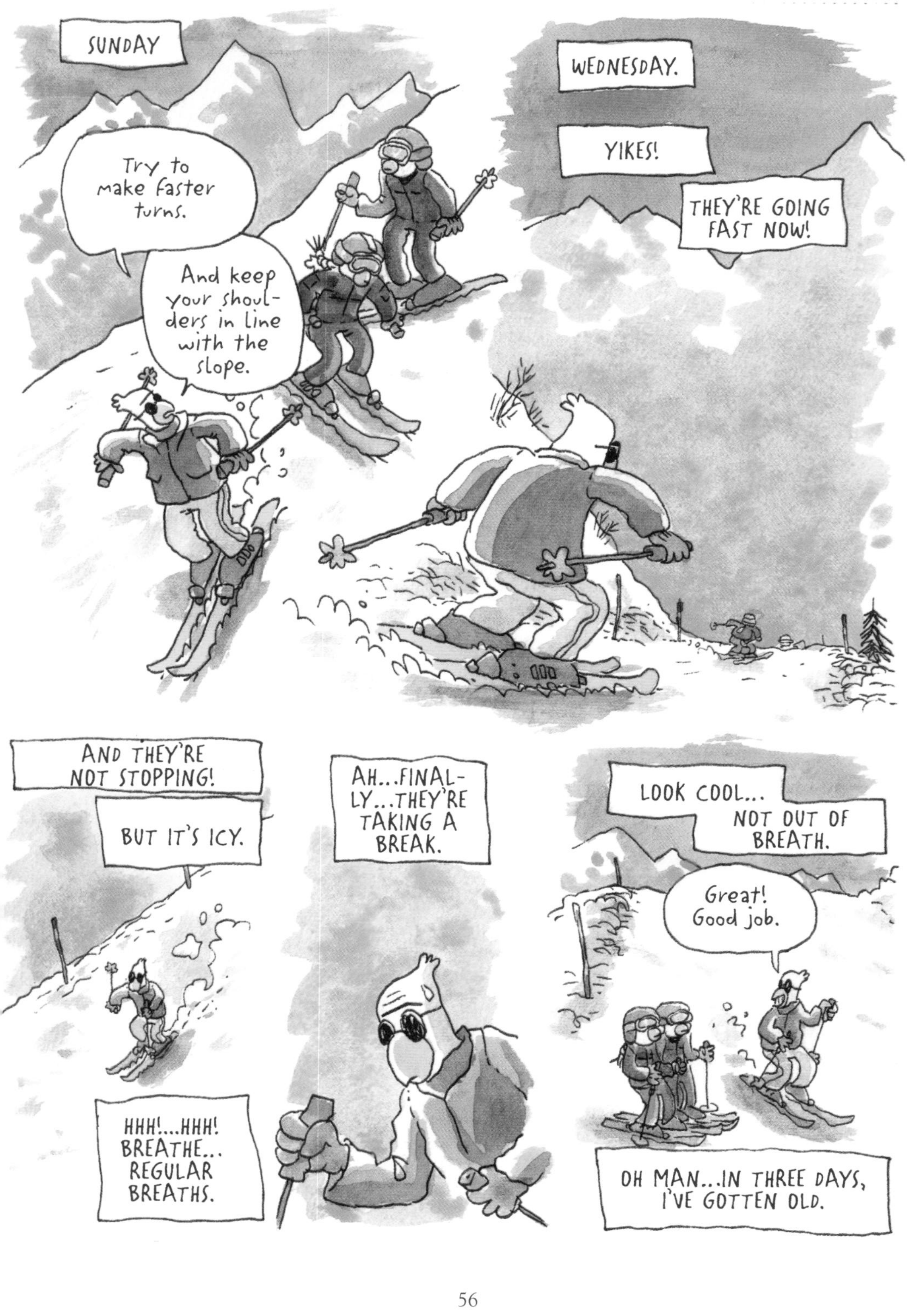
SUNDAY
Try to make faster turns.
And keep your shoulders in line with the slope.
WEDNESDAY.
YIKES!
THEY'RE GOING FAST NOW!
AND THEY'RE NOT STOPPING!
BUT IT'S ICY.
HHH!...HHH! BREATHE... REGULAR BREATHS.
AH...FINALLY...THEY'RE TAKING A BREAK.
LOOK COOL...
NOT OUT OF BREATH.
Great! Good job.
OH MAN...IN THREE DAYS, I'VE GOTTEN OLD.

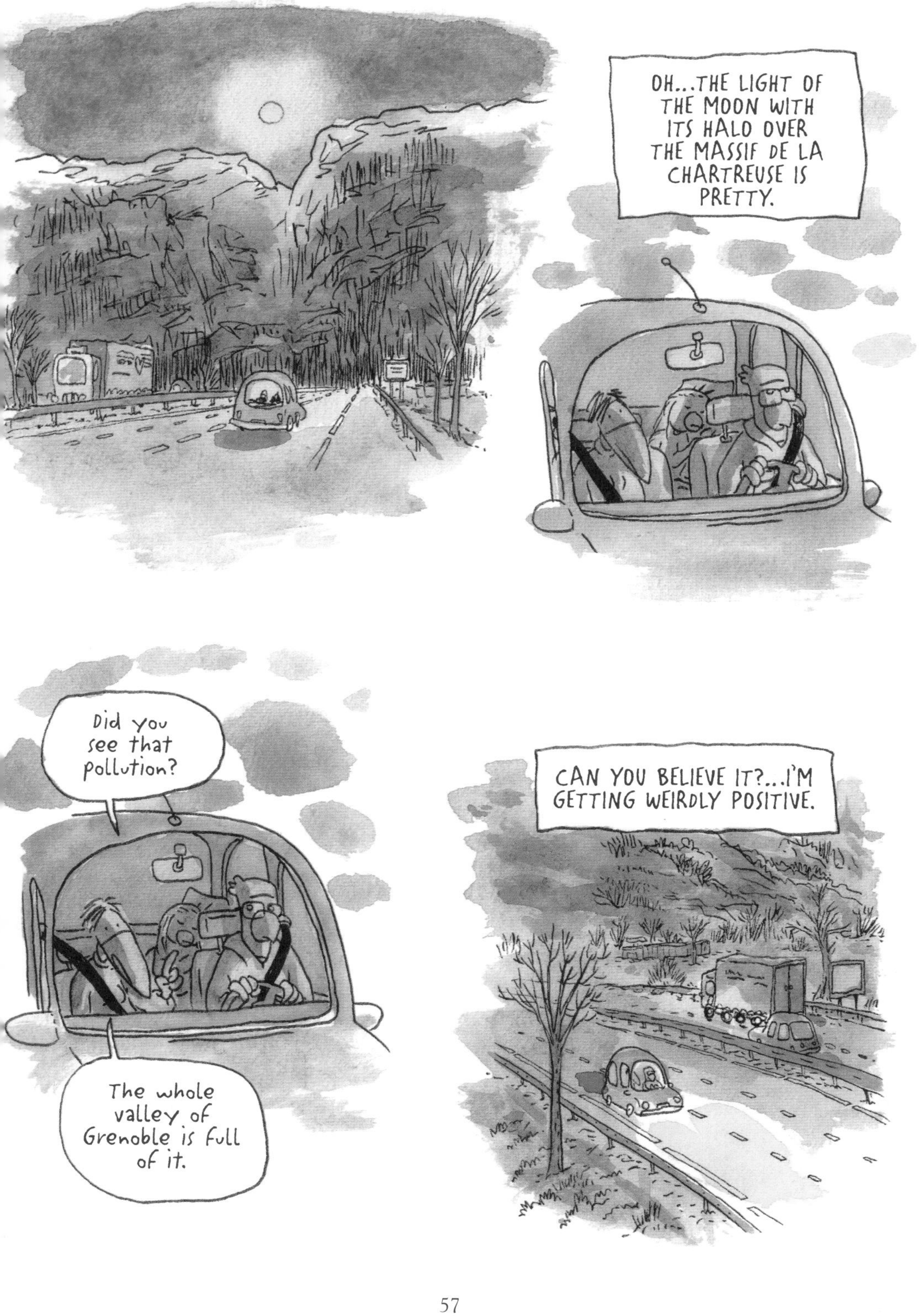
OH...THE LIGHT OF THE MOON WITH ITS HALO OVER THE MASSIF DE LA CHARTREUSE IS PRETTY.
Did you see that pollution?
The whole valley of Grenoble is full of it.
CAN YOU BELIEVE IT?...I'M GETTING WEIRDLY POSITIVE.

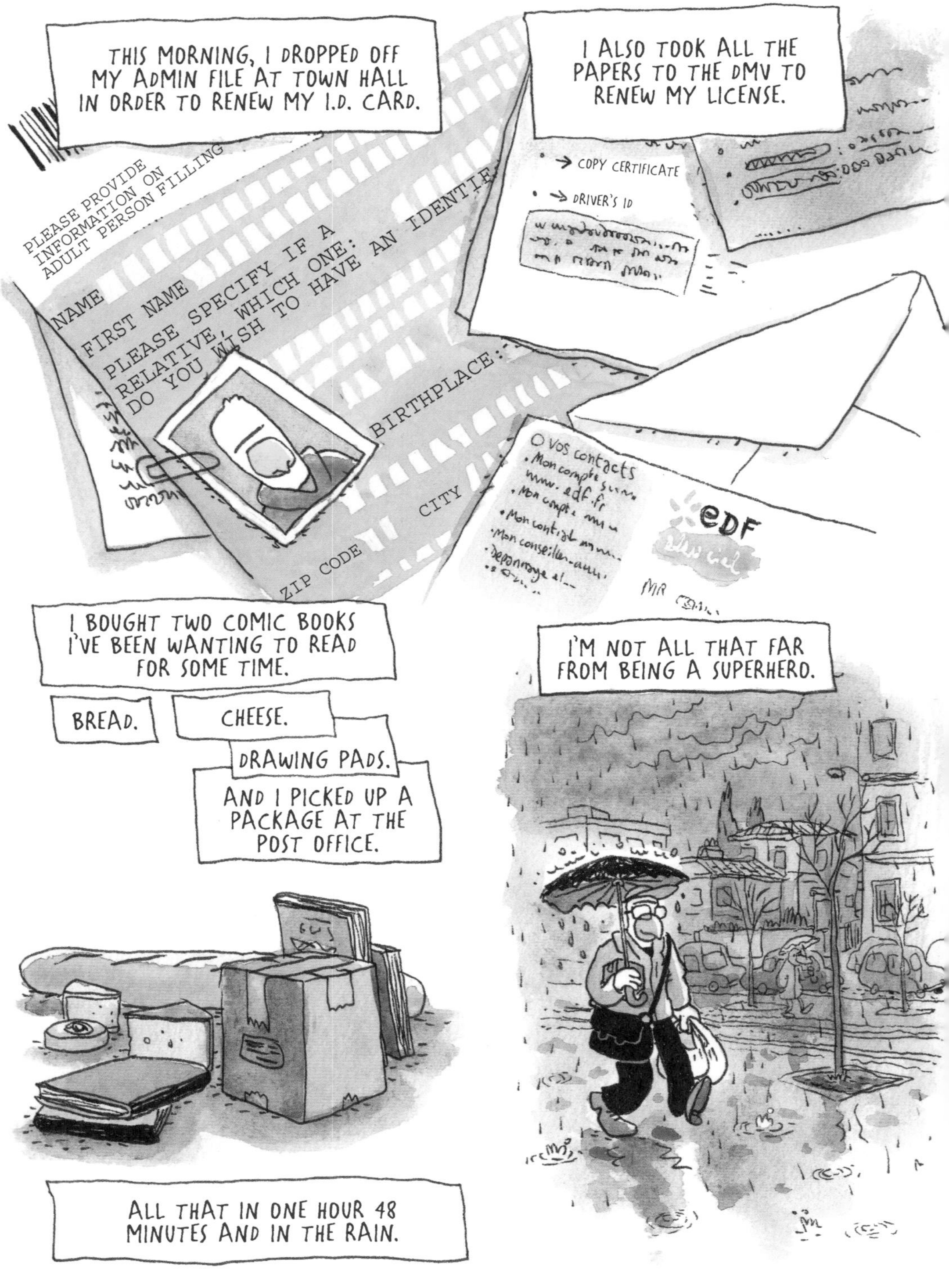
THIS MORNING, I DROPPED OFF MY ADMIN FILE AT TOWN HALL IN ORDER TO RENEW MY I.D. CARD.
PLEASE PROVIDE INFORMATION ON ADULT PERSON FILLING
NAME
FIRST NAME
PLEASE SPECIFY IF A RELATIVE, WHICH ONE:
DO YOU WISH TO HAVE AN IDENTIE
BIRTHPLACE:
CITY
ZIP CODE
I ALSO TOOK ALL THE PAPERS TO THE DMV TO RENEW MY LICENSE.
→ COPY CERTIFICATE
→ DRIVER'S ID
Vos contacts
• Mon compte
www.edf.fr
edf
MR
I BOUGHT TWO COMIC BOOKS I'VE BEEN WANTING TO READ FOR SOME TIME.
BREAD.
CHEESE.
DRAWING PADS.
AND I PICKED UP A PACKAGE AT THE POST OFFICE.
ALL THAT IN ONE HOUR 48 MINUTES AND IN THE RAIN.
I'M NOT ALL THAT FAR FROM BEING A SUPERHERO.

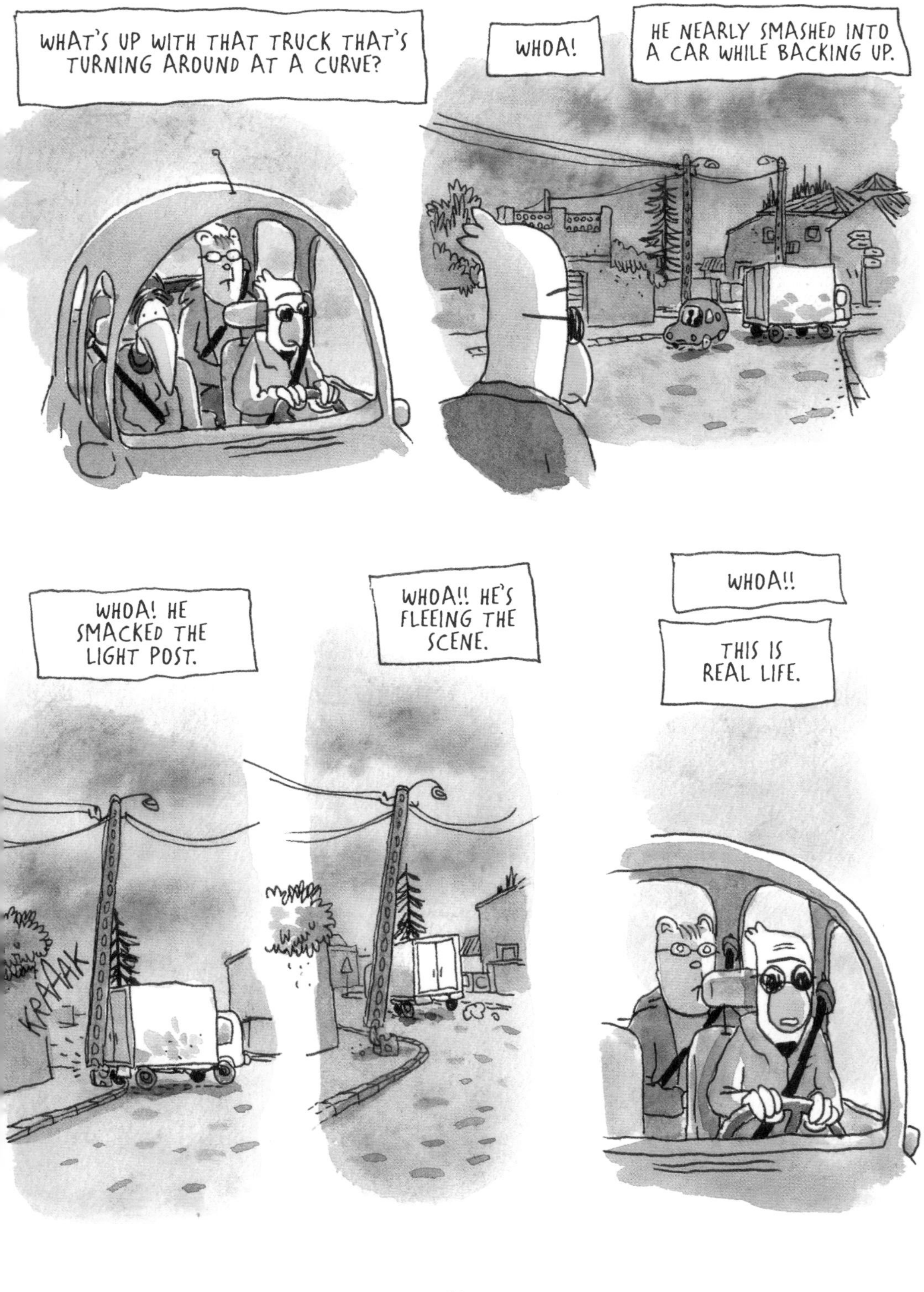
WHAT'S UP WITH THAT TRUCK THAT'S TURNING AROUND AT A CURVE?
WHOA!
HE NEARLY SMASHED INTO A CAR WHILE BACKING UP.
WHOA! HE SMACKED THE LIGHT POST.
KRAAAK
WHOA!! HE'S FLEEING THE SCENE.
WHOA!!
THIS IS REAL LIFE.

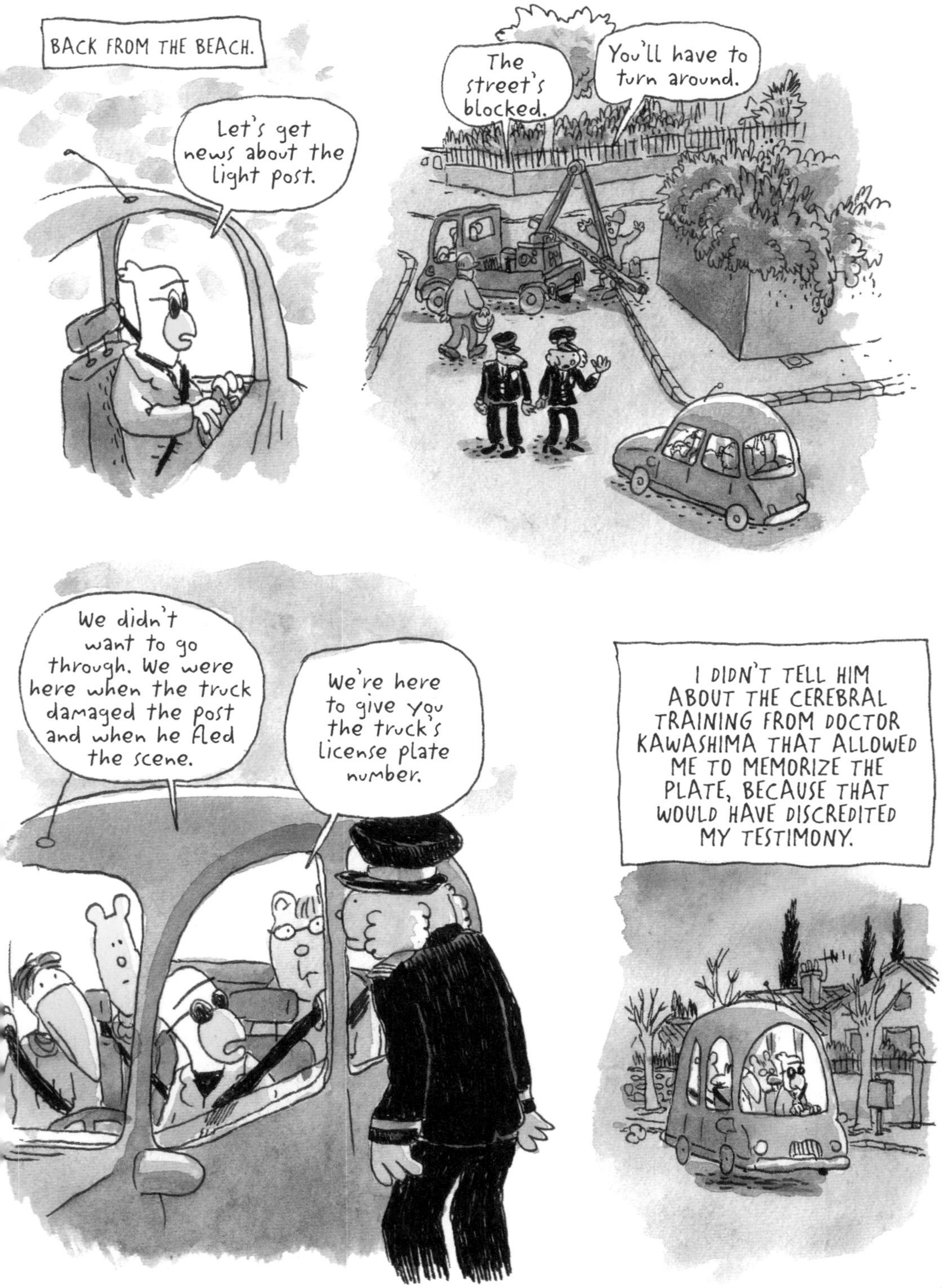
BACK FROM THE BEACH.
Let's get news about the light post.
The street's blocked.
You'll have to turn around.
We didn't want to go through. We were here when the truck damaged the post and when he fled the scene.
We're here to give you the truck's license plate number.
I DIDN'T TELL HIM ABOUT THE CEREBRAL TRAINING FROM DOCTOR KAWASHIMA THAT ALLOWED ME TO MEMORIZE THE PLATE, BECAUSE THAT WOULD HAVE DISCREDITED MY TESTIMONY.

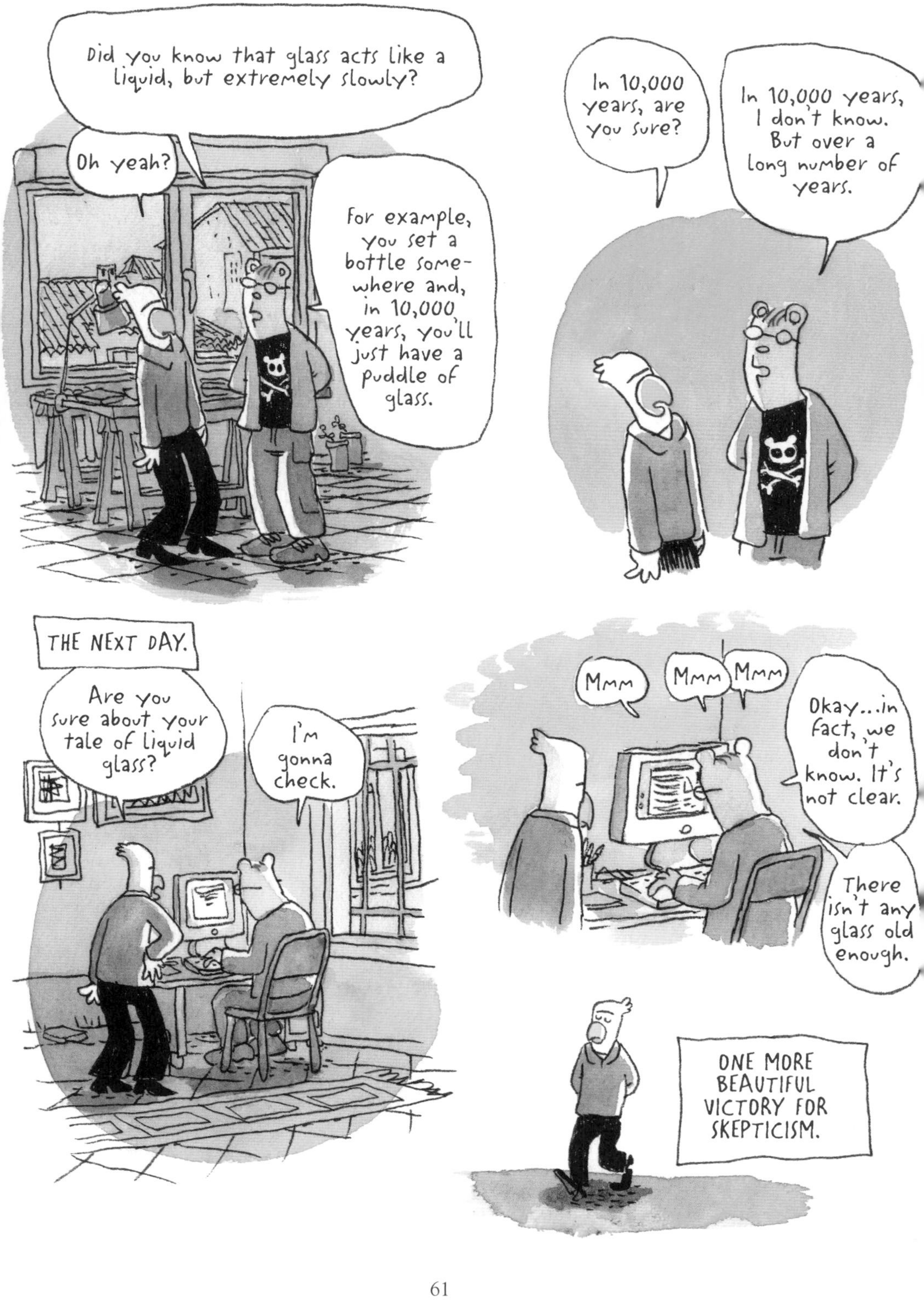

Did you know that glass acts like a liquid, but extremely slowly?
Oh yeah?
For example, you set a bottle somewhere and, in 10,000 years, you'll just have a puddle of glass.
In 10,000 years, are you sure?
In 10,000 years, I don't know. But over a long number of years.
THE NEXT DAY.
Are you sure about your tale of liquid glass?
I'm gonna check.
Mmm
Mmm
Mmm
Okay...in fact, we don't know. It's not clear.
There isn't any glass old enough.
ONE MORE BEAUTIFUL VICTORY FOR SKEPTICISM.

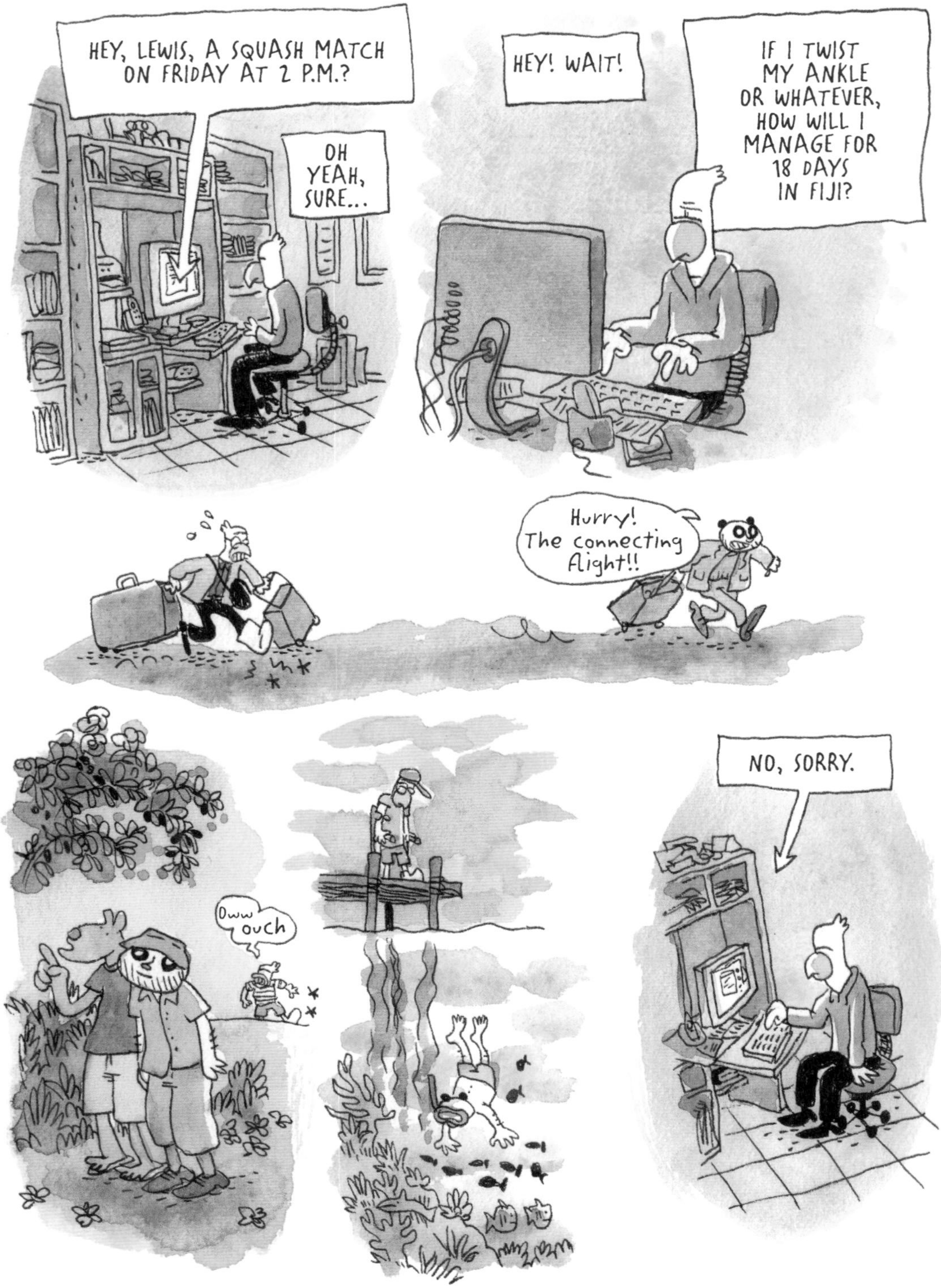
HEY, LEWIS, A SQUASH MATCH ON FRIDAY AT 2 P.M.?
OH YEAH, SURE...
HEY! WAIT!
IF I TWIST MY ANKLE OR WHATEVER, HOW WILL I MANAGE FOR 18 DAYS IN FIJI?
Hurry! The connecting flight!!
Oww ouch
NO, SORRY.

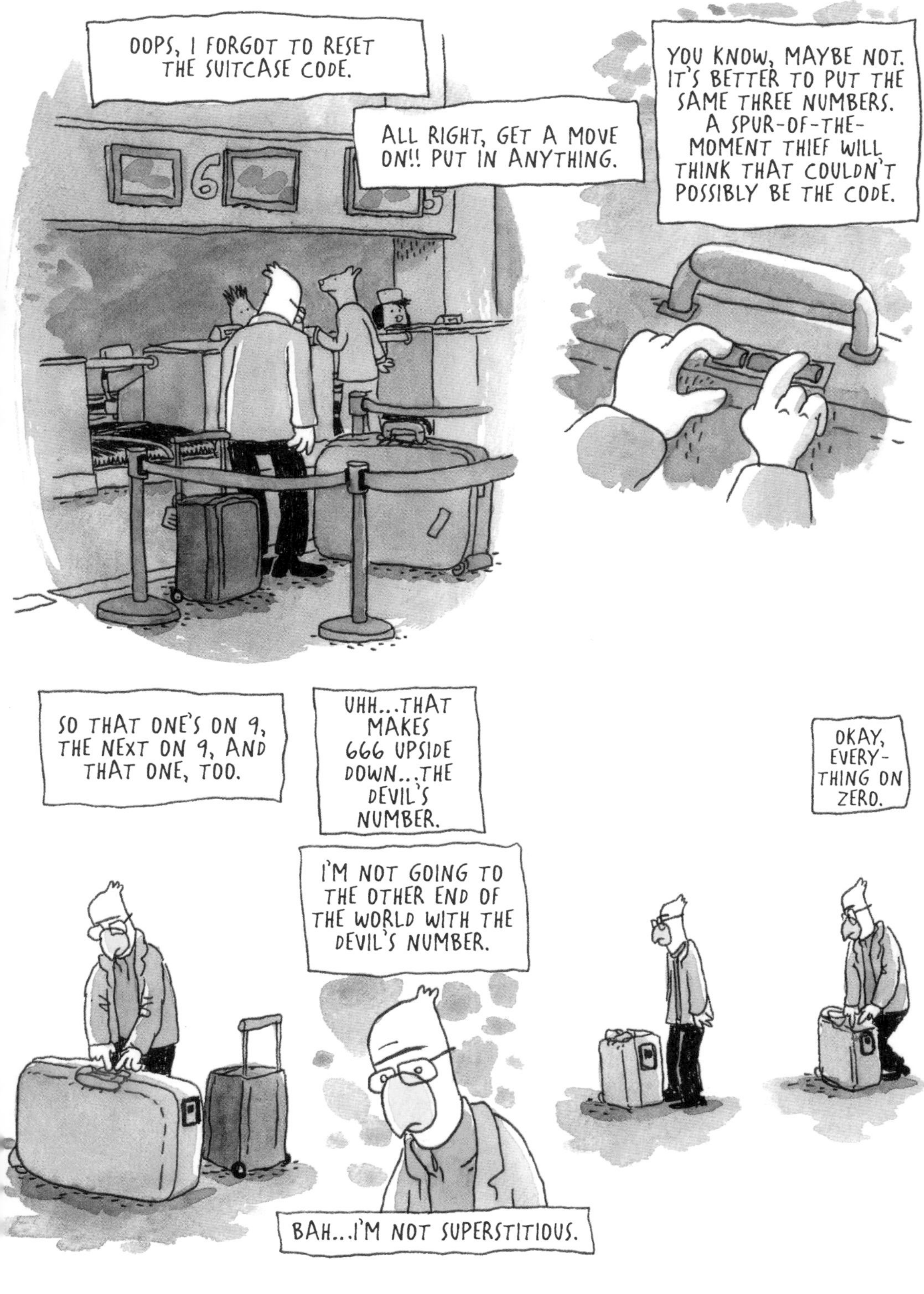
OOPS, I FORGOT TO RESET THE SUITCASE CODE.
ALL RIGHT, GET A MOVE ON!! PUT IN ANYTHING.
YOU KNOW, MAYBE NOT. IT'S BETTER TO PUT THE SAME THREE NUMBERS. A SPUR-OF-THE-MOMENT THIEF WILL THINK THAT COULDN'T POSSIBLY BE THE CODE.
SO THAT ONE'S ON 9, THE NEXT ON 9, AND THAT ONE, TOO.
UHH...THAT MAKES 666 UPSIDE DOWN...THE DEVIL'S NUMBER.
I'M NOT GOING TO THE OTHER END OF THE WORLD WITH THE DEVIL'S NUMBER.
BAH...I'M NOT SUPERSTITIOUS.
OKAY, EVERY-THING ON ZERO.

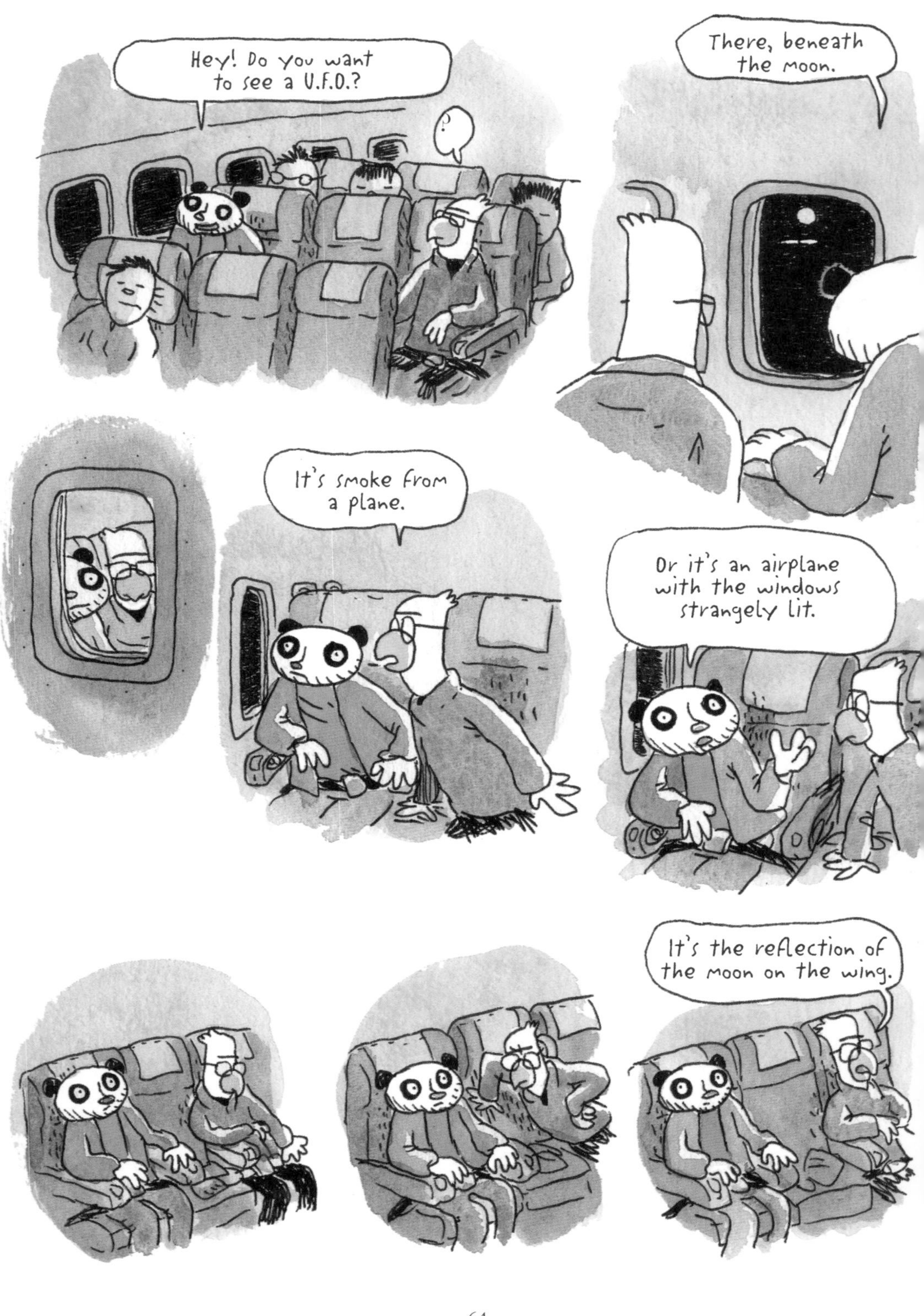
Hey! Do you want to see a U.F.O.?
?
There, beneath the moon.
It's smoke from a plane.
Or it's an airplane with the windows strangely lit.
It's the reflection of the moon on the wing.

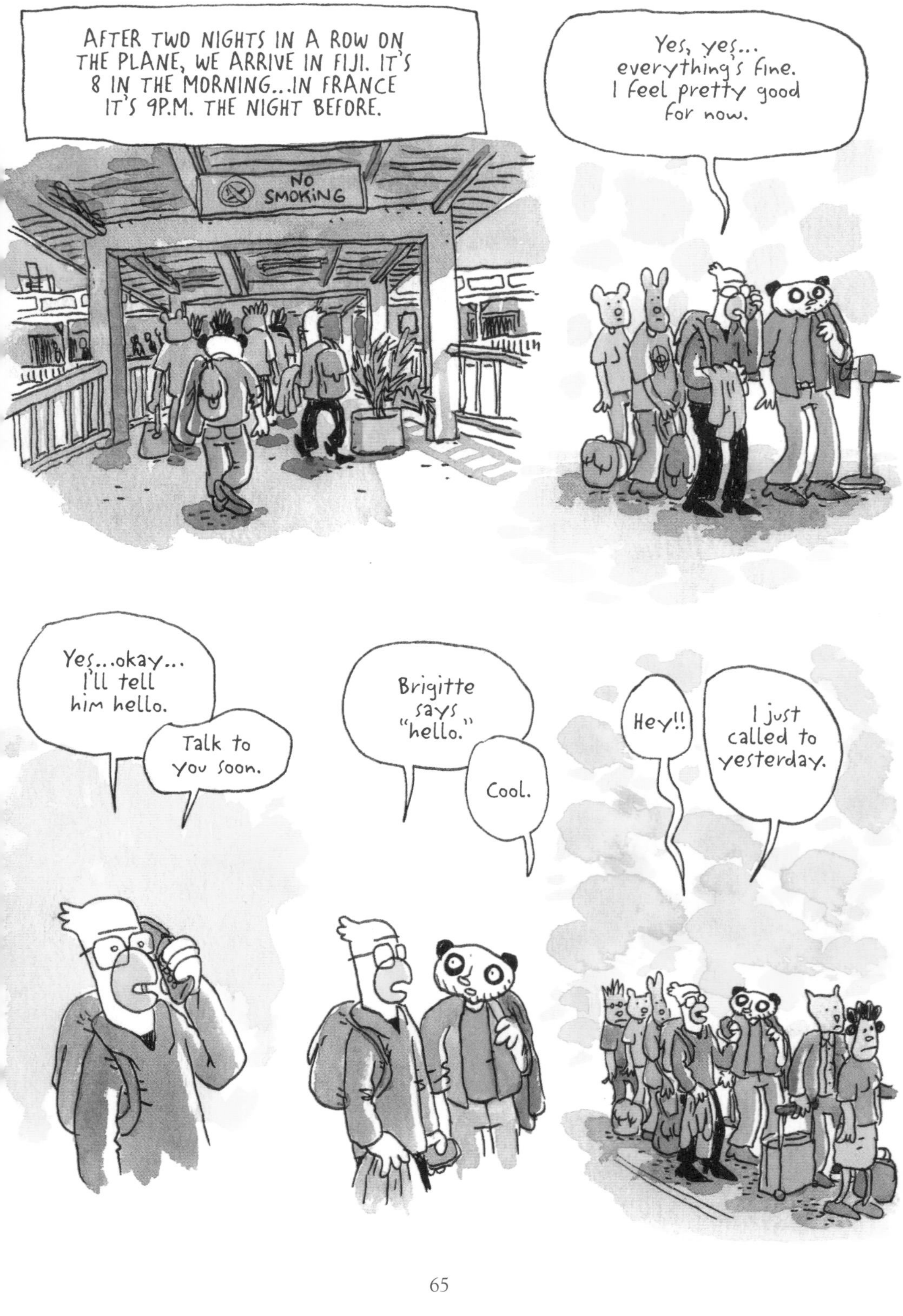
AFTER TWO NIGHTS IN A ROW ON THE PLANE, WE ARRIVE IN FIJI. IT'S 8 IN THE MORNING...IN FRANCE IT'S 9P.M. THE NIGHT BEFORE.
NO SMOKING
Yes, yes... everything's fine. I feel pretty good for now.
Yes...okay... I'll tell him hello.
Talk to you soon.
Brigitte says "hello."
Cool.
Hey!!
I just called to yesterday.

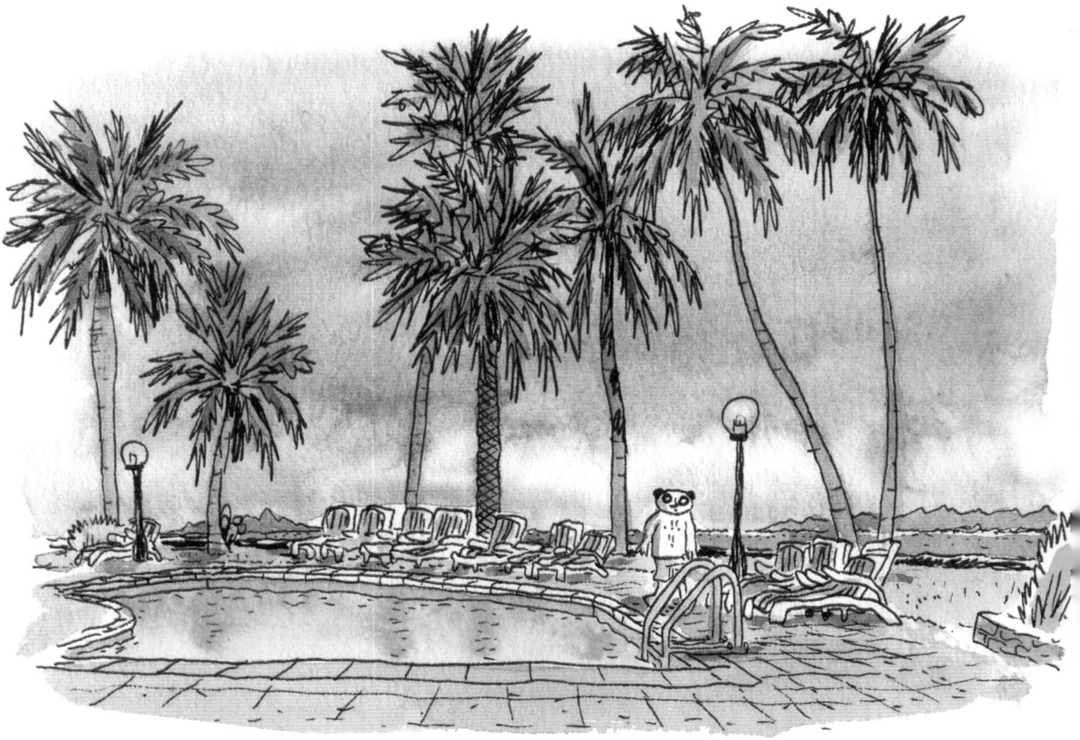

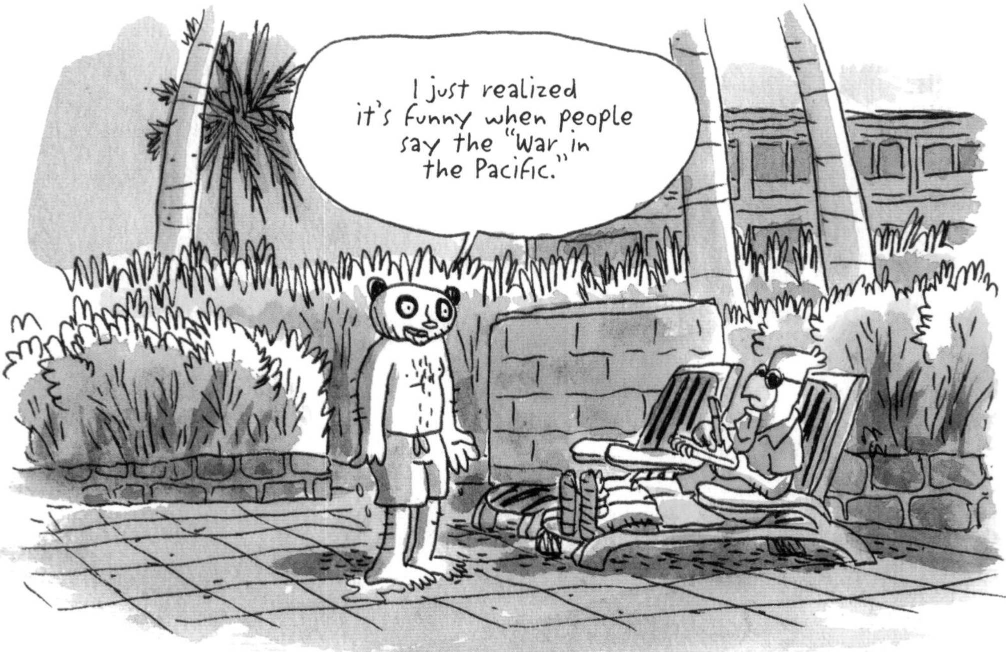
I just realized it's funny when people say the "War in the Pacific."

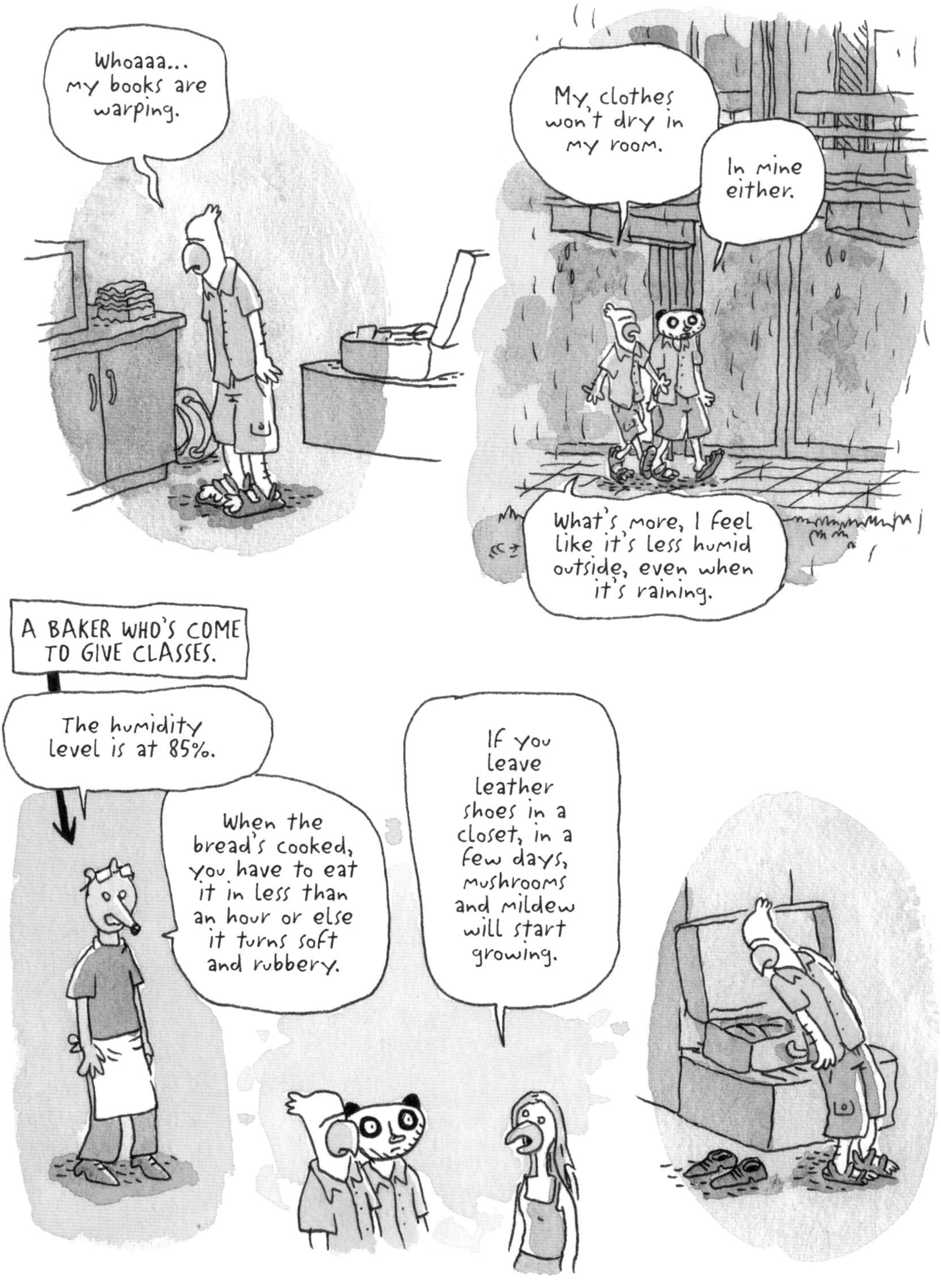
Whoaaa... my books are warping.
My clothes won't dry in my room.
In mine either.
What's more, I feel like it's less humid outside, even when it's raining.
A BAKER WHO'S COME TO GIVE CLASSES.
The humidity level is at 85%.
When the bread's cooked, you have to eat it in less than an hour or else it turns soft and rubbery.
If you leave leather shoes in a closet, in a few days, mushrooms and mildew will start growing.

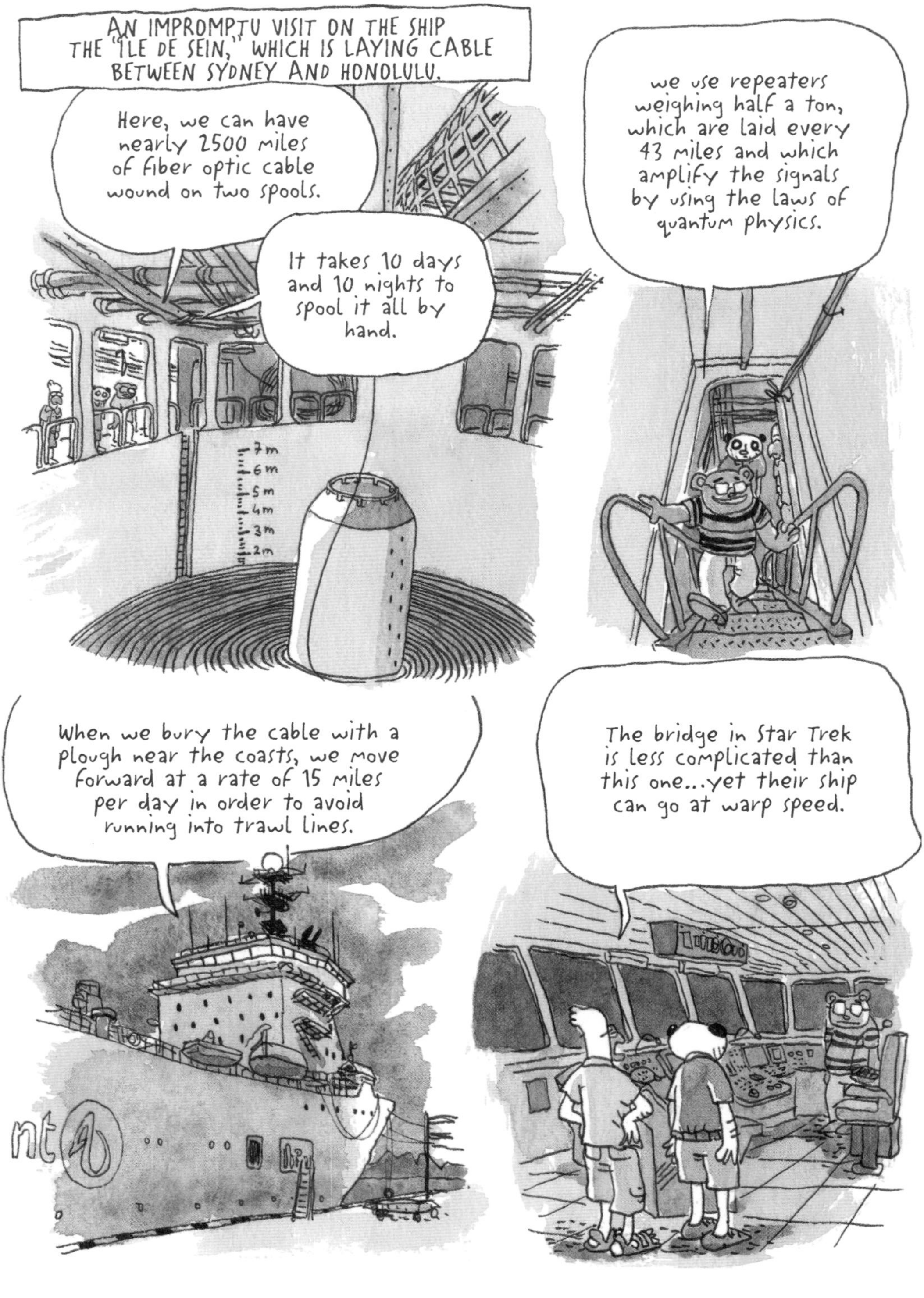
AN IMPROMPTU VISIT ON THE SHIP THE "ÎLE DE SEIN," WHICH IS LAYING CABLE BETWEEN SYDNEY AND HONOLULU.
Here, we can have nearly 2500 miles of fiber optic cable wound on two spools.
It takes 10 days and 10 nights to spool it all by hand.
7m
6m
5m
4m
3m
2m
we use repeaters weighing half a ton, which are laid every 43 miles and which amplify the signals by using the laws of quantum physics.
When we bury the cable with a plough near the coasts, we move forward at a rate of 15 miles per day in order to avoid running into trawl lines.
The bridge in Star Trek is less complicated than this one...yet their ship can go at warp speed.

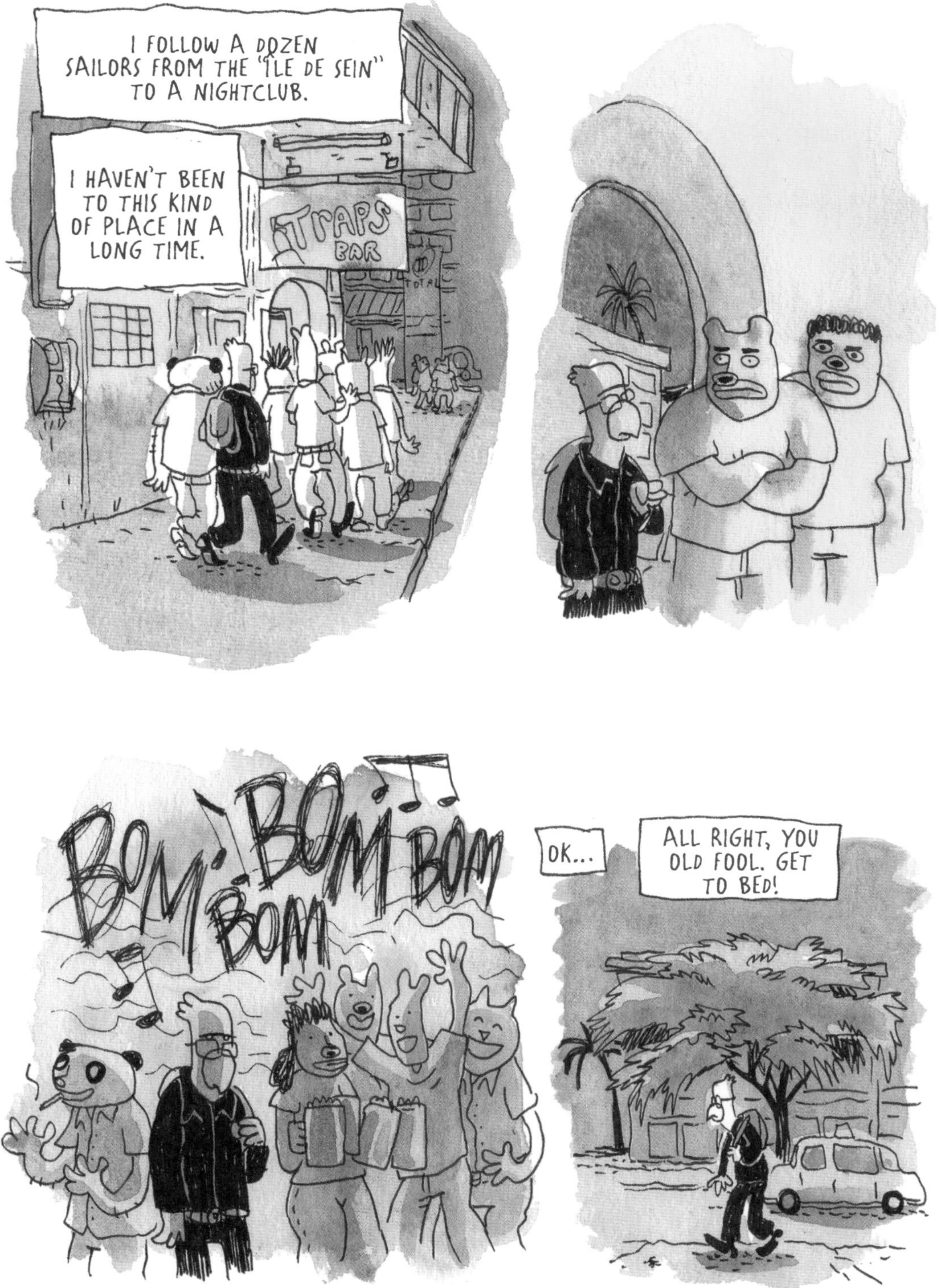
I FOLLOW A DOZEN SAILORS FROM THE "ÎLE DE SEIN" TO A NIGHTCLUB.
I HAVEN'T BEEN TO THIS KIND OF PLACE IN A LONG TIME.
TRAPS BAR
TOTAL
BOM BOM BOM BOM BOM
OK...
ALL RIGHT, YOU OLD FOOL. GET TO BED!

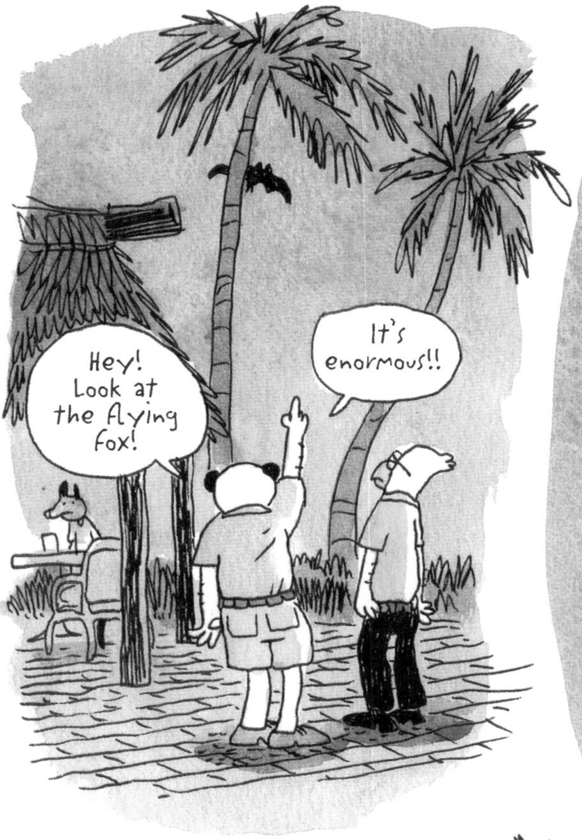
Hey! Look at the flying fox!
It's enormous!!

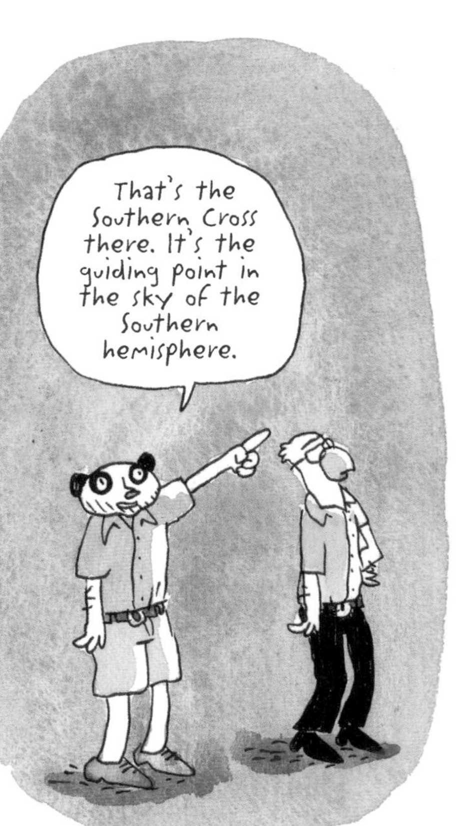
That's the Southern Cross there. It's the guiding point in the sky of the Southern hemisphere.

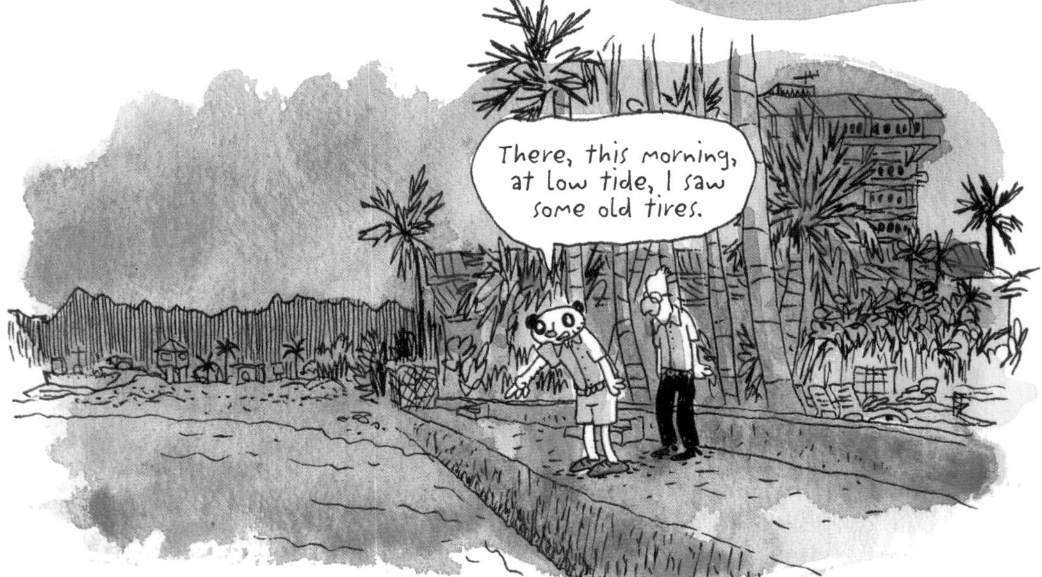
There, this morning, at low tide, I saw some old tires.

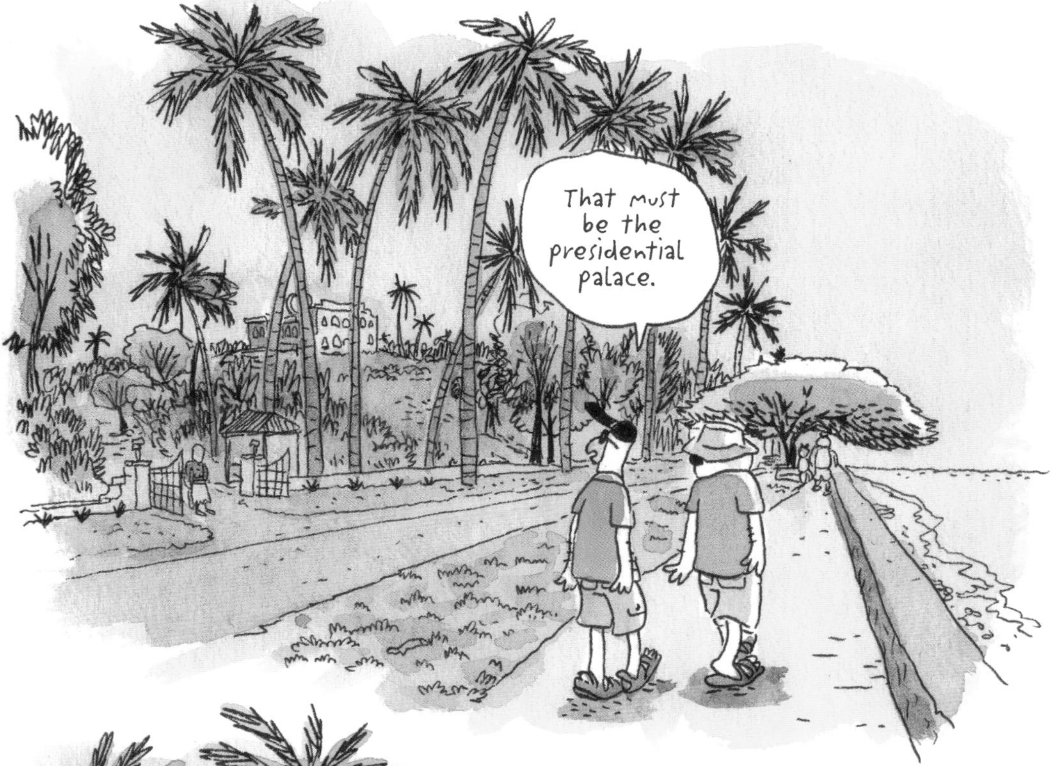
That must be the presidential palace.

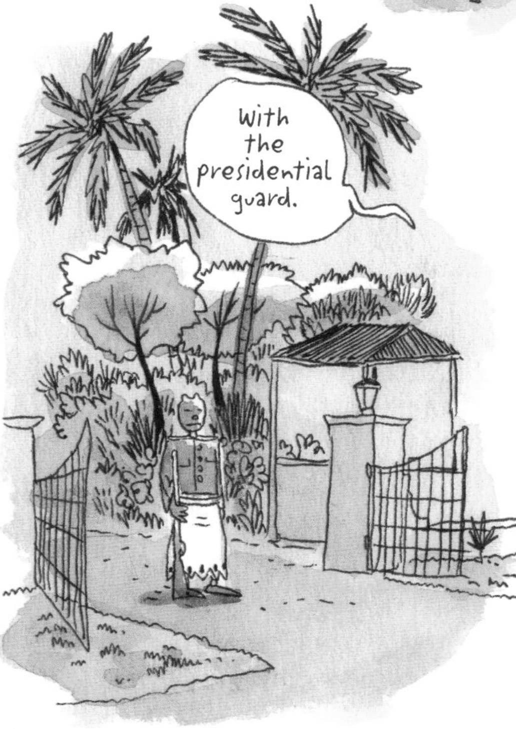
With the presidential guard.

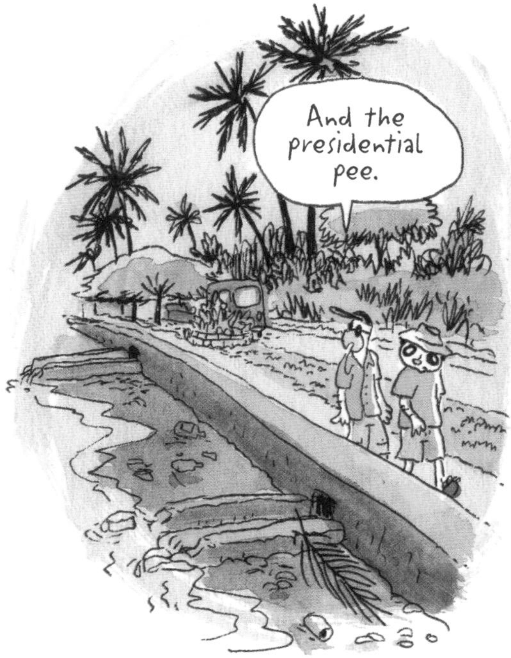
And the presidential pee.

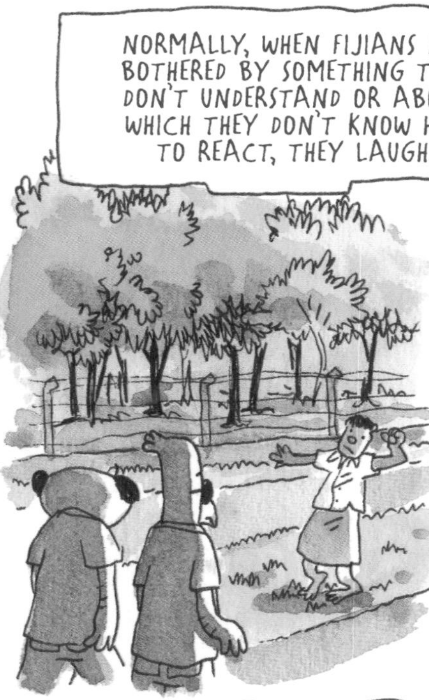
NORMALLY, WHEN FIJIANS ARE BOTHERED BY SOMETHING THEY DON'T UNDERSTAND OR ABOUT WHICH THEY DON'T KNOW HOW TO REACT, THEY LAUGH.

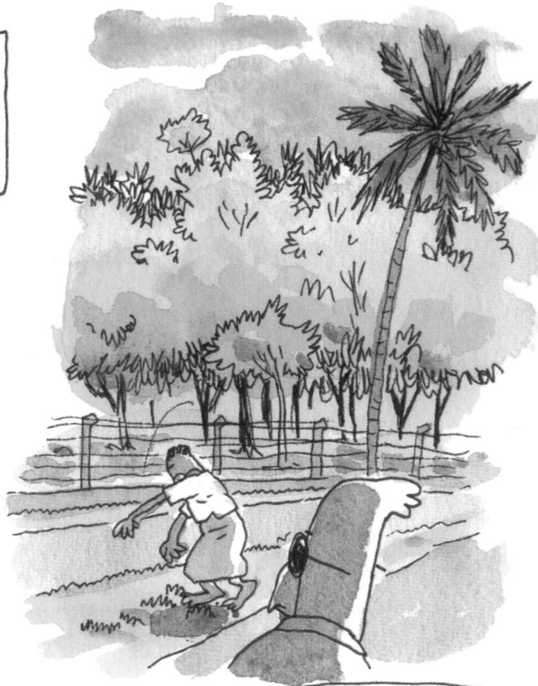

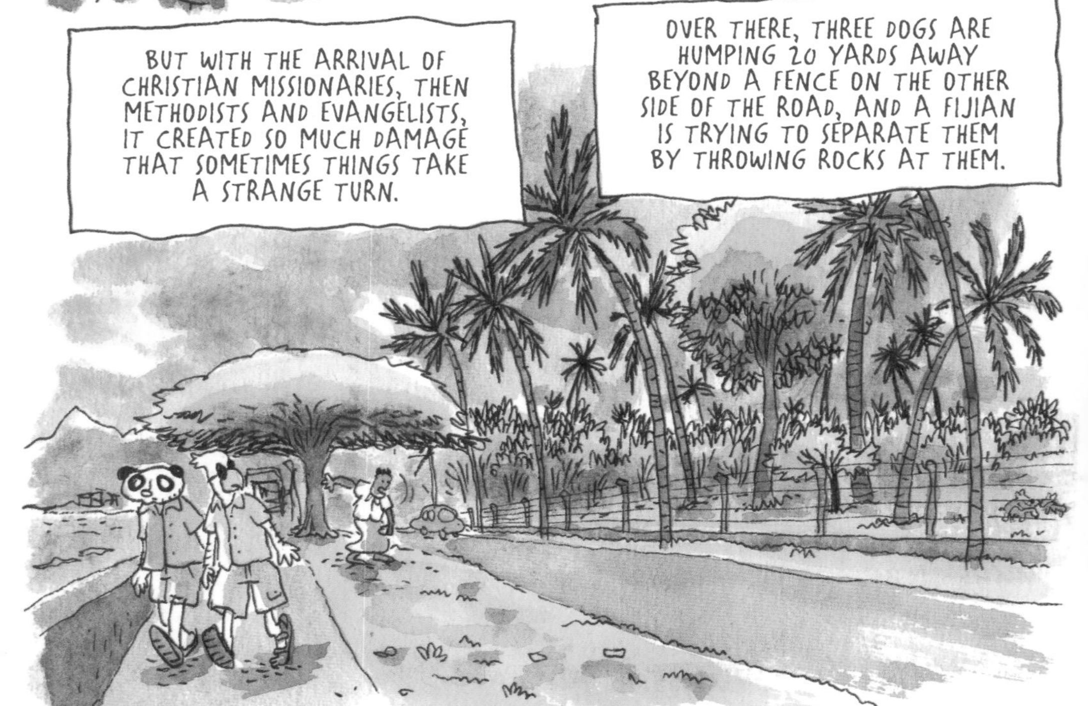
BUT WITH THE ARRIVAL OF CHRISTIAN MISSIONARIES, THEN METHODISTS AND EVANGELISTS, IT CREATED SO MUCH DAMAGE THAT SOMETIMES THINGS TAKE A STRANGE TURN.
OVER THERE, THREE DOGS ARE HUMPING 20 YARDS AWAY BEYOND A FENCE ON THE OTHER SIDE OF THE ROAD, AND A FIJIAN IS TRYING TO SEPARATE THEM BY THROWING ROCKS AT THEM.

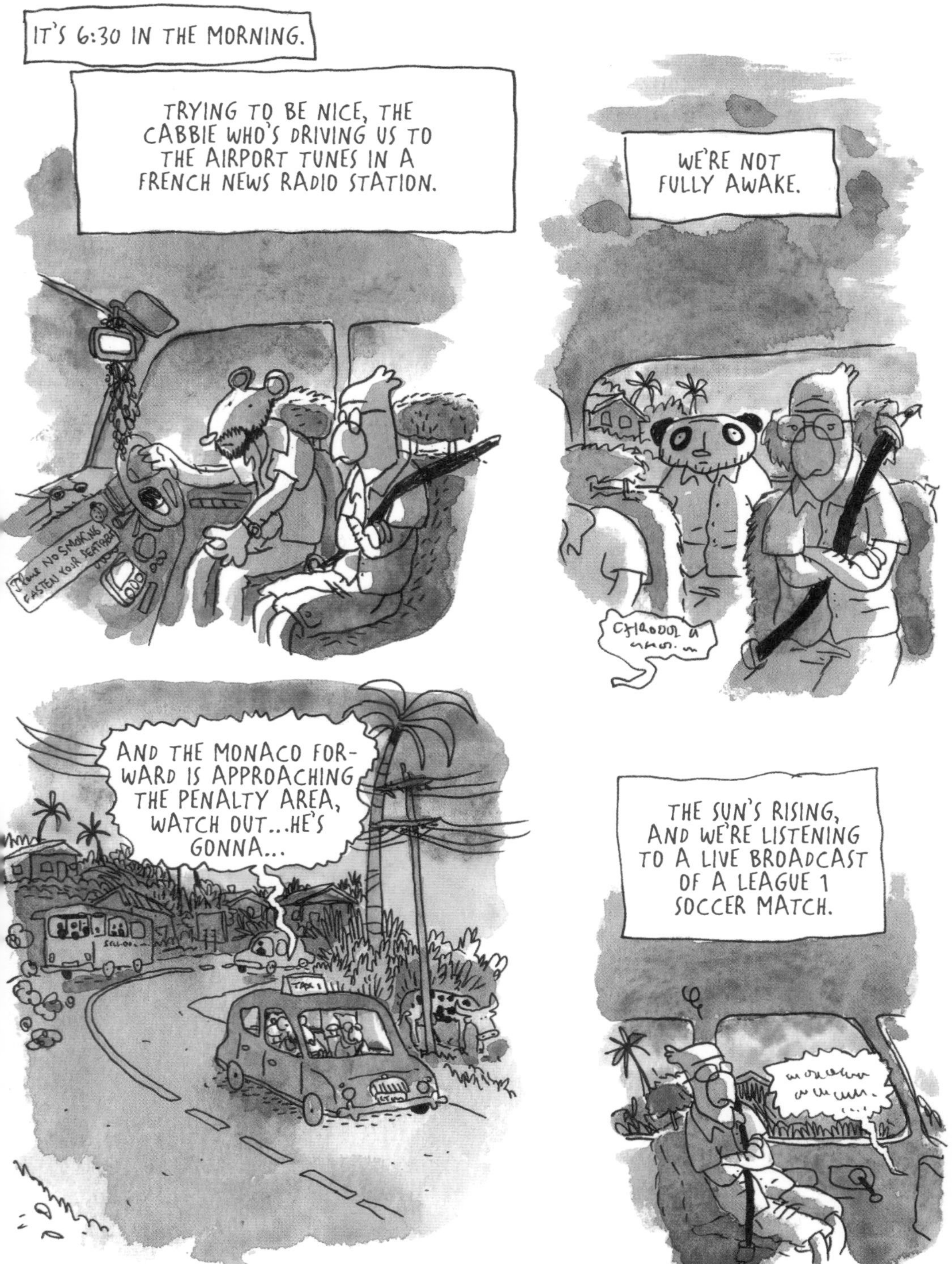
IT'S 6:30 IN THE MORNING.
TRYING TO BE NICE, THE CABBIE WHO'S DRIVING US TO THE AIRPORT TUNES IN A FRENCH NEWS RADIO STATION.
WE'RE NOT FULLY AWAKE.
AND THE MONACO FOR-WARD IS APPROACHING THE PENALTY AREA, WATCH OUT...HE'S GONNA...
THE SUN'S RISING, AND WE'RE LISTENING TO A LIVE BROADCAST OF A LEAGUE 1 SOCCER MATCH.

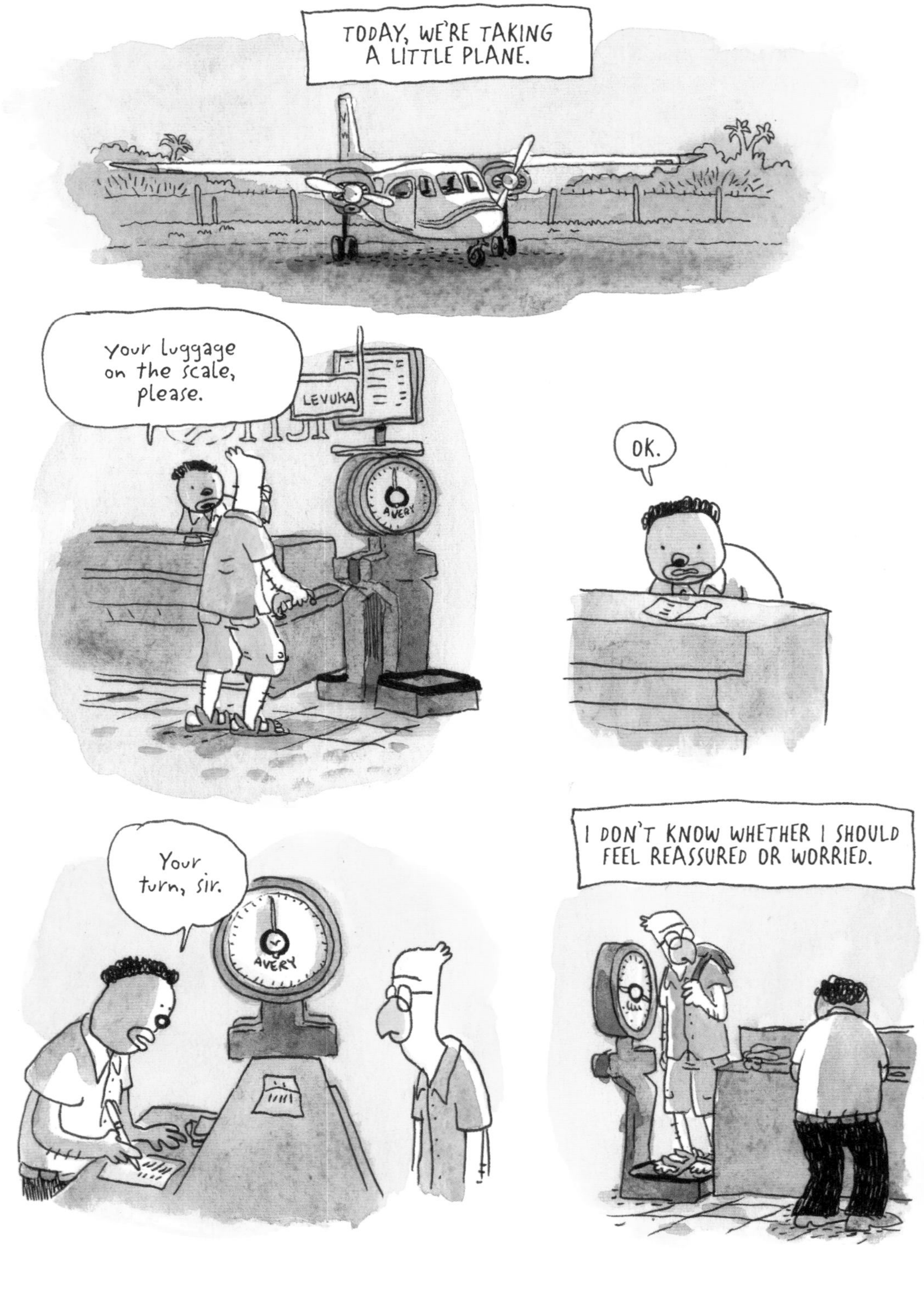
TODAY, WE'RE TAKING A LITTLE PLANE.
Your luggage on the scale, please.
LEVUKA
AVERY
OK.
Your turn, sir.
AVERY
I DON'T KNOW WHETHER I SHOULD FEEL REASSURED OR WORRIED.

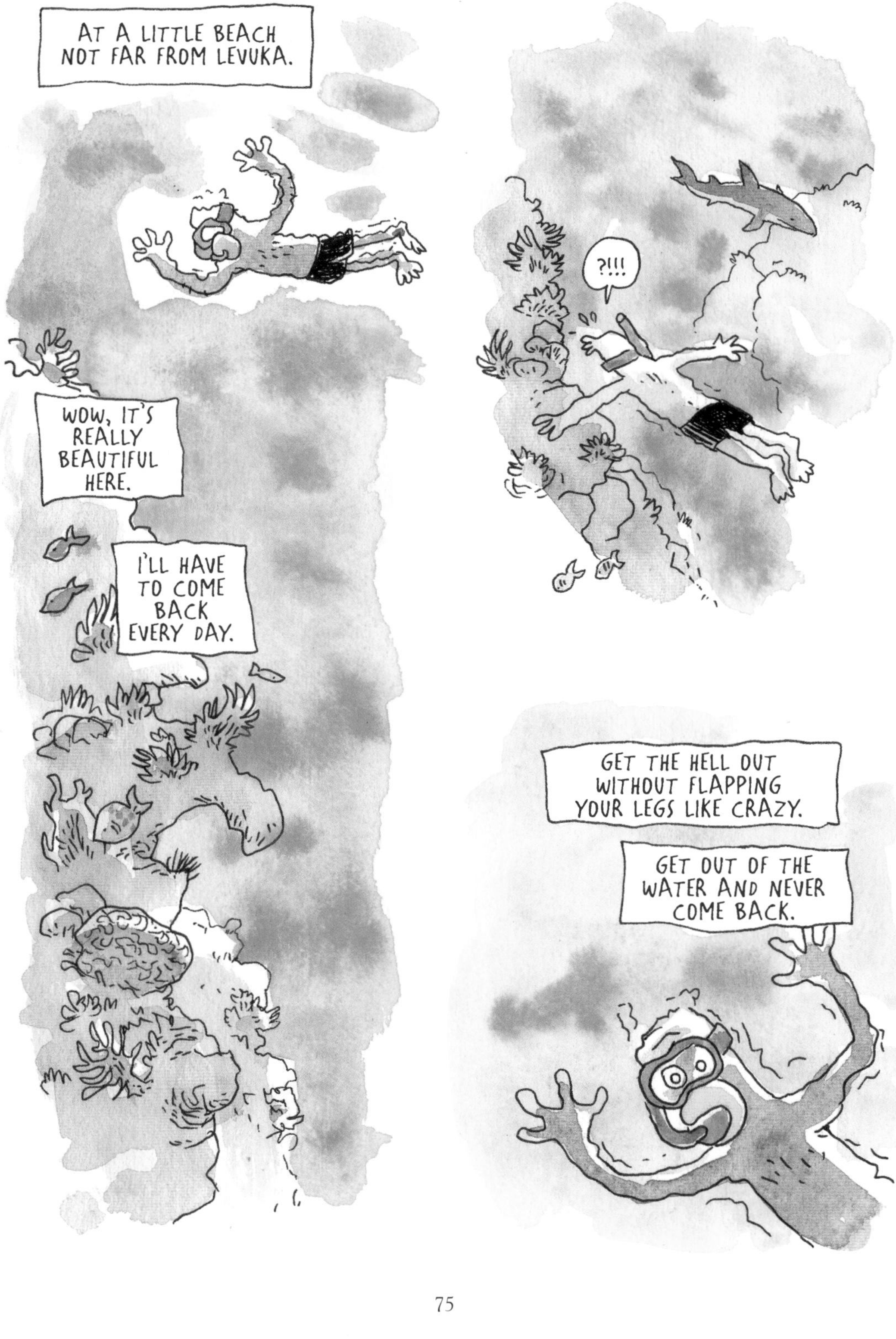
AT A LITTLE BEACH NOT FAR FROM LEVUKA.
WOW, IT'S REALLY BEAUTIFUL HERE.
I'LL HAVE TO COME BACK EVERY DAY.
?!!!
GET THE HELL OUT WITHOUT FLAPPING YOUR LEGS LIKE CRAZY.
GET OUT OF THE WATER AND NEVER COME BACK.

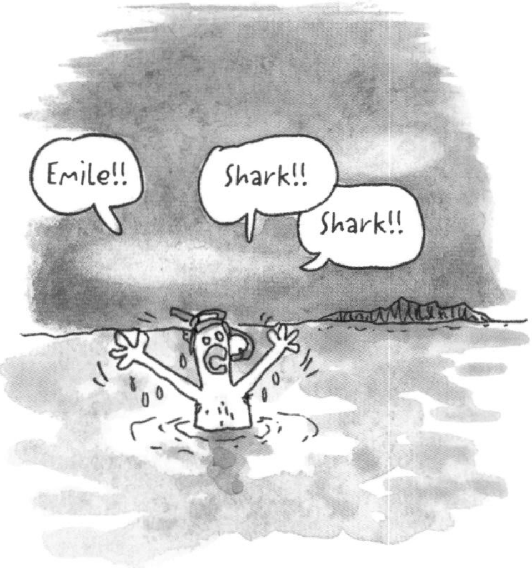
Emile!!
Shark!!
Shark!!

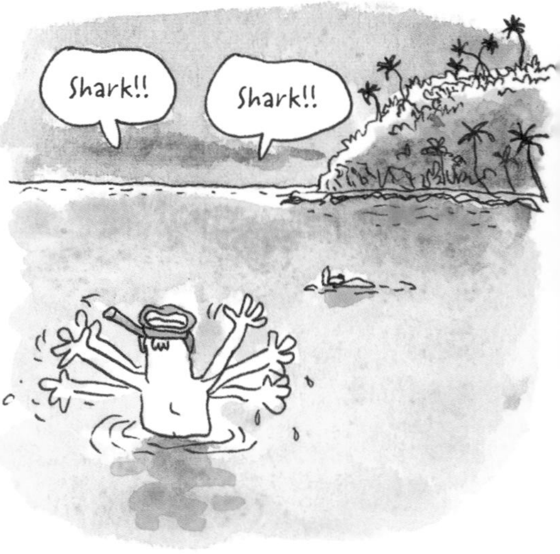
Shark!!
Shark!!

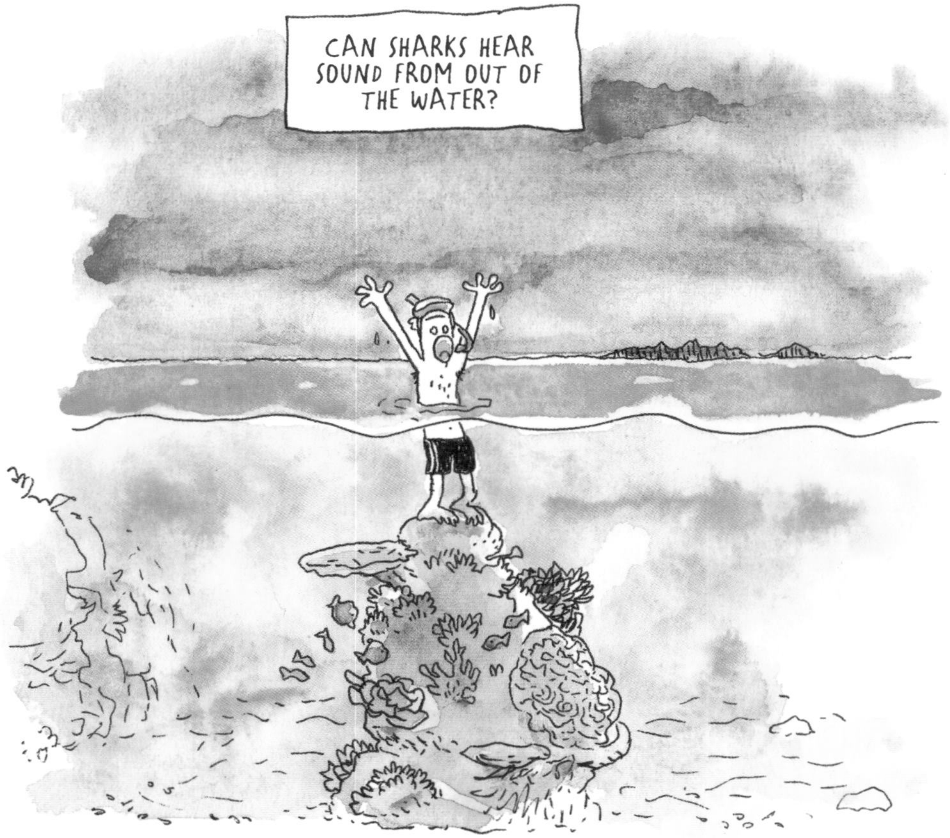
CAN SHARKS HEAR SOUND FROM OUT OF THE WATER?

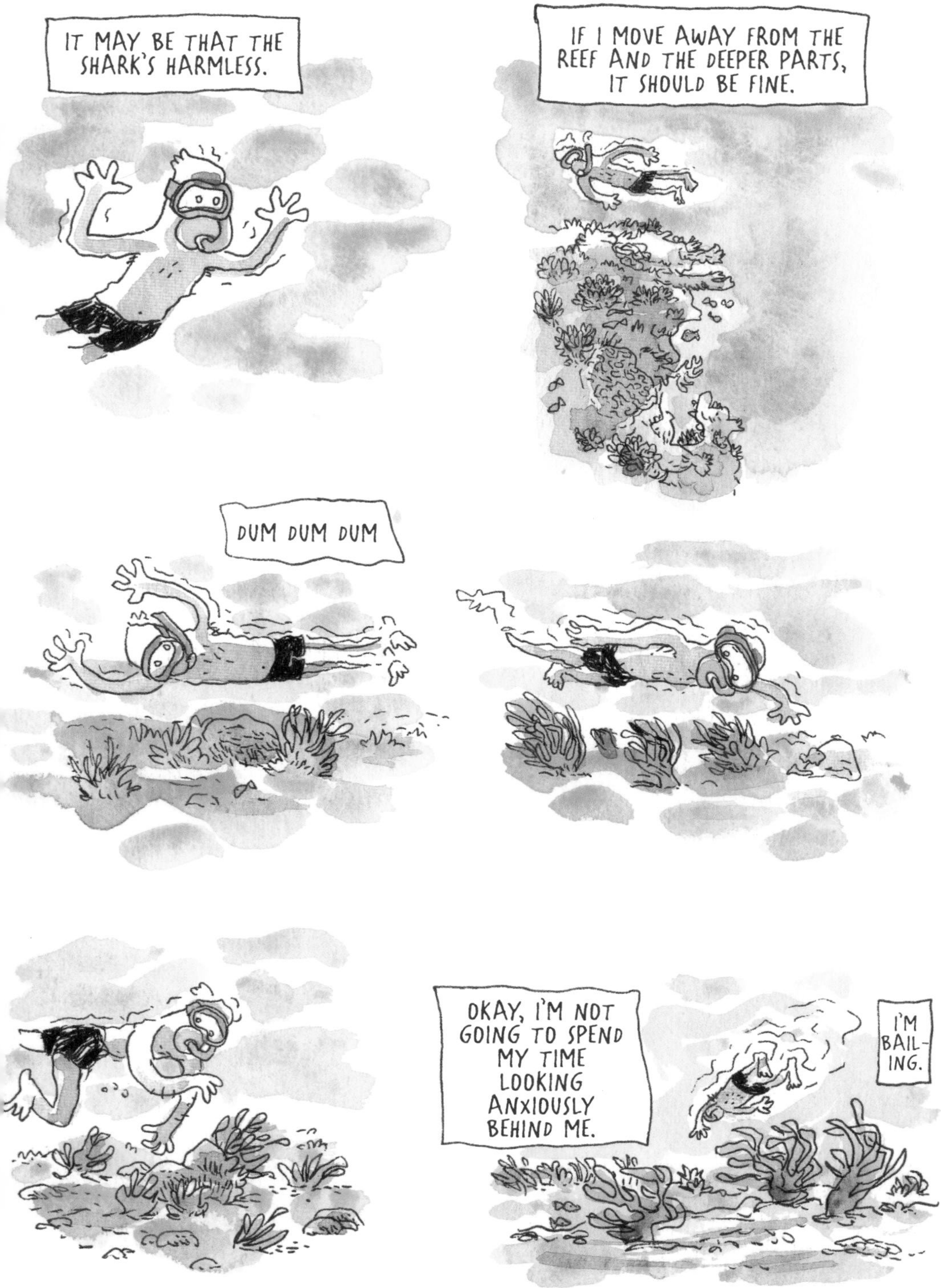
IT MAY BE THAT THE SHARK'S HARMLESS.
IF I MOVE AWAY FROM THE REEF AND THE DEEPER PARTS, IT SHOULD BE FINE.
DUM DUM DUM
OKAY, I'M NOT GOING TO SPEND MY TIME LOOKING ANXIOUSLY BEHIND ME.
I'M BAIL-ING.

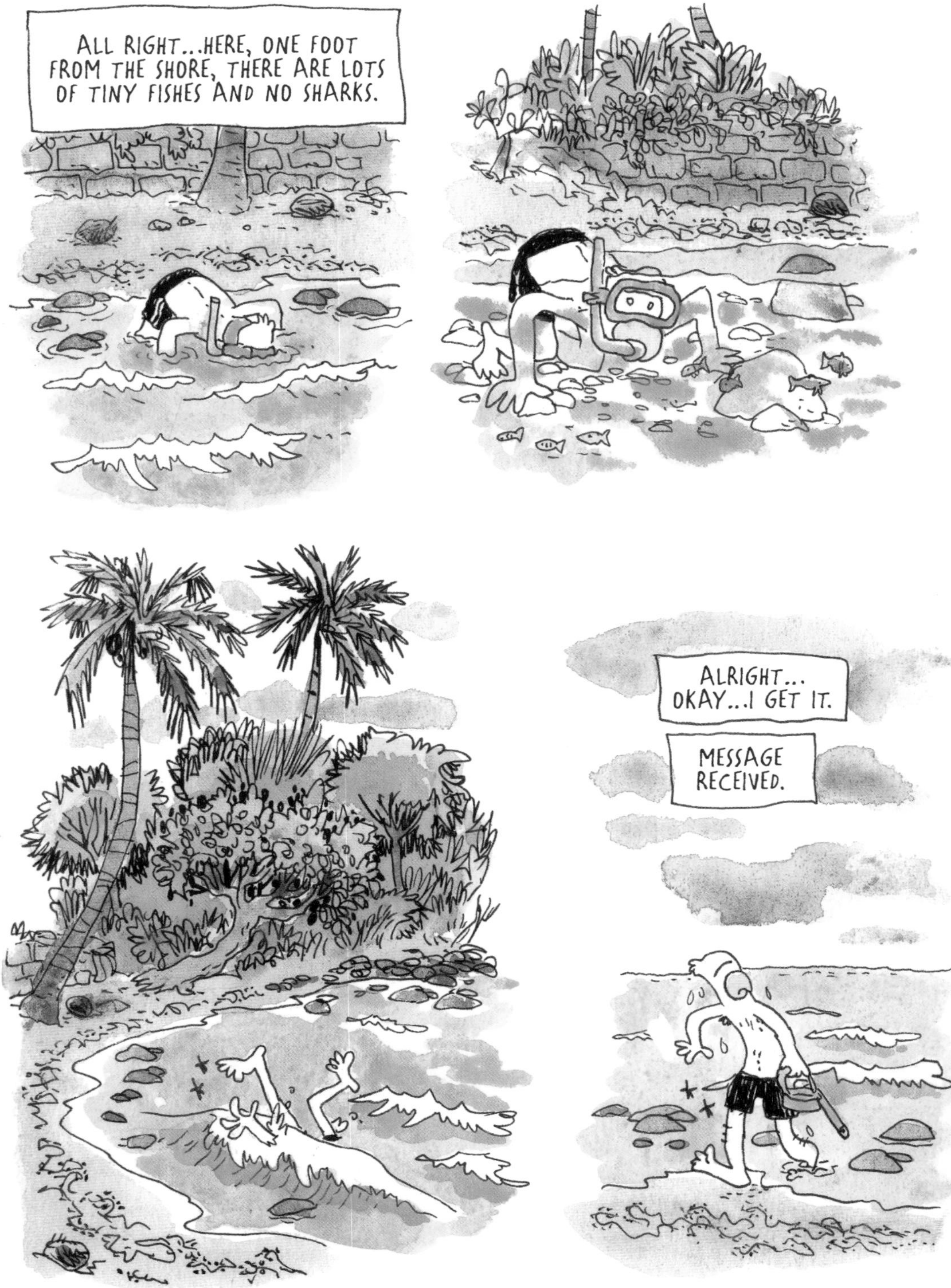
ALL RIGHT...HERE, ONE FOOT FROM THE SHORE, THERE ARE LOTS OF TINY FISHES AND NO SHARKS.
ALRIGHT... OKAY...I GET IT.
MESSAGE RECEIVED.

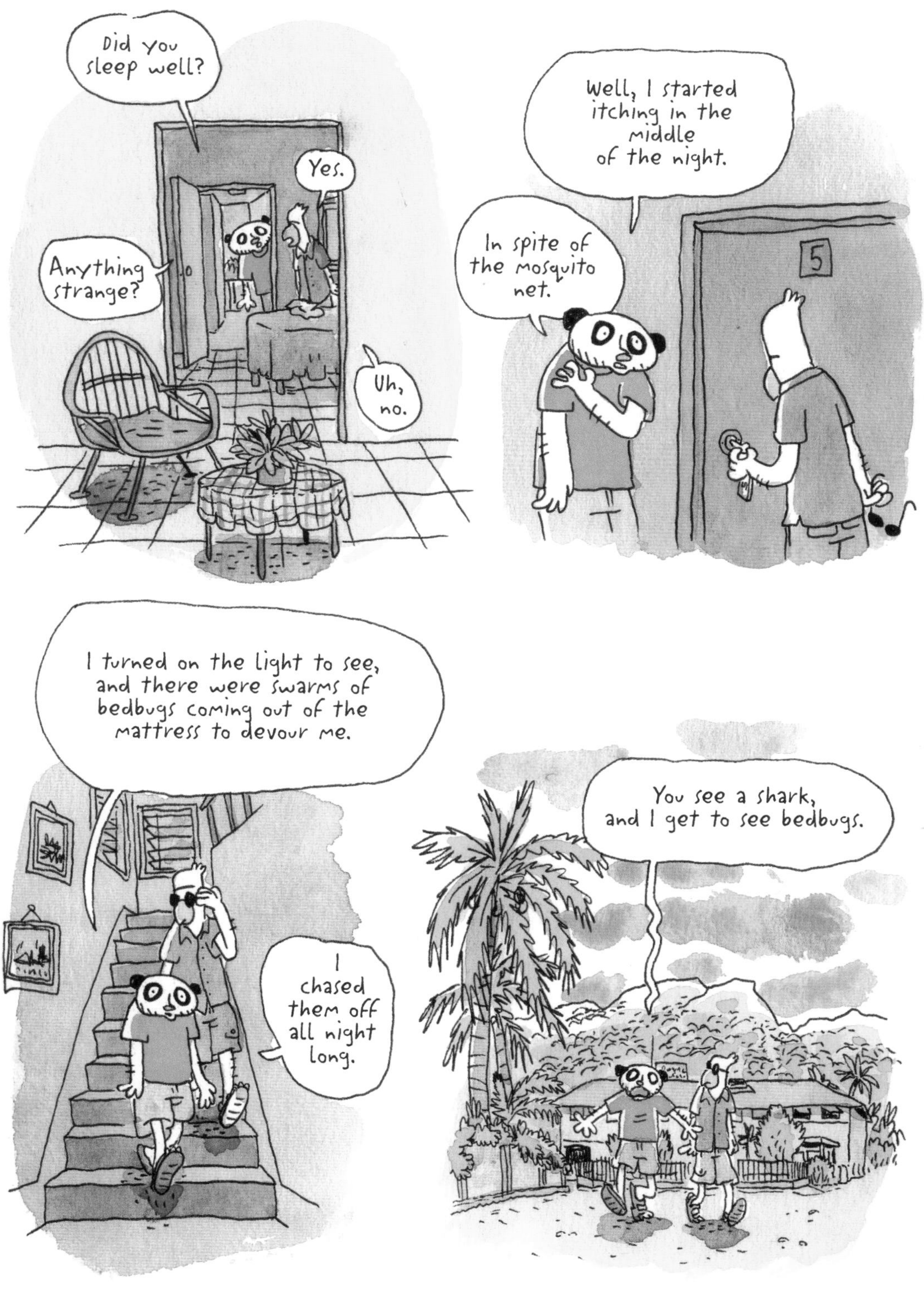
Did you sleep well?
Yes.
Anything strange?
Uh, no.
Well, I started itching in the middle of the night.
In spite of the mosquito net.
5
I turned on the light to see, and there were swarms of bedbugs coming out of the mattress to devour me.
I chased them off all night long.
You see a shark, and I get to see bedbugs.

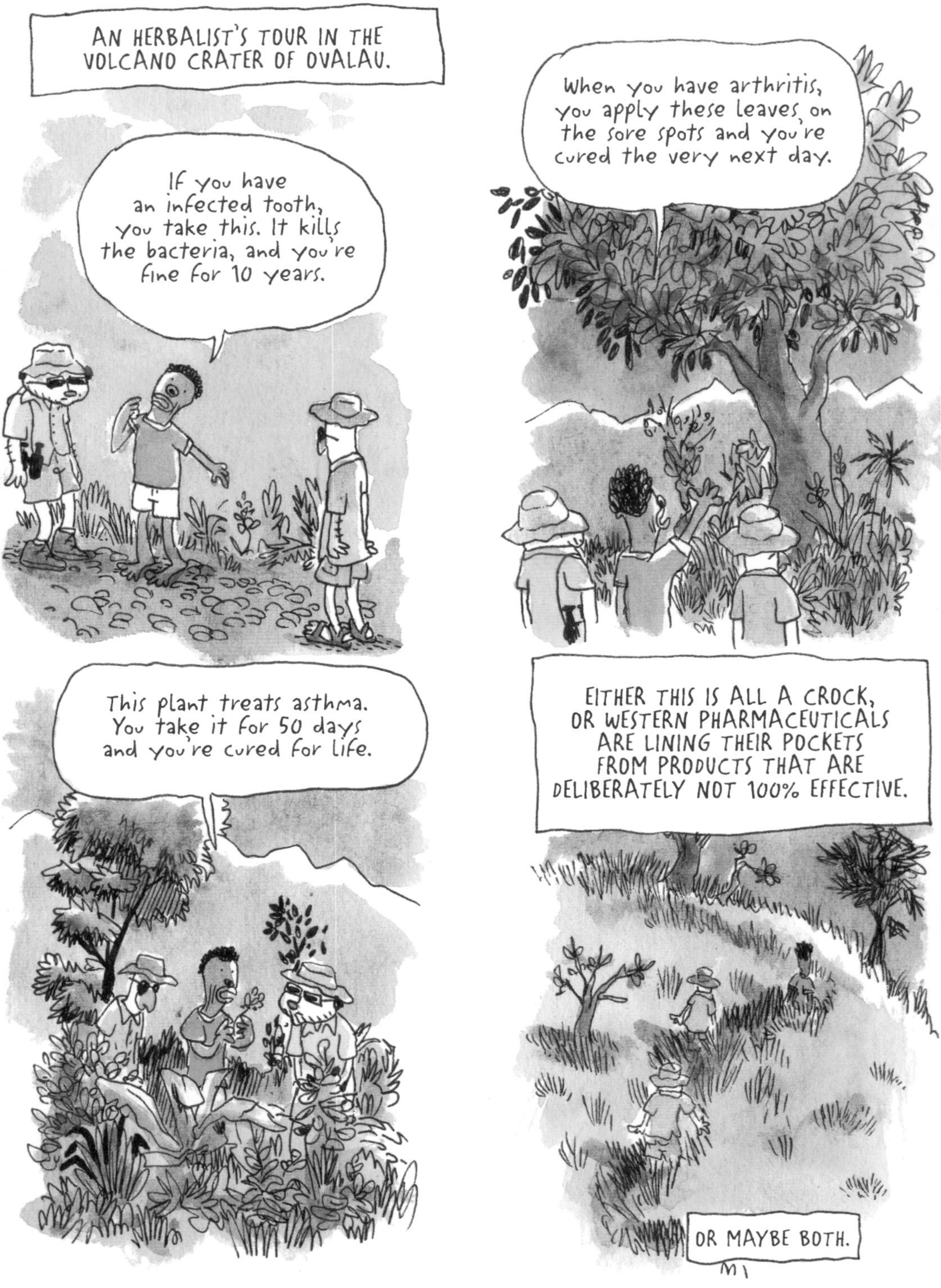
AN HERBALIST'S TOUR IN THE VOLCANO CRATER OF OVALAU.
If you have an infected tooth, you take this. It kills the bacteria, and you're fine for 10 years.
When you have arthritis, you apply these leaves on the sore spots and you're cured the very next day.
This plant treats asthma. You take it for 50 days and you're cured for life.
EITHER THIS IS ALL A CROCK, OR WESTERN PHARMACEUTICALS ARE LINING THEIR POCKETS FROM PRODUCTS THAT ARE DELIBERATELY NOT 100% EFFECTIVE.
OR MAYBE BOTH.

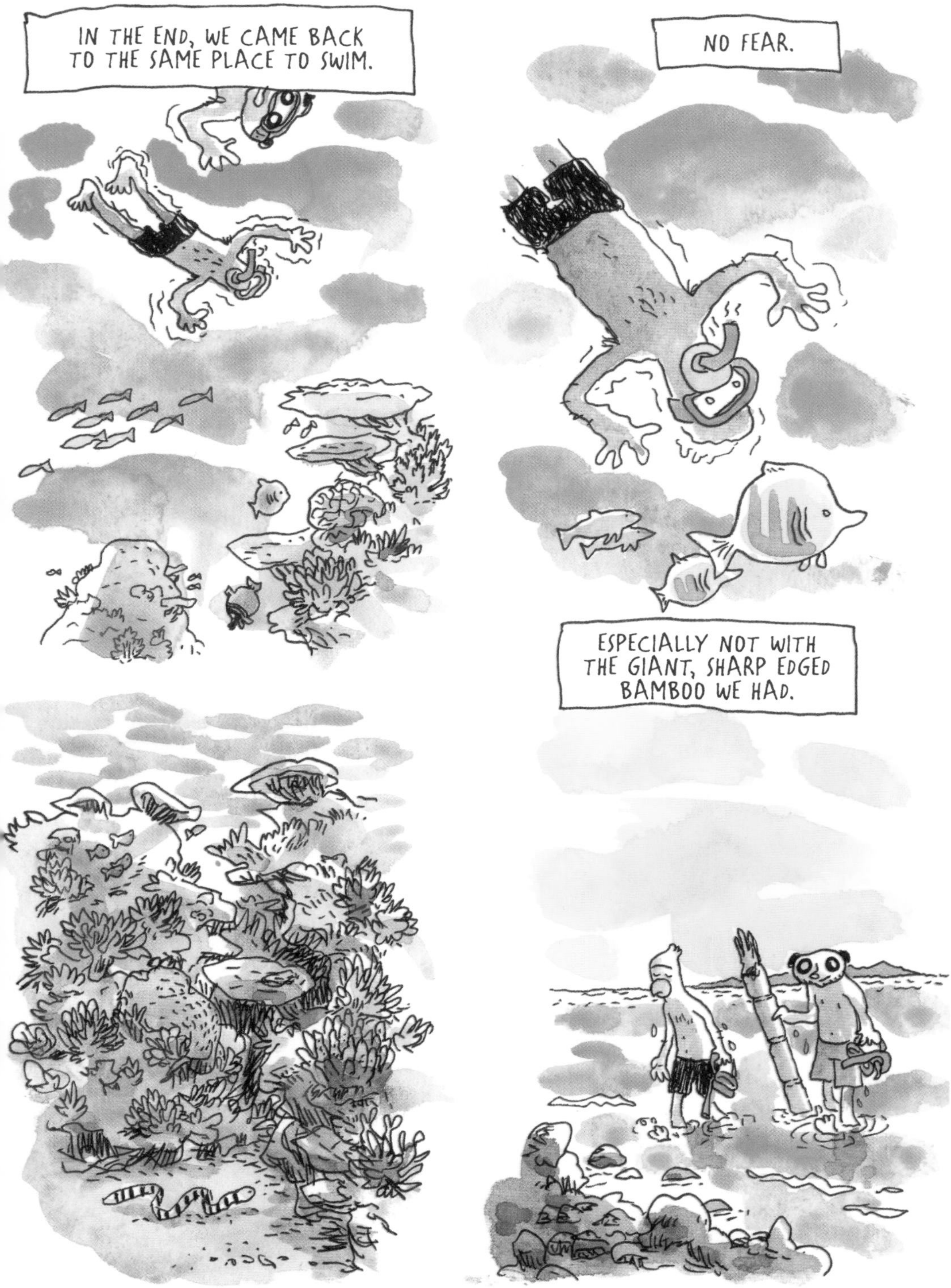
IN THE END, WE CAME BACK TO THE SAME PLACE TO SWIM.
NO FEAR.
ESPECIALLY NOT WITH THE GIANT, SHARP EDGED BAMBOO WE HAD.

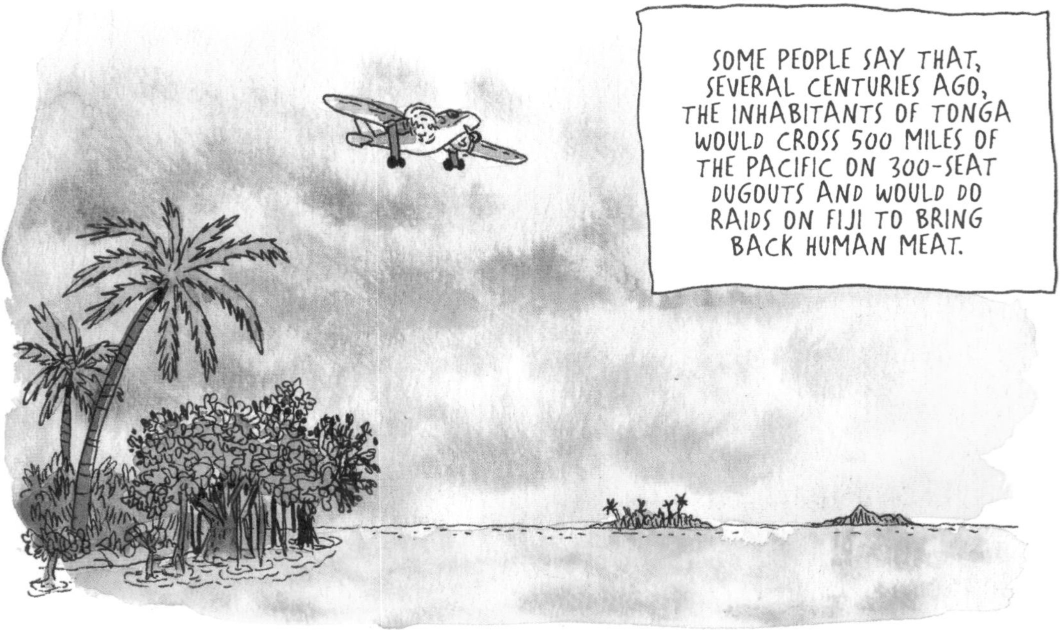
SOME PEOPLE SAY THAT, SEVERAL CENTURIES AGO, THE INHABITANTS OF TONGA WOULD CROSS 500 MILES OF THE PACIFIC ON 300-SEAT DUGOUTS AND WOULD DO RAIDS ON FIJI TO BRING BACK HUMAN MEAT.

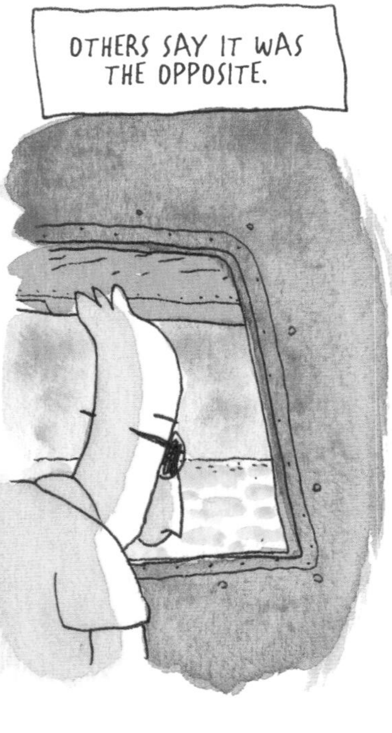
OTHERS SAY IT WAS THE OPPOSITE.

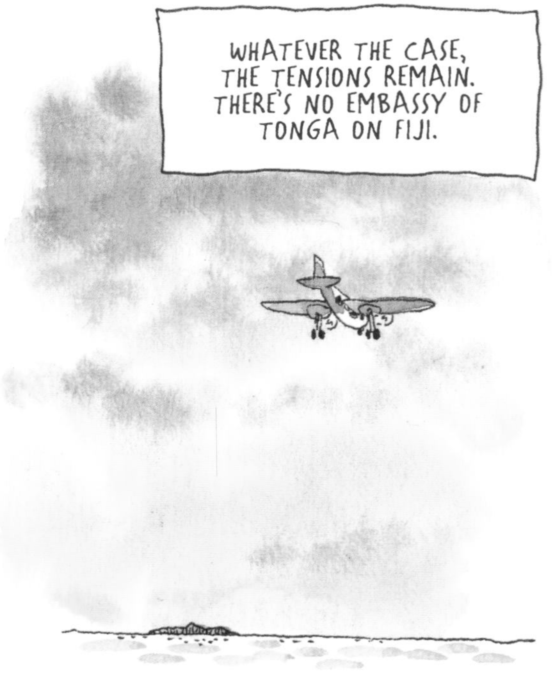
WHATEVER THE CASE, THE TENSIONS REMAIN. THERE'S NO EMBASSY OF TONGA ON FIJI.

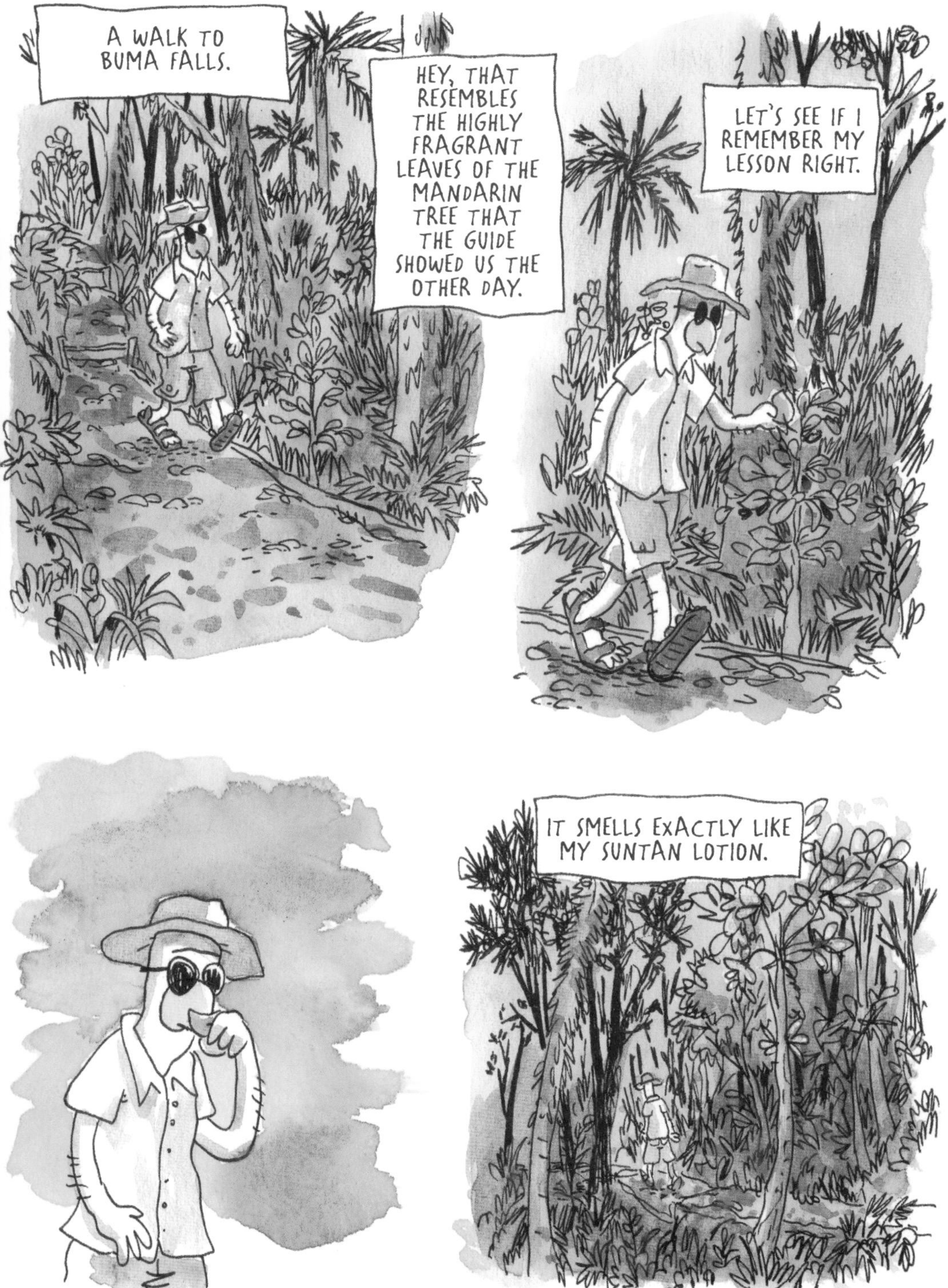
A WALK TO BUMA FALLS.
HEY, THAT RESEMBLES THE HIGHLY FRAGRANT LEAVES OF THE MANDARIN TREE THAT THE GUIDE SHOWED US THE OTHER DAY.
LET'S SEE IF I REMEMBER MY LESSON RIGHT.
IT SMELLS EXACTLY LIKE MY SUNTAN LOTION.

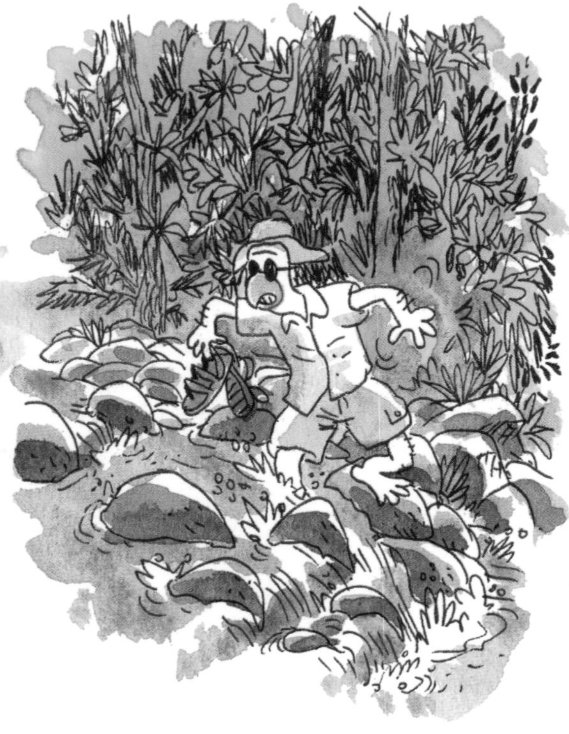

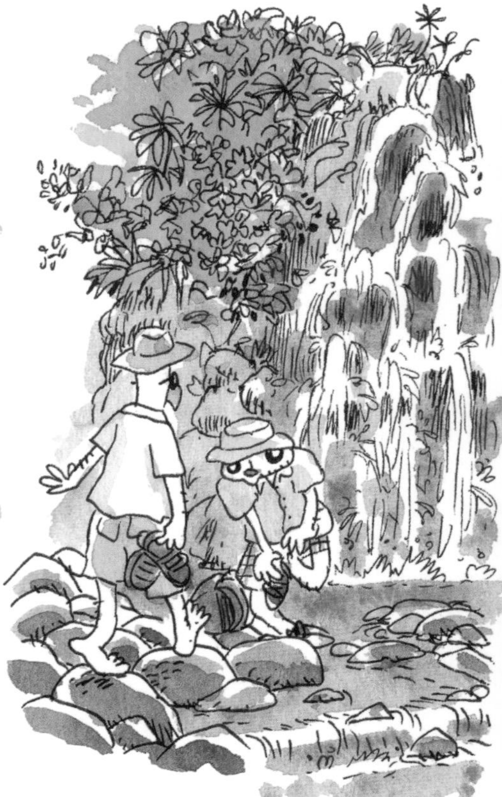

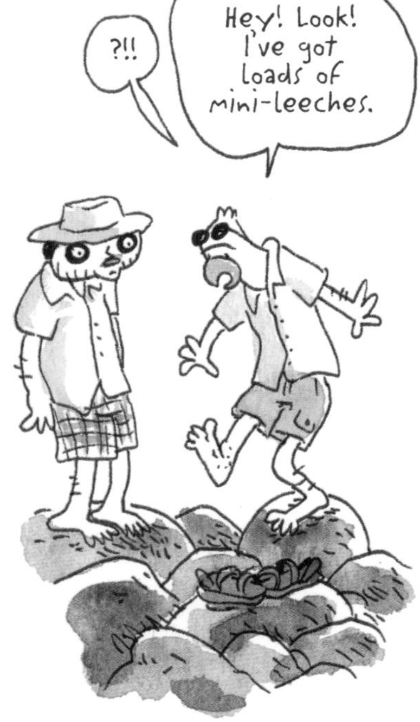
?!!
Hey! Look! I've got loads of mini-leeches.

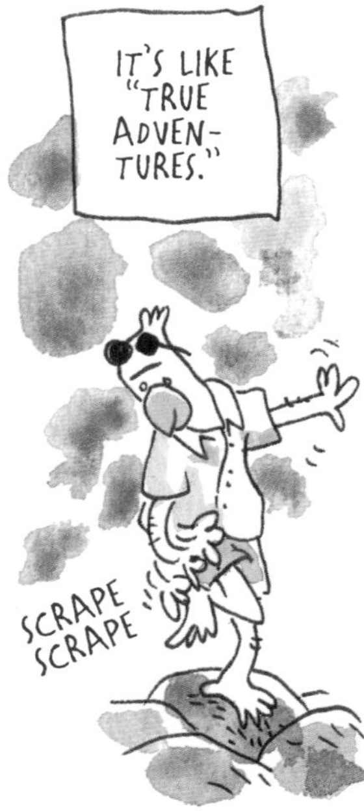
IT'S LIKE "TRUE ADVEN-TURES."
SCRAPE SCRAPE

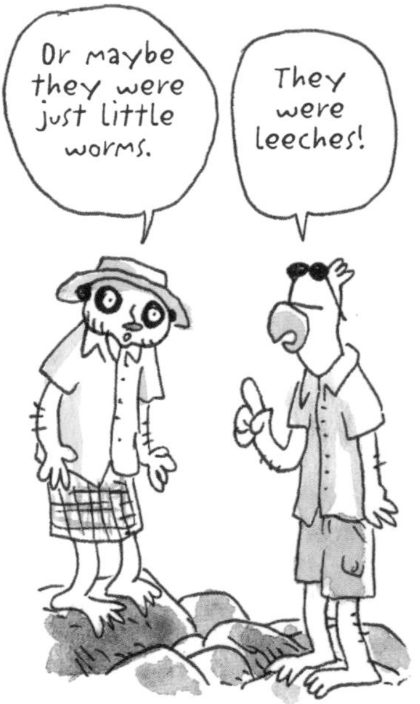
Or maybe they were just little worms.
They were leeches!

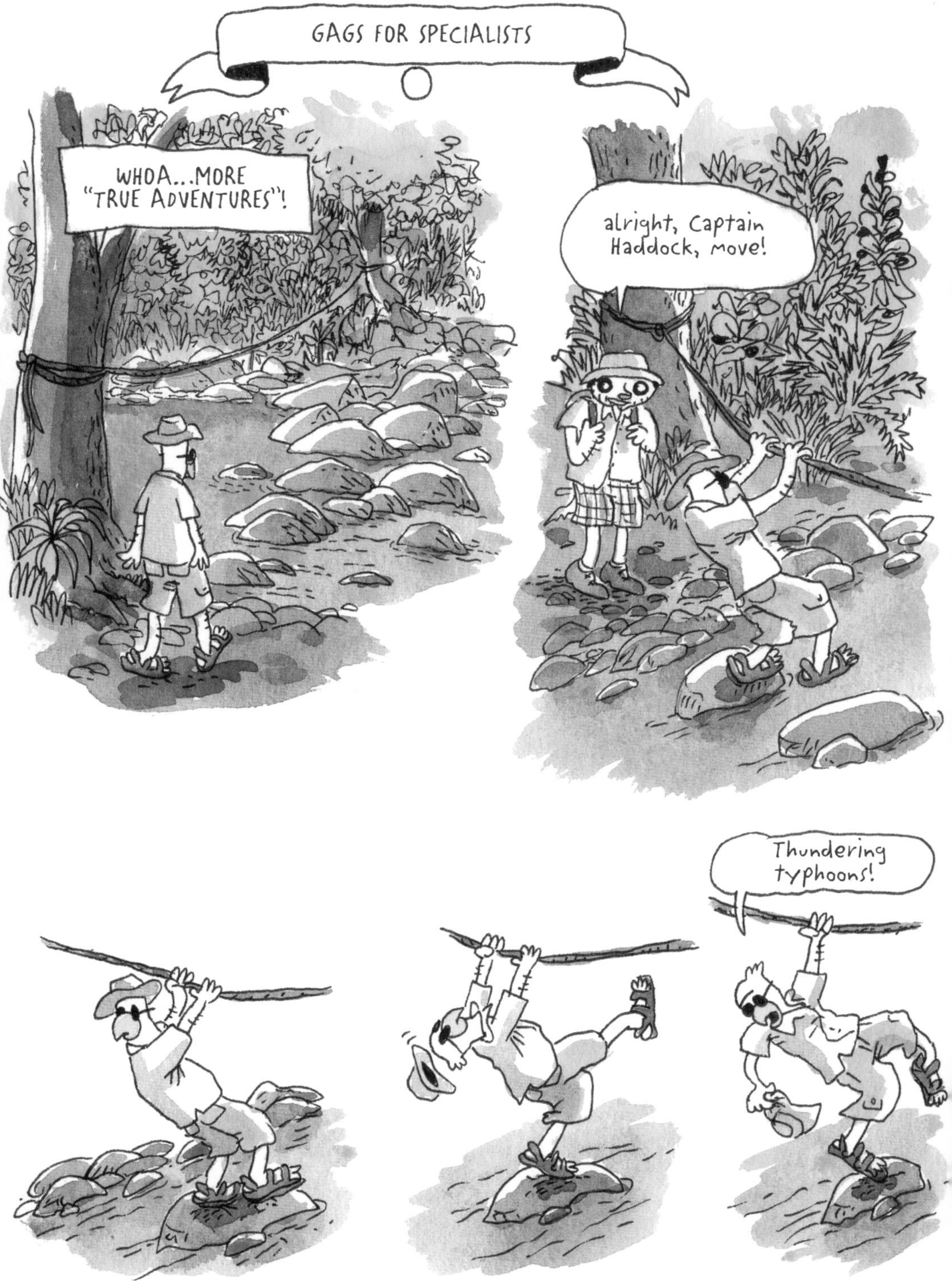
GAGS FOR SPECIALISTS
WHOA...MORE "TRUE ADVENTURES"!
alright, Captain Haddock, move!
Thundering typhoons!

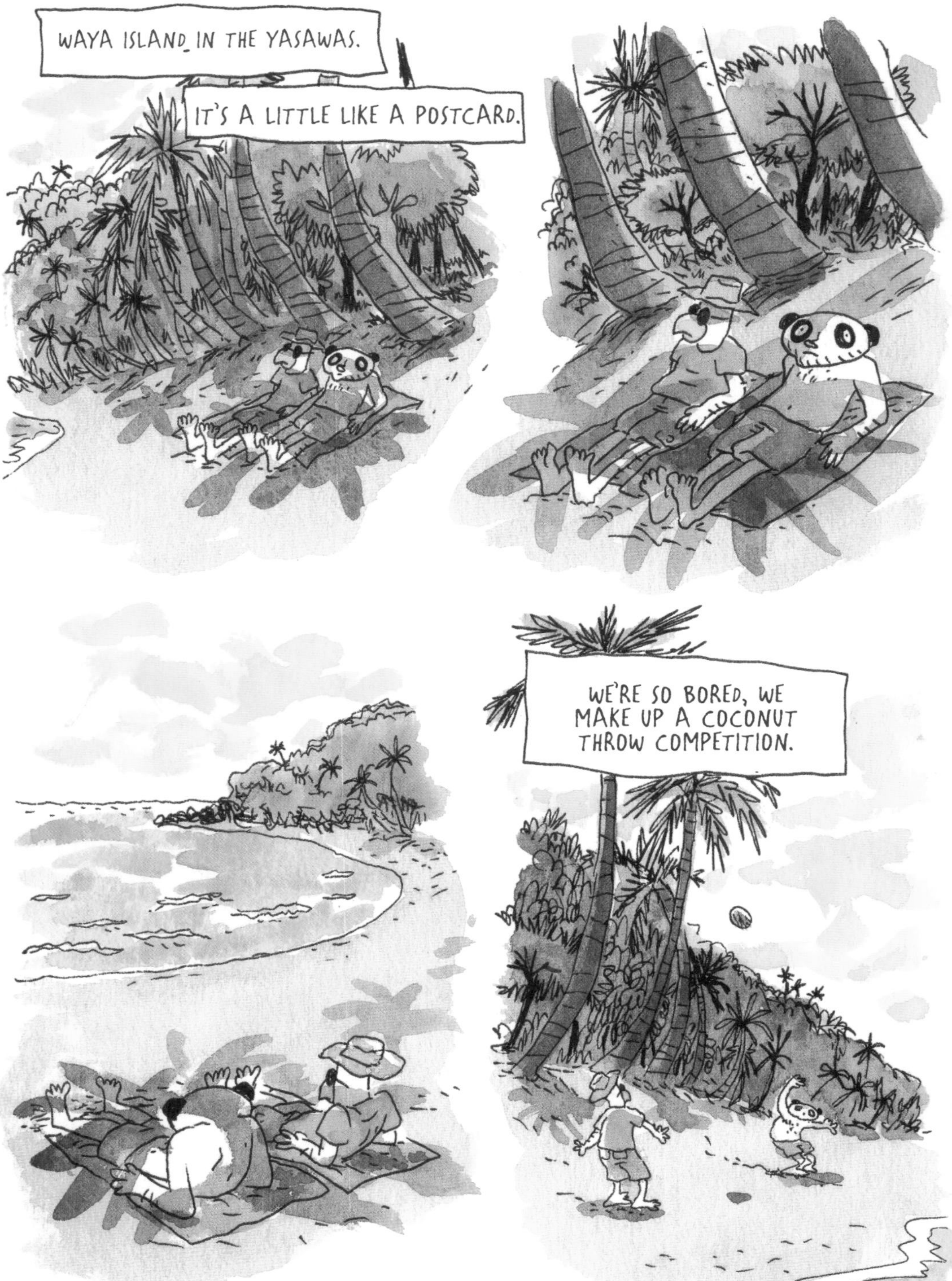

WAYA ISLAND, IN THE YASAWAS.
IT'S A LITTLE LIKE A POSTCARD.
WE'RE SO BORED, WE MAKE UP A COCONUT THROW COMPETITION.

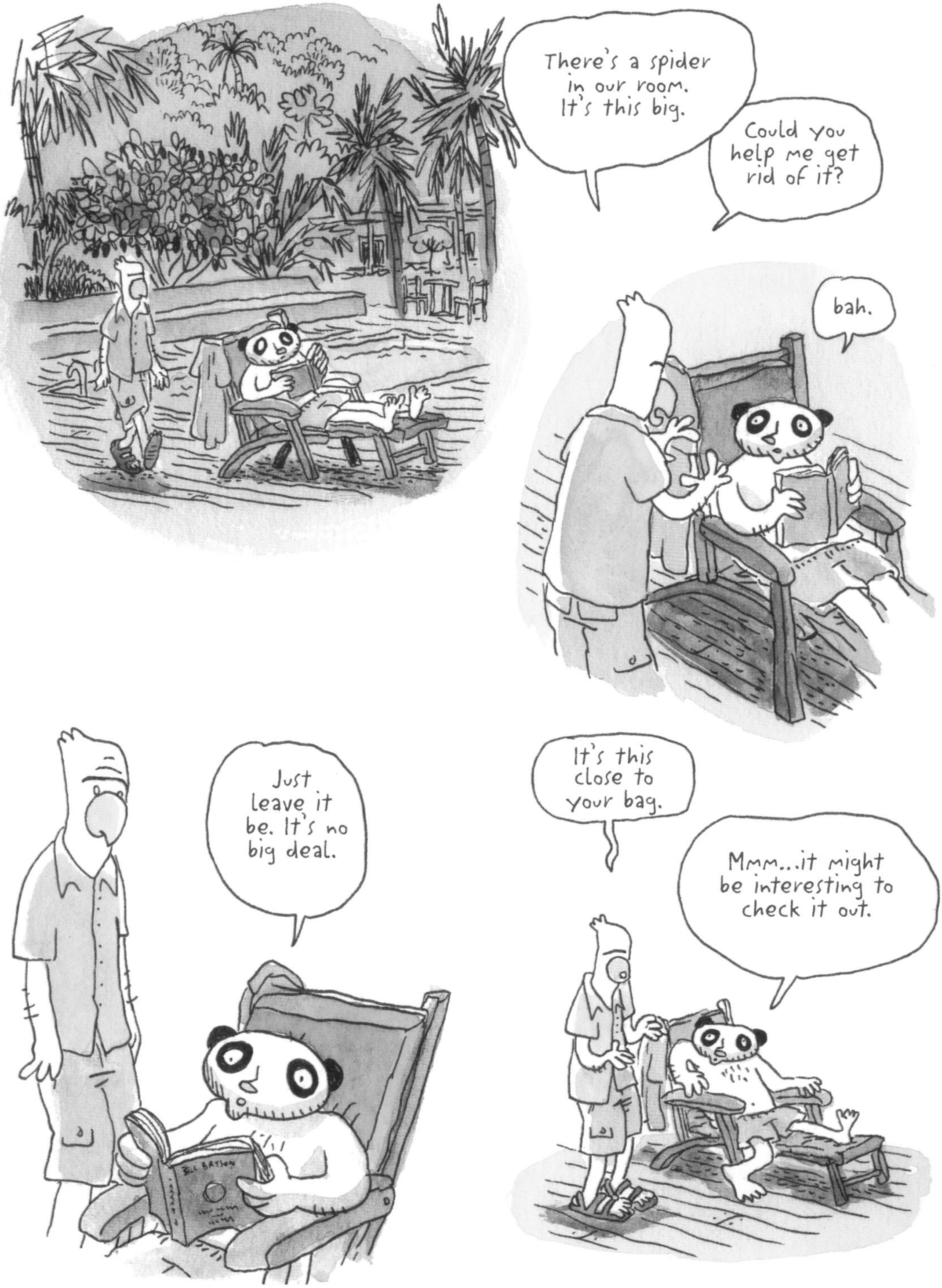
There's a spider in our room. It's this big.
Could you help me get rid of it?
bah.
Just leave it be. It's no big deal.
It's this close to your bag.
Mmm...it might be interesting to check it out.

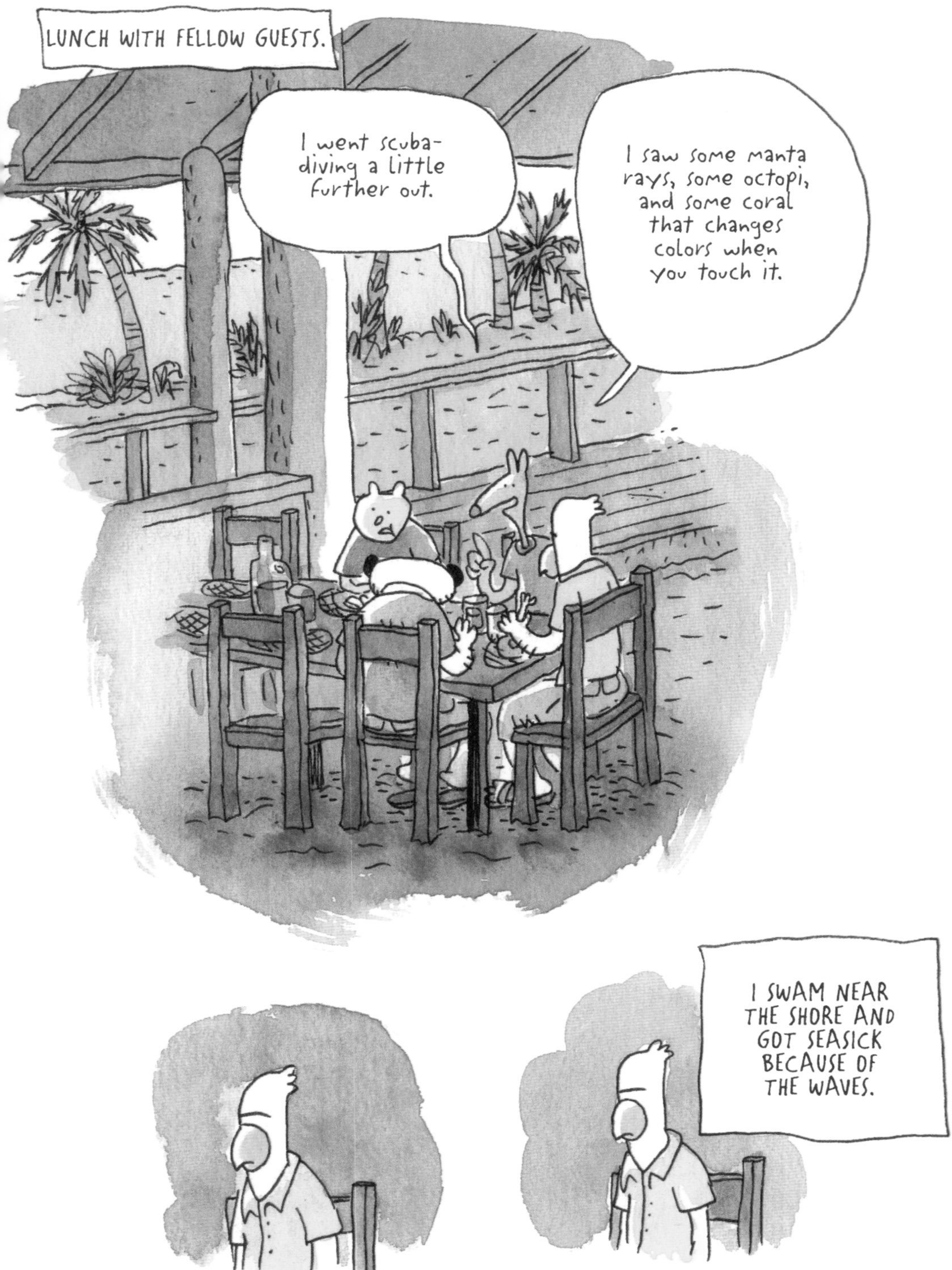
LUNCH WITH FELLOW GUESTS.
I went scuba-diving a little further out.
I saw some manta rays, some octopi, and some coral that changes colors when you touch it.
I SWAM NEAR THE SHORE AND GOT SEASICK BECAUSE OF THE WAVES.

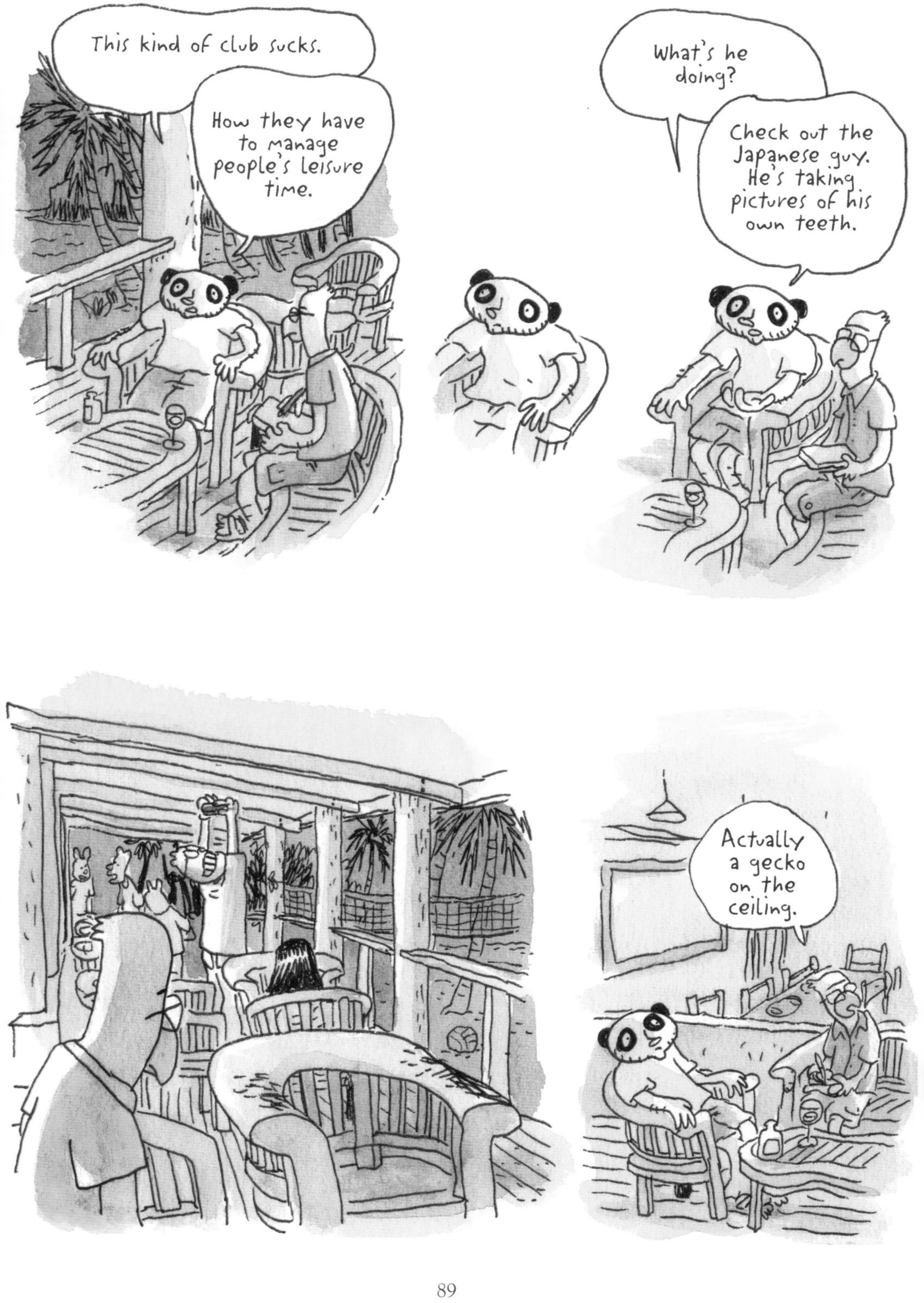
This kind of club sucks.
How they have to manage people's leisure time.
What's he doing?
Check out the Japanese guy. He's taking pictures of his own teeth.
Actually a gecko on the ceiling.

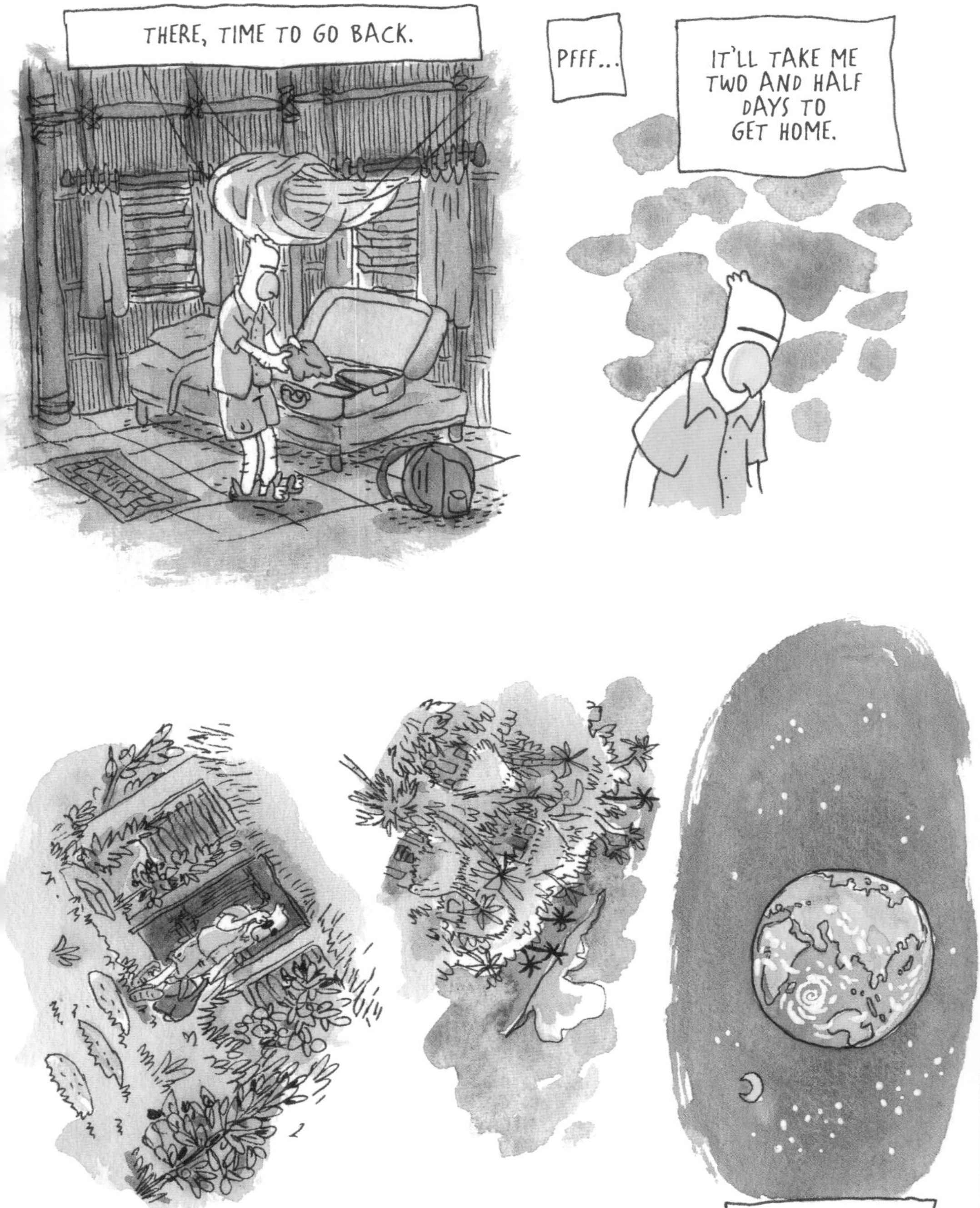
THERE, TIME TO GO BACK.
PFFF...
IT'LL TAKE ME TWO AND HALF DAYS TO GET HOME.
EVEN IF IT ISN'T ALL THAT MUCH.

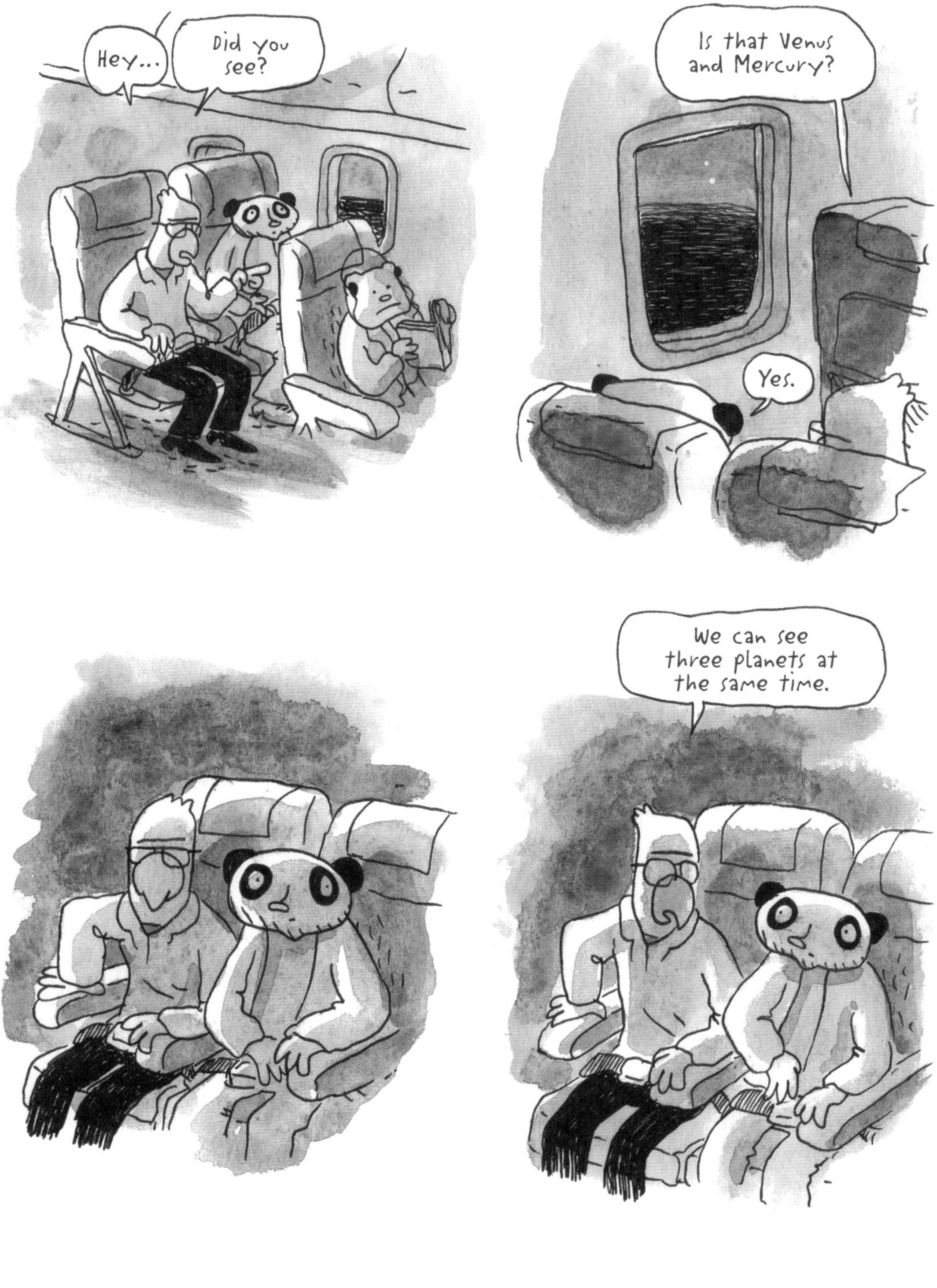
Hey...
Did you see?
Is that Venus and Mercury?
Yes.
We can see three planets at the same time.

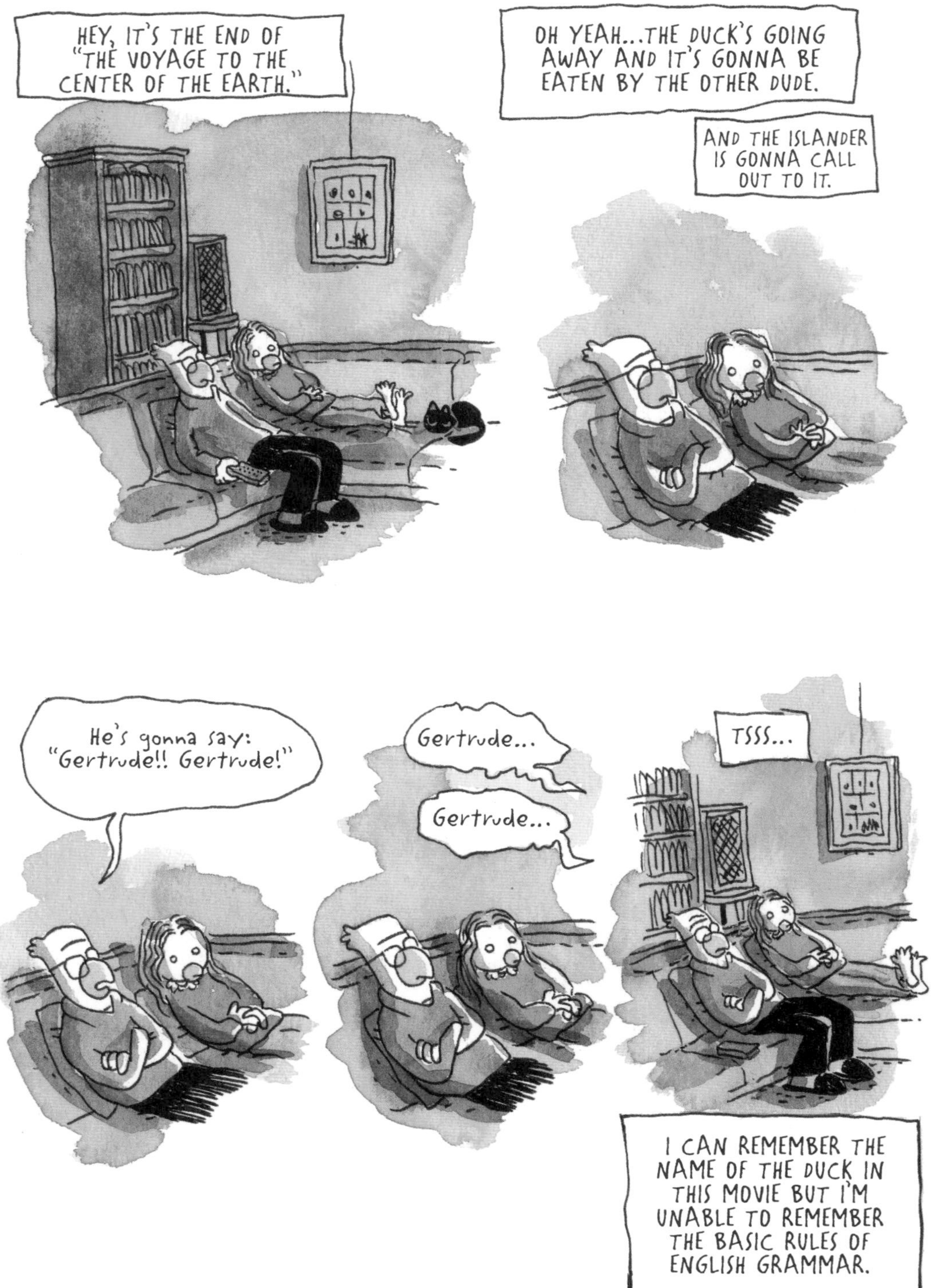
HEY, IT'S THE END OF "THE VOYAGE TO THE CENTER OF THE EARTH."
OH YEAH...THE DUCK'S GOING AWAY AND IT'S GONNA BE EATEN BY THE OTHER DUDE.
AND THE ISLANDER IS GONNA CALL OUT TO IT.
He's gonna say: "Gertrude!! Gertrude!"
Gertrude...
Gertrude...
TSSS...
I CAN REMEMBER THE NAME OF THE DUCK IN THIS MOVIE BUT I'M UNABLE TO REMEMBER THE BASIC RULES OF ENGLISH GRAMMAR.

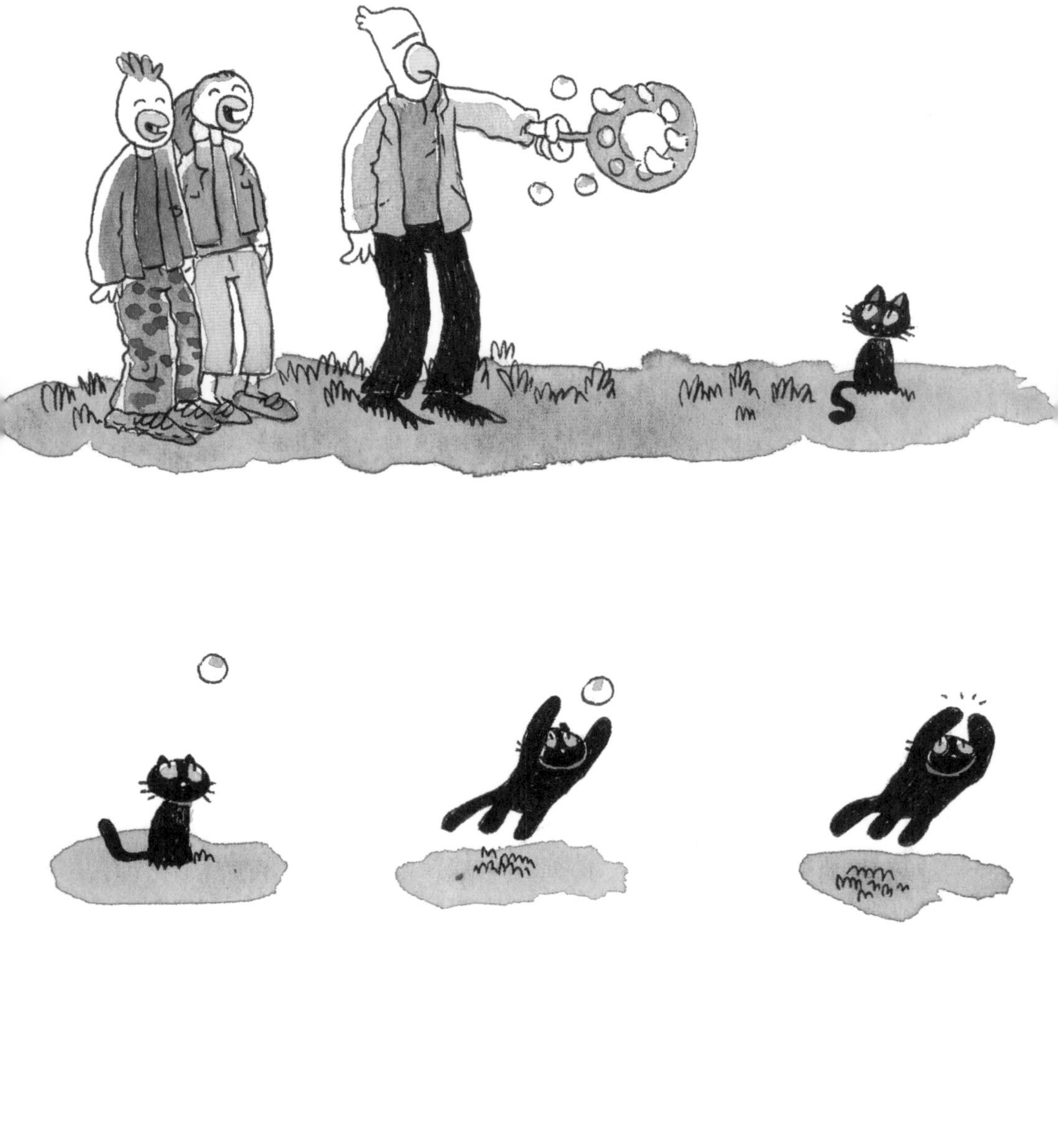

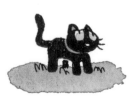

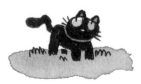

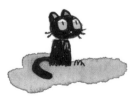

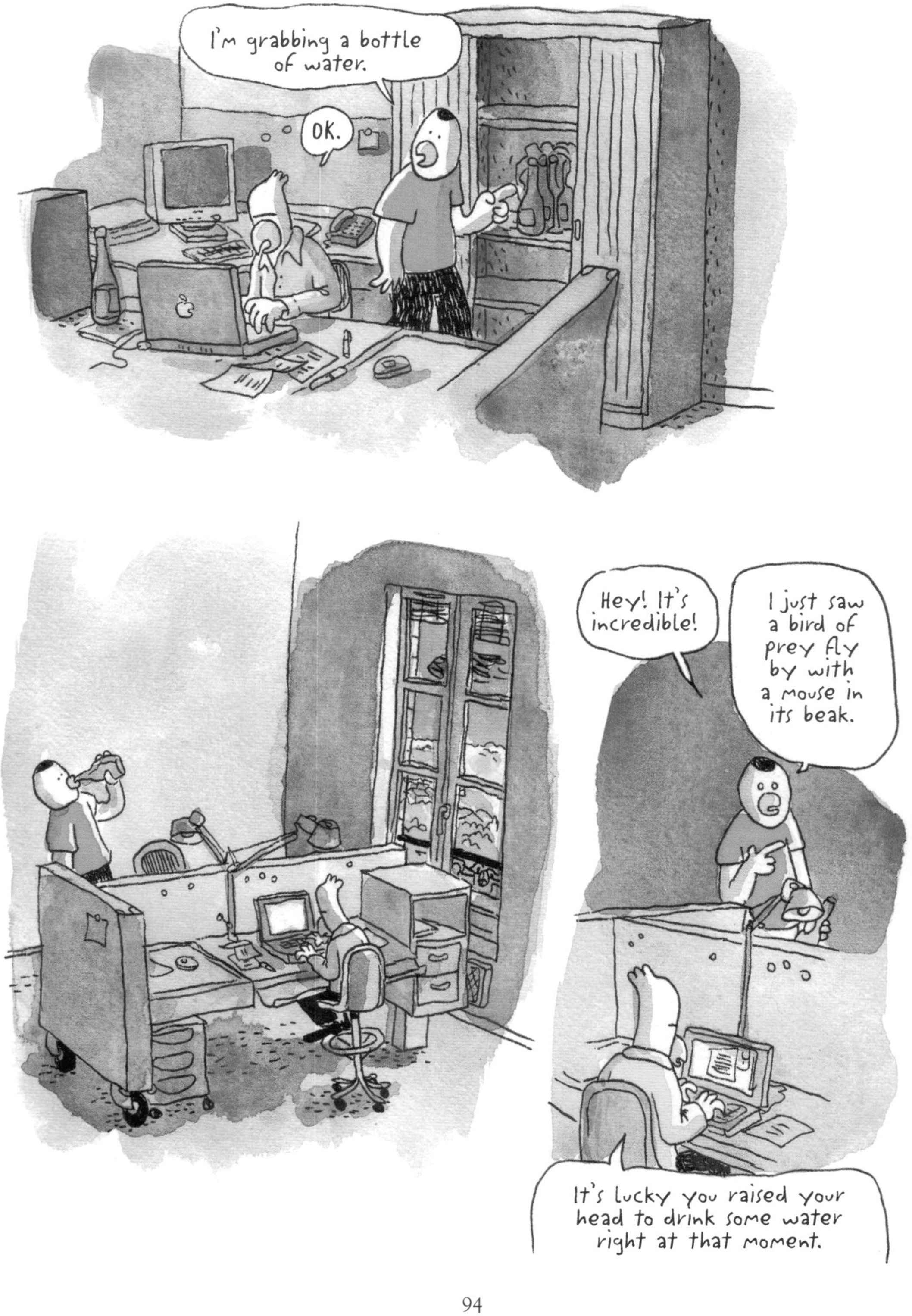
I'm grabbing a bottle of water.
OK.
Hey! It's incredible!
I just saw a bird of prey fly by with a mouse in its beak.
It's lucky you raised your head to drink some water right at that moment.

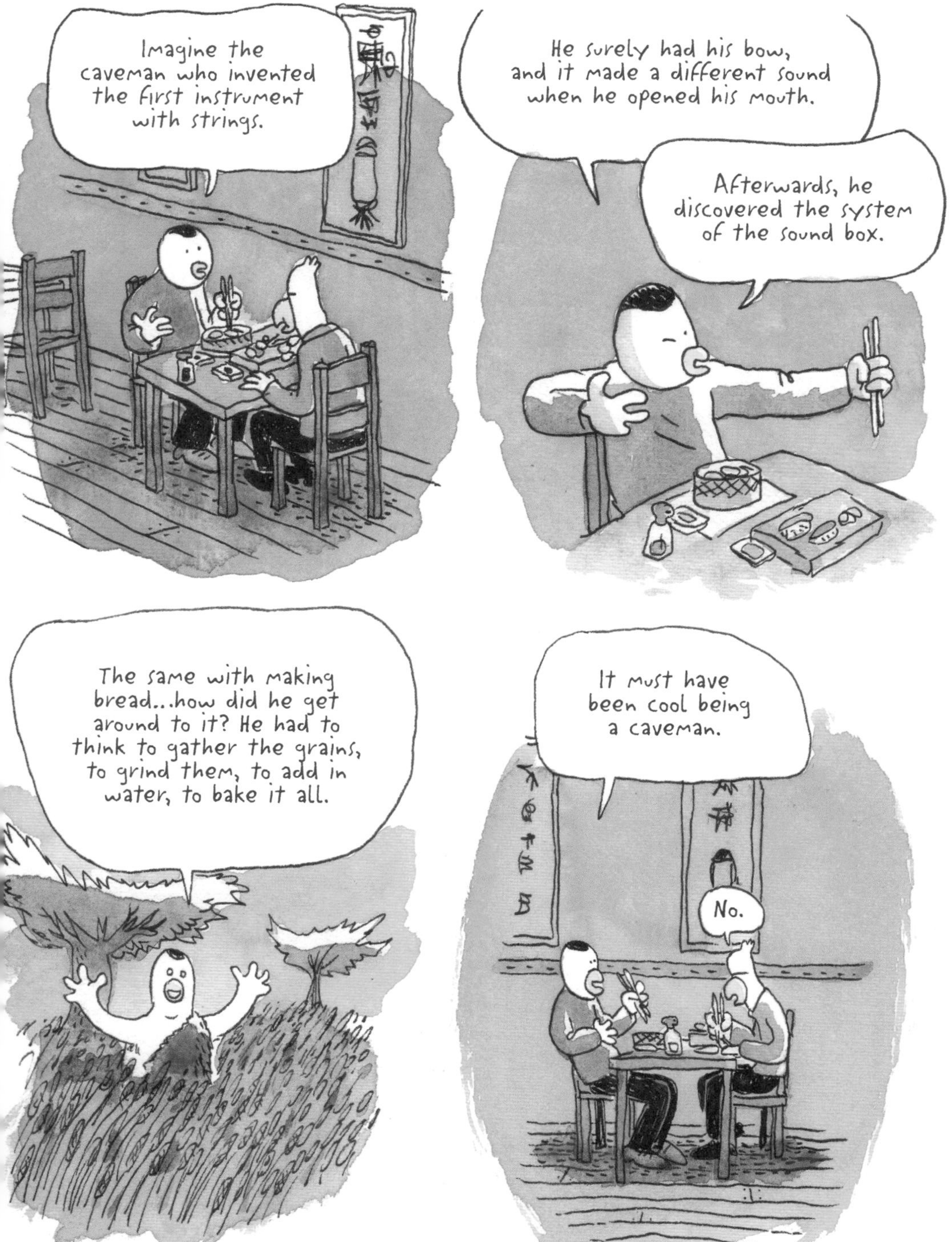
Imagine the caveman who invented the first instrument with strings.
He surely had his bow, and it made a different sound when he opened his mouth.
Afterwards, he discovered the system of the sound box.
The same with making bread...how did he get around to it? He had to think to gather the grains, to grind them, to add in water, to bake it all.
It must have been cool being a caveman.
No.

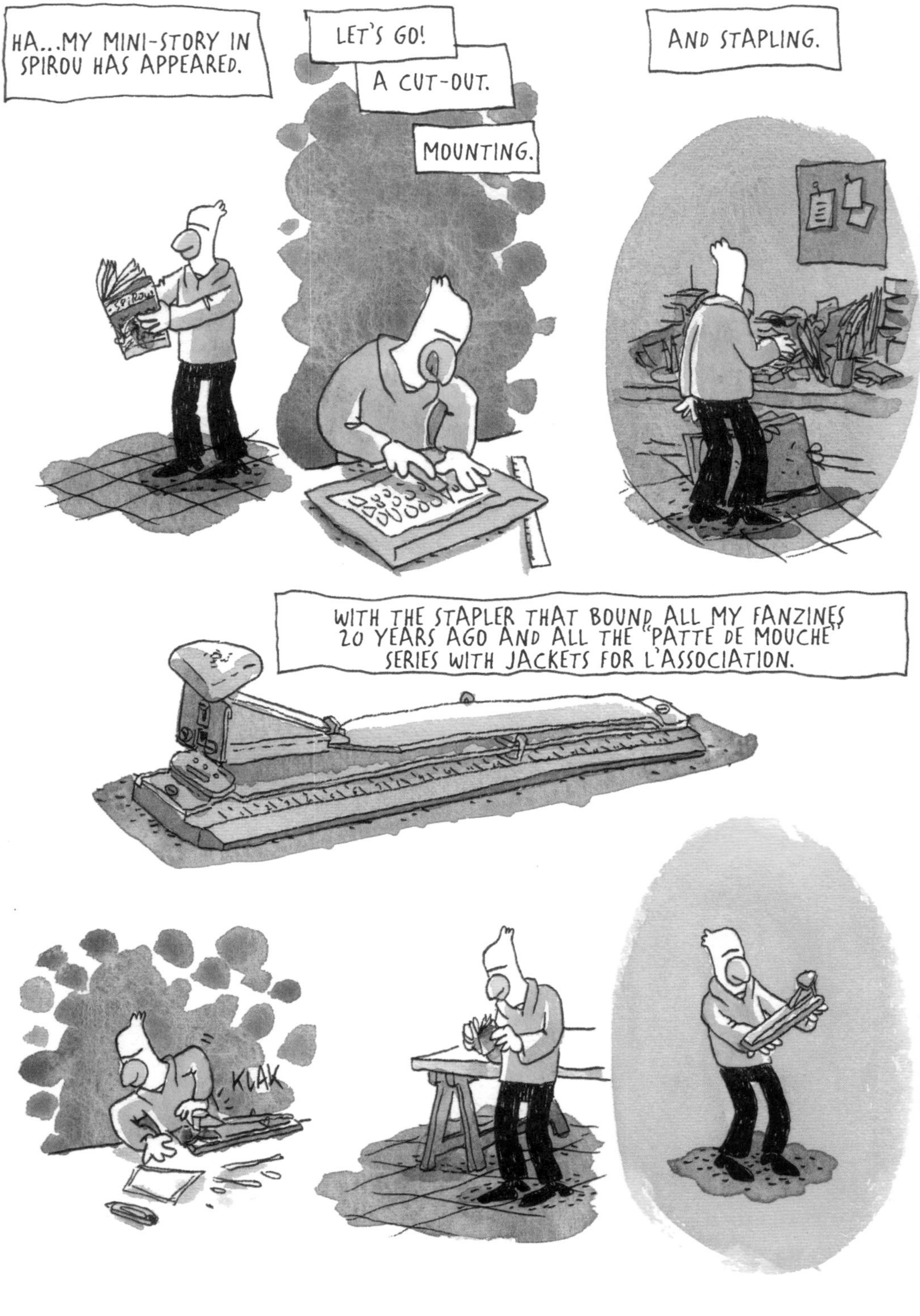
HA...MY MINI-STORY IN SPIROU HAS APPEARED.
LET'S GO!
A CUT-OUT.
MOUNTING.
AND STAPLING.
WITH THE STAPLER THAT BOUND ALL MY FANZINES 20 YEARS AGO AND ALL THE "PATTE DE MOUCHE" SERIES WITH JACKETS FOR L'ASSOCIATION.
KLAK

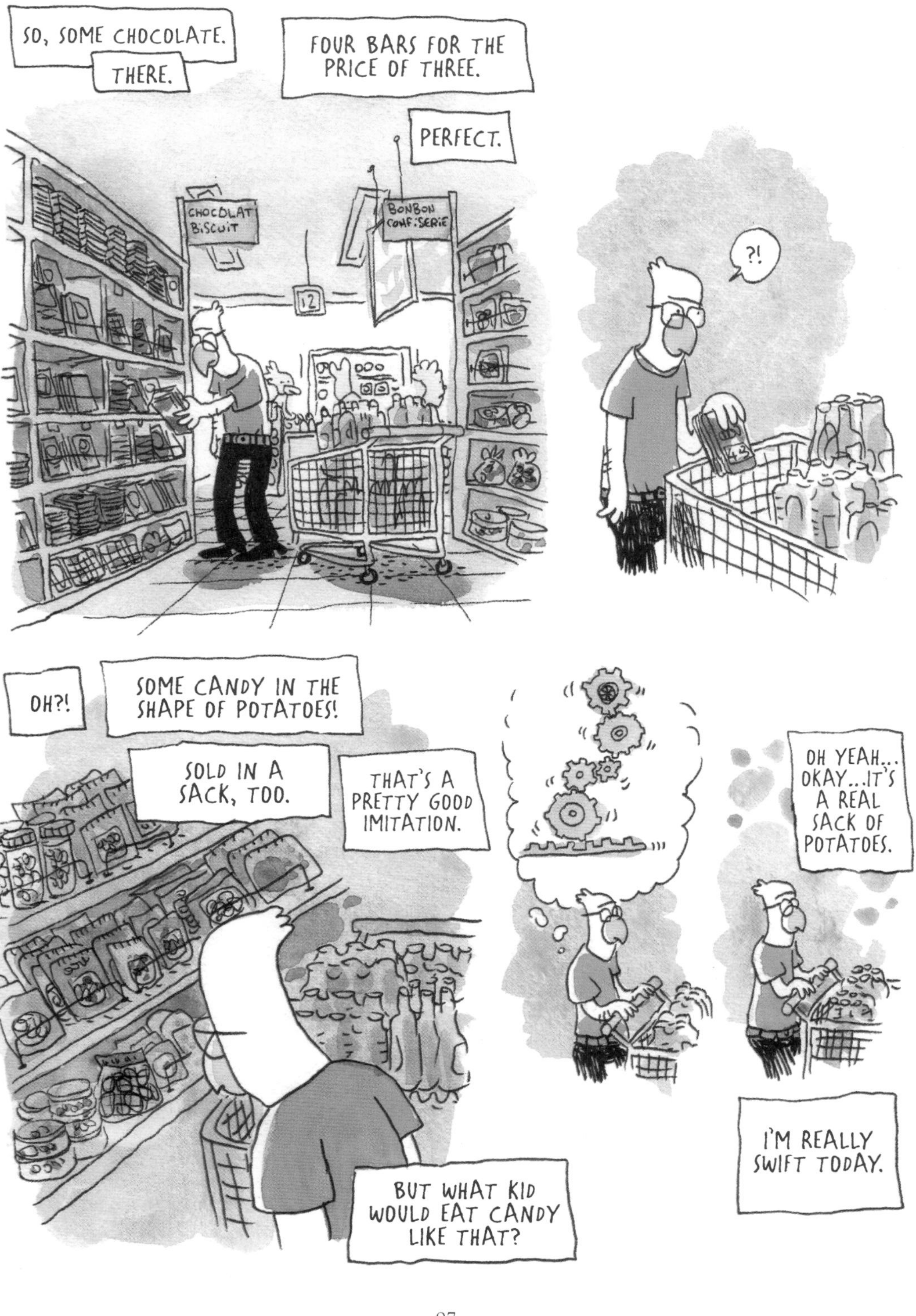
SO, SOME CHOCOLATE.
THERE.
FOUR BARS FOR THE PRICE OF THREE.
PERFECT.
CHOCOLAT BISCUIT
BONBON CONFISERIE
12
?!
OH?!
SOME CANDY IN THE SHAPE OF POTATOES!
SOLD IN A SACK, TOO.
THAT'S A PRETTY GOOD IMITATION.
BUT WHAT KID WOULD EAT CANDY LIKE THAT?
OH YEAH... OKAY...IT'S A REAL SACK OF POTATOES.
I'M REALLY SWIFT TODAY.

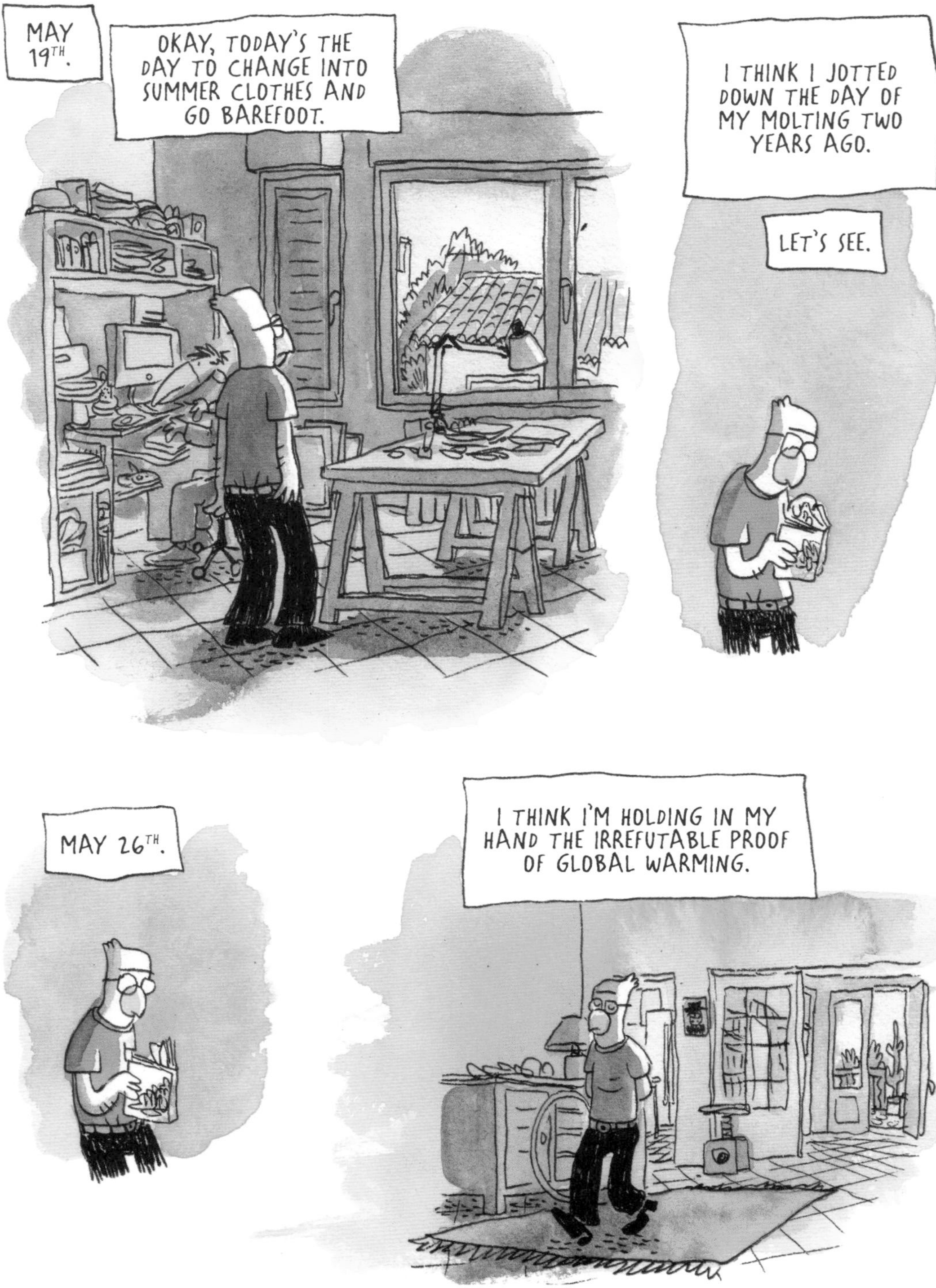
MAY 19TH.
OKAY, TODAY'S THE DAY TO CHANGE INTO SUMMER CLOTHES AND GO BAREFOOT.
I THINK I JOTTED DOWN THE DAY OF MY MOLTING TWO YEARS AGO.
LET'S SEE.
MAY 26TH.
I THINK I'M HOLDING IN MY HAND THE IRREFUTABLE PROOF OF GLOBAL WARMING.

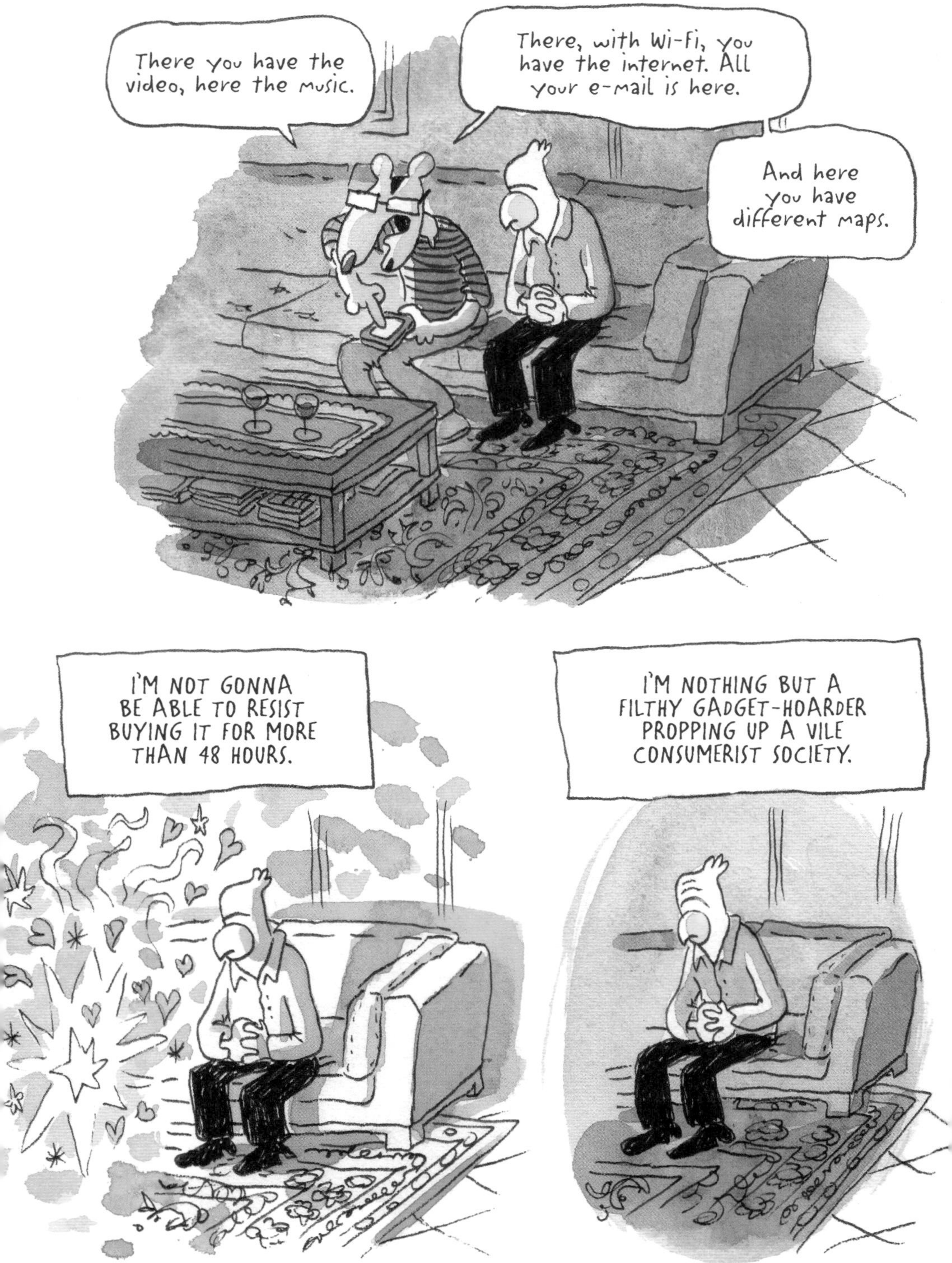
There you have the video, here the music.
There, with Wi-Fi, you have the internet. All your e-mail is here.
And here you have different maps.
I'M NOT GONNA BE ABLE TO RESIST BUYING IT FOR MORE THAN 48 HOURS.
I'M NOTHING BUT A FILTHY GADGET-HOARDER PROPPING UP A VILE CONSUMERIST SOCIETY.

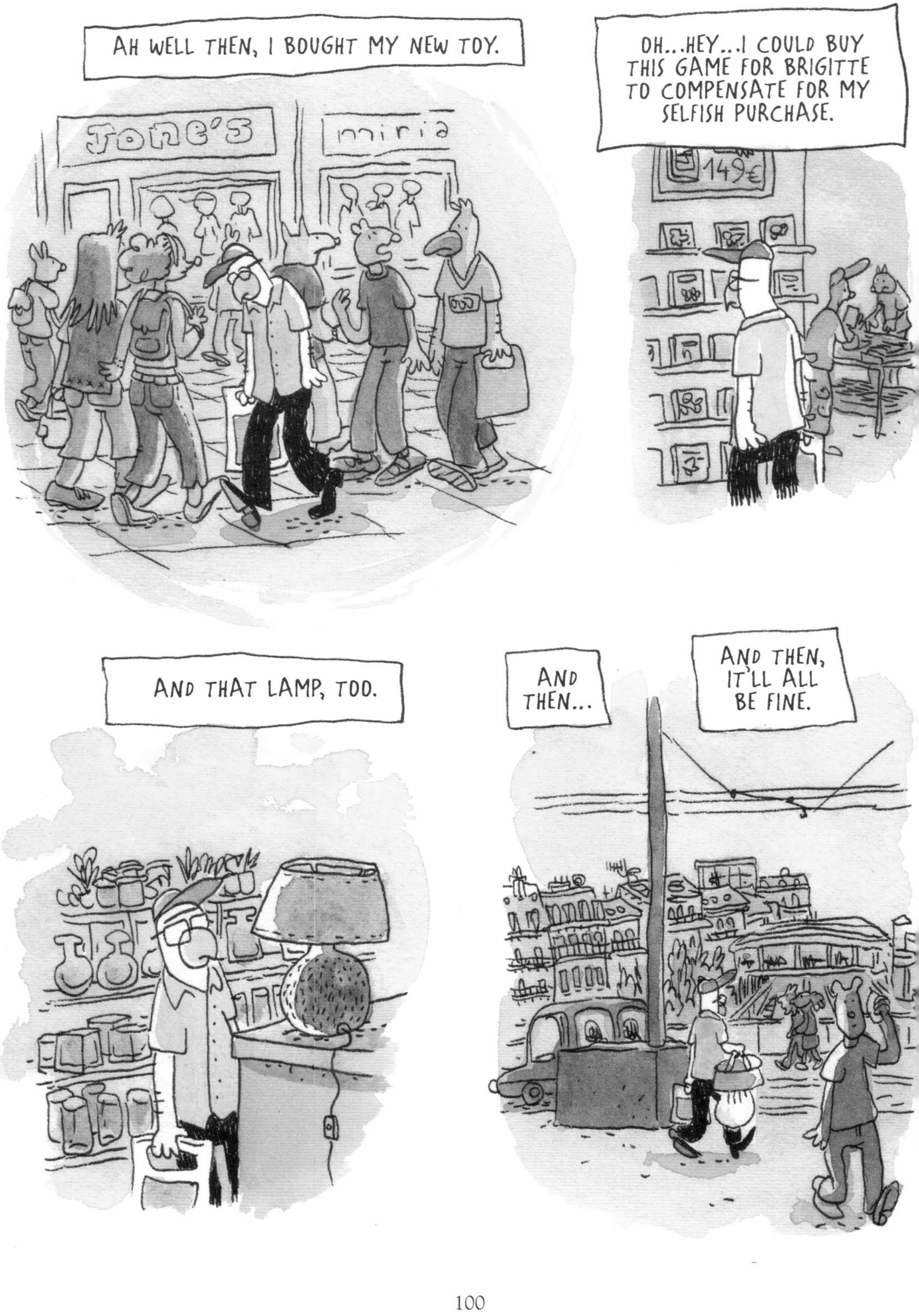
AH WELL THEN, I BOUGHT MY NEW TOY.
OH...HEY...I COULD BUY THIS GAME FOR BRIGITTE TO COMPENSATE FOR MY SELFISH PURCHASE.
149€
AND THAT LAMP, TOO.
AND THEN...
AND THEN, IT'LL ALL BE FINE.

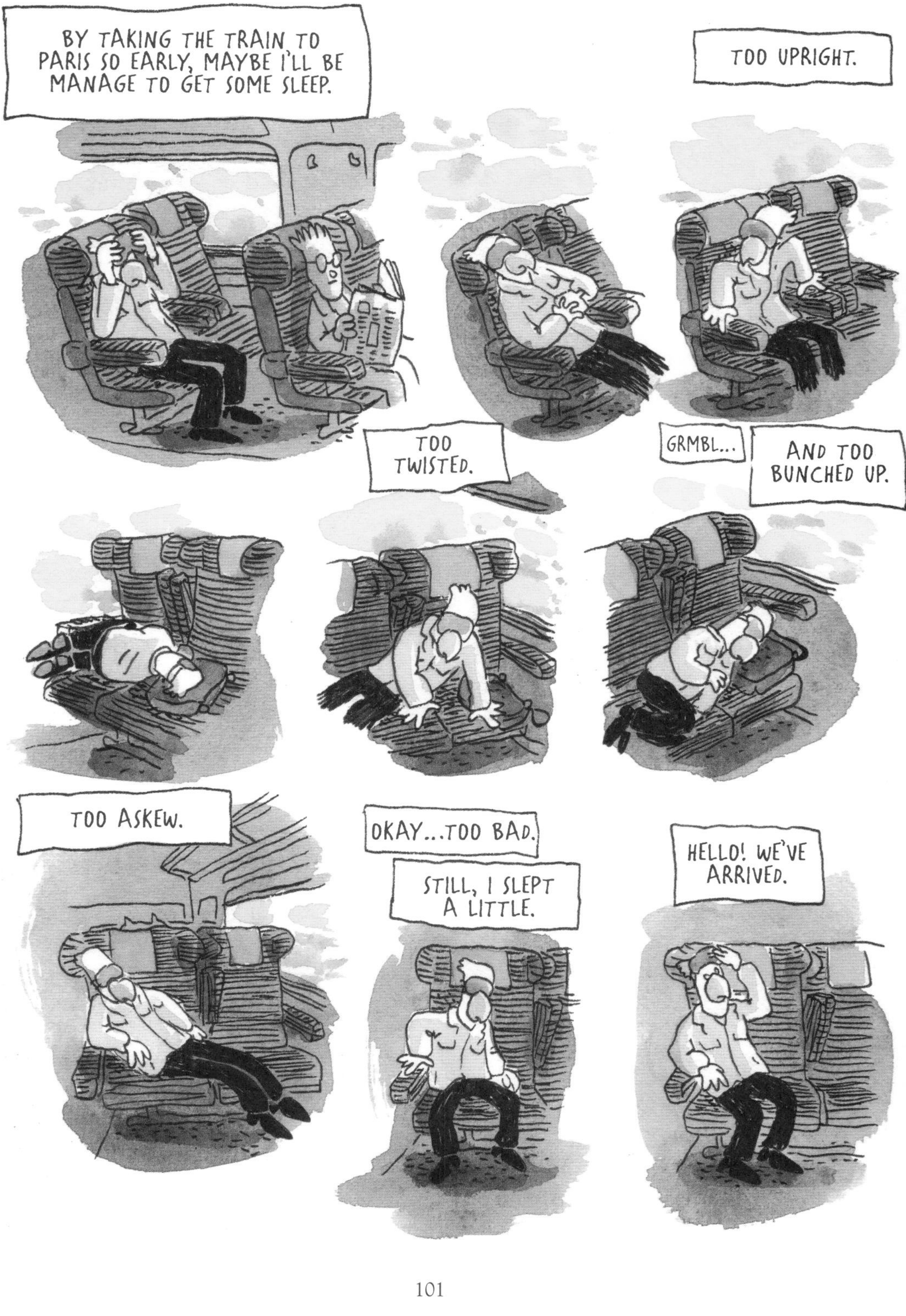
BY TAKING THE TRAIN TO PARIS SO EARLY, MAYBE I'LL BE MANAGE TO GET SOME SLEEP.
TOO UPRIGHT.
TOO TWISTED.
GRMBL...
AND TOO BUNCHED UP.
TOO ASKEW.
OKAY...TOO BAD.
STILL, I SLEPT A LITTLE.
HELLO! WE'VE ARRIVED.

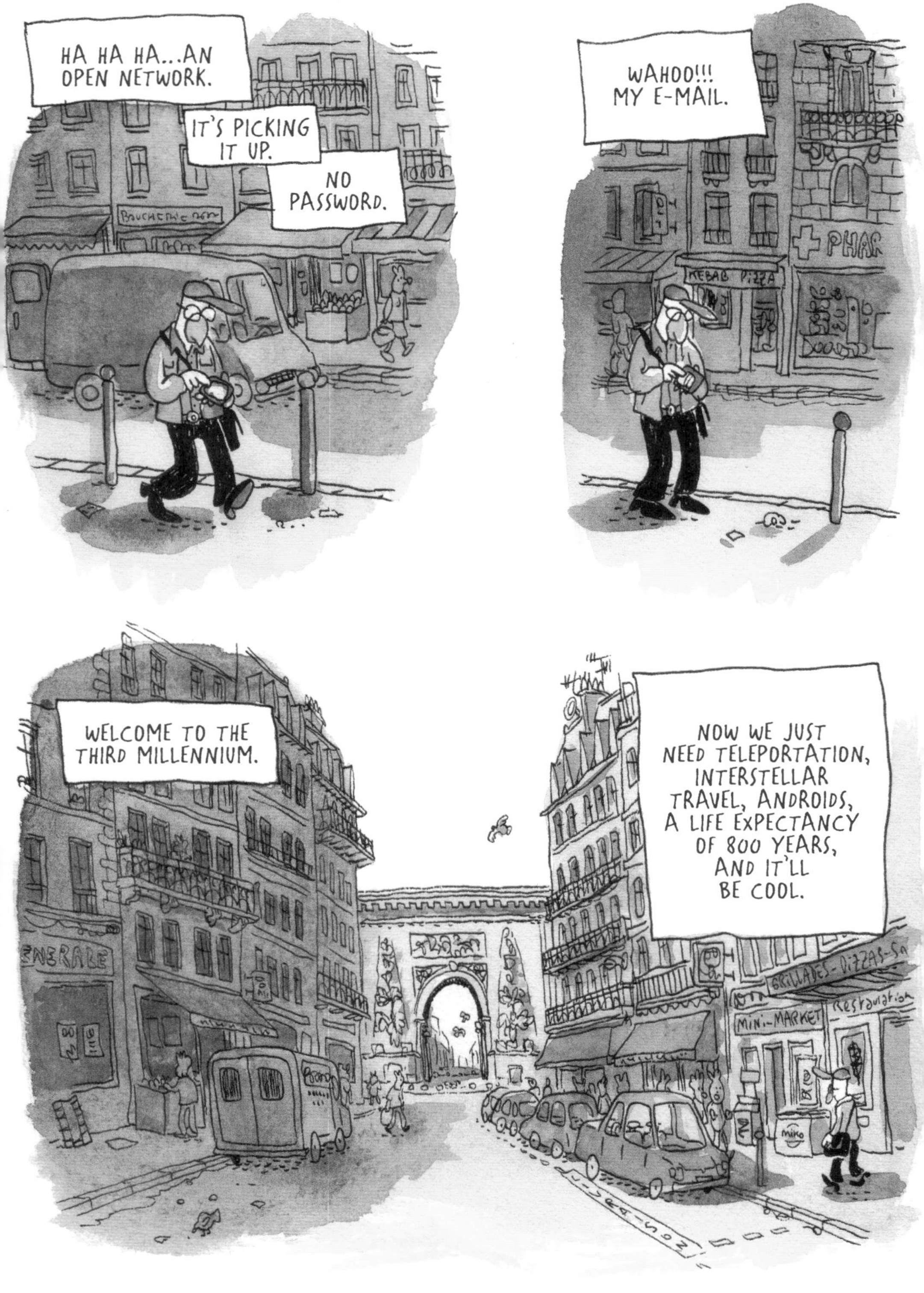
HA HA HA...AN OPEN NETWORK.
IT'S PICKING IT UP.
NO PASSWORD.
KEBAB PIZZA
PHAR
WAHOO!!! MY E-MAIL.
WELCOME TO THE THIRD MILLENNIUM.
NOW WE JUST NEED TELEPORTATION, INTERSTELLAR TRAVEL, ANDROIDS, A LIFE EXPECTANCY OF 800 YEARS, AND IT'LL BE COOL.
GRILLADES - PIZZAS
MINI-MARKET
Restauration

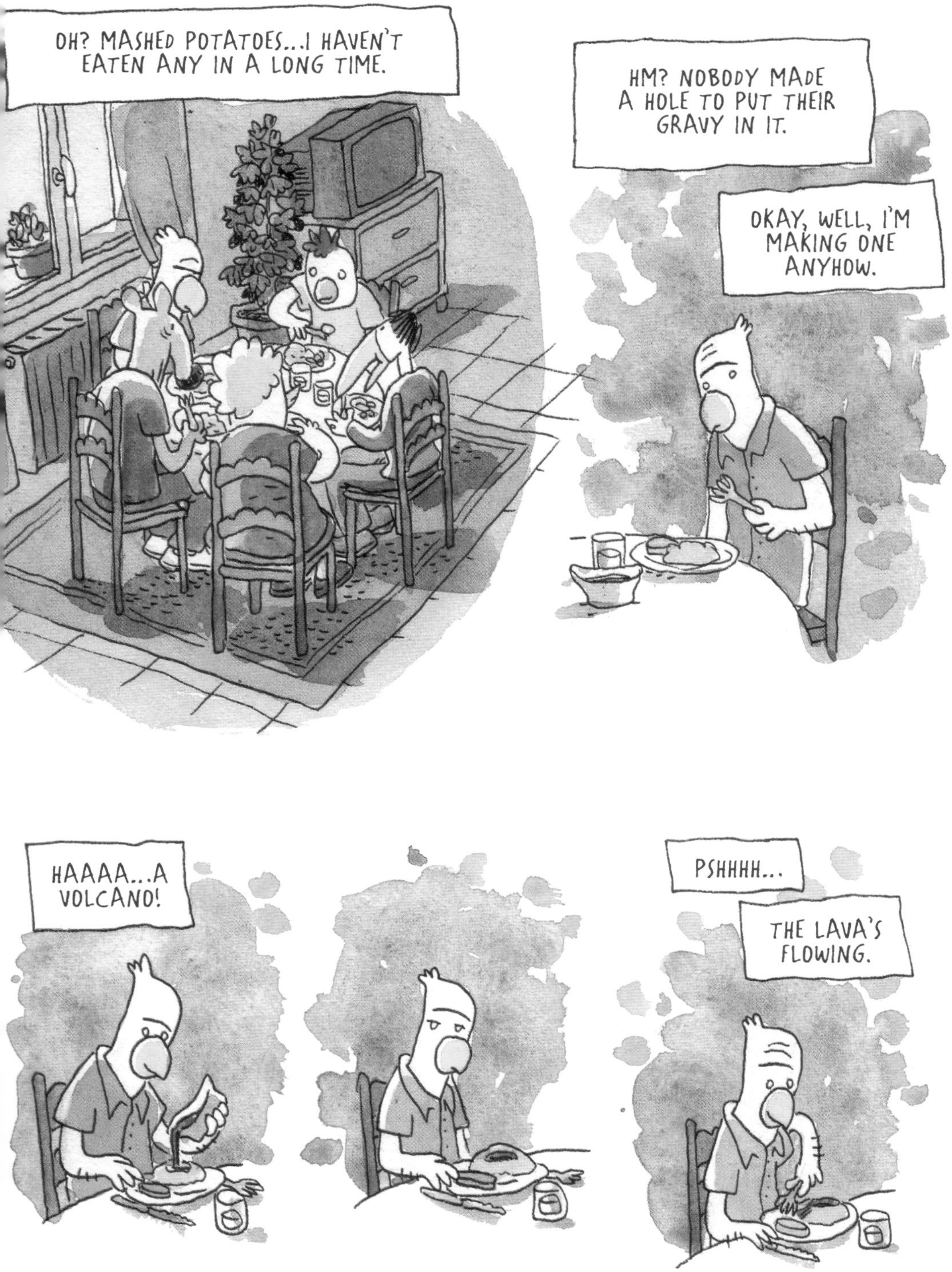
OH? MASHED POTATOES...I HAVEN'T EATEN ANY IN A LONG TIME.
HM? NOBODY MADE A HOLE TO PUT THEIR GRAVY IN IT.
OKAY, WELL, I'M MAKING ONE ANYHOW.
HAAAA...A VOLCANO!
PSHHHH...
THE LAVA'S FLOWING.

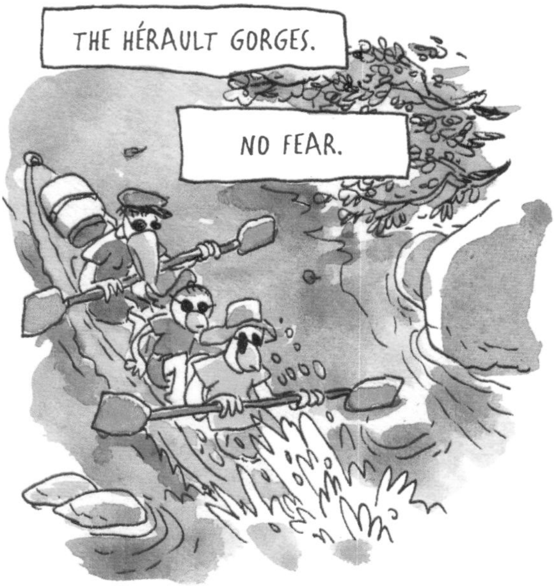
THE HÉRAULT GORGES.
NO FEAR.

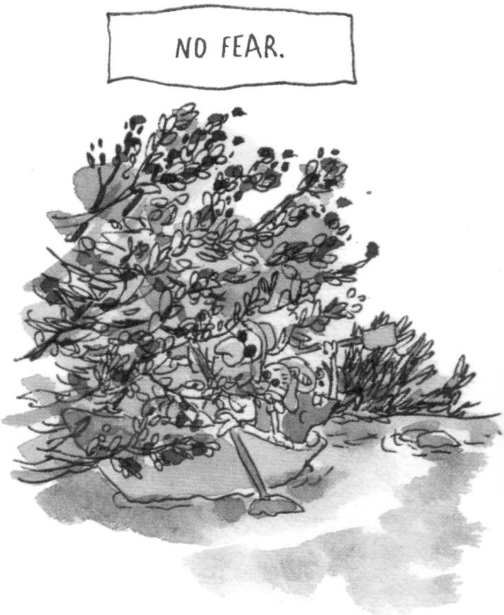
NO FEAR.

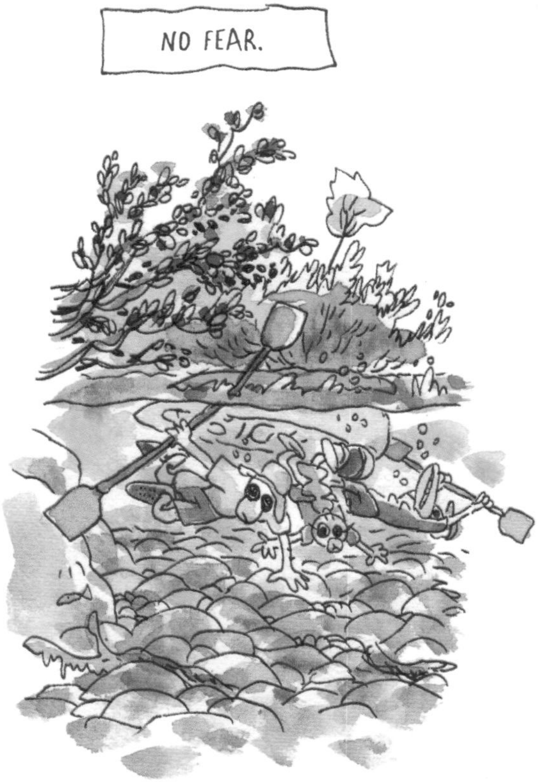
NO FEAR.

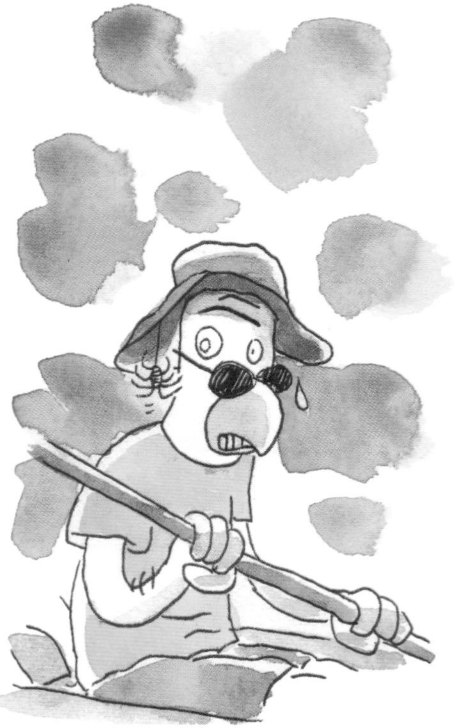

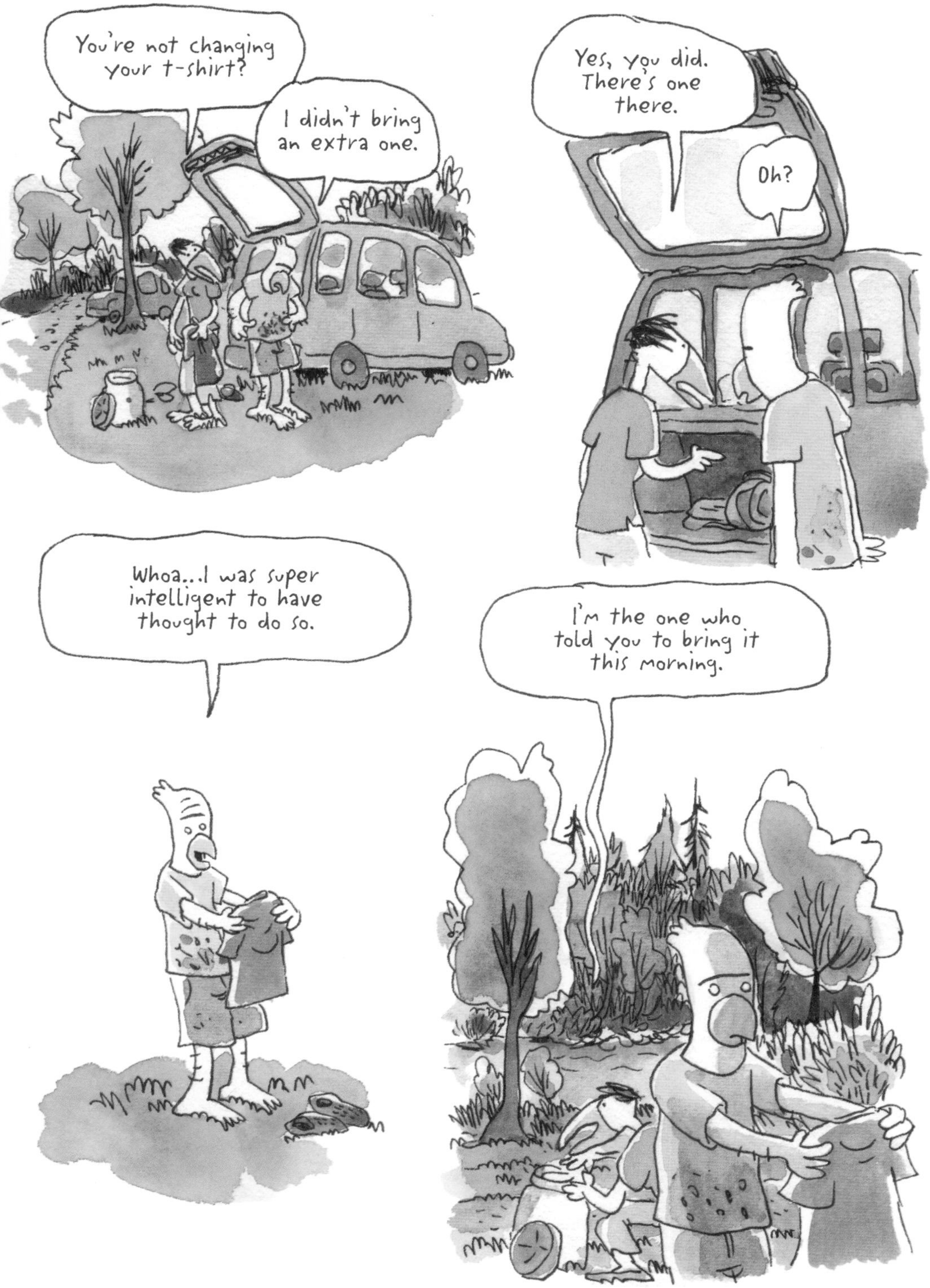
You're not changing your t-shirt?
I didn't bring an extra one.
Yes, you did. There's one there.
Oh?
Whoa...I was super intelligent to have thought to do so.
I'm the one who told you to bring it this morning.

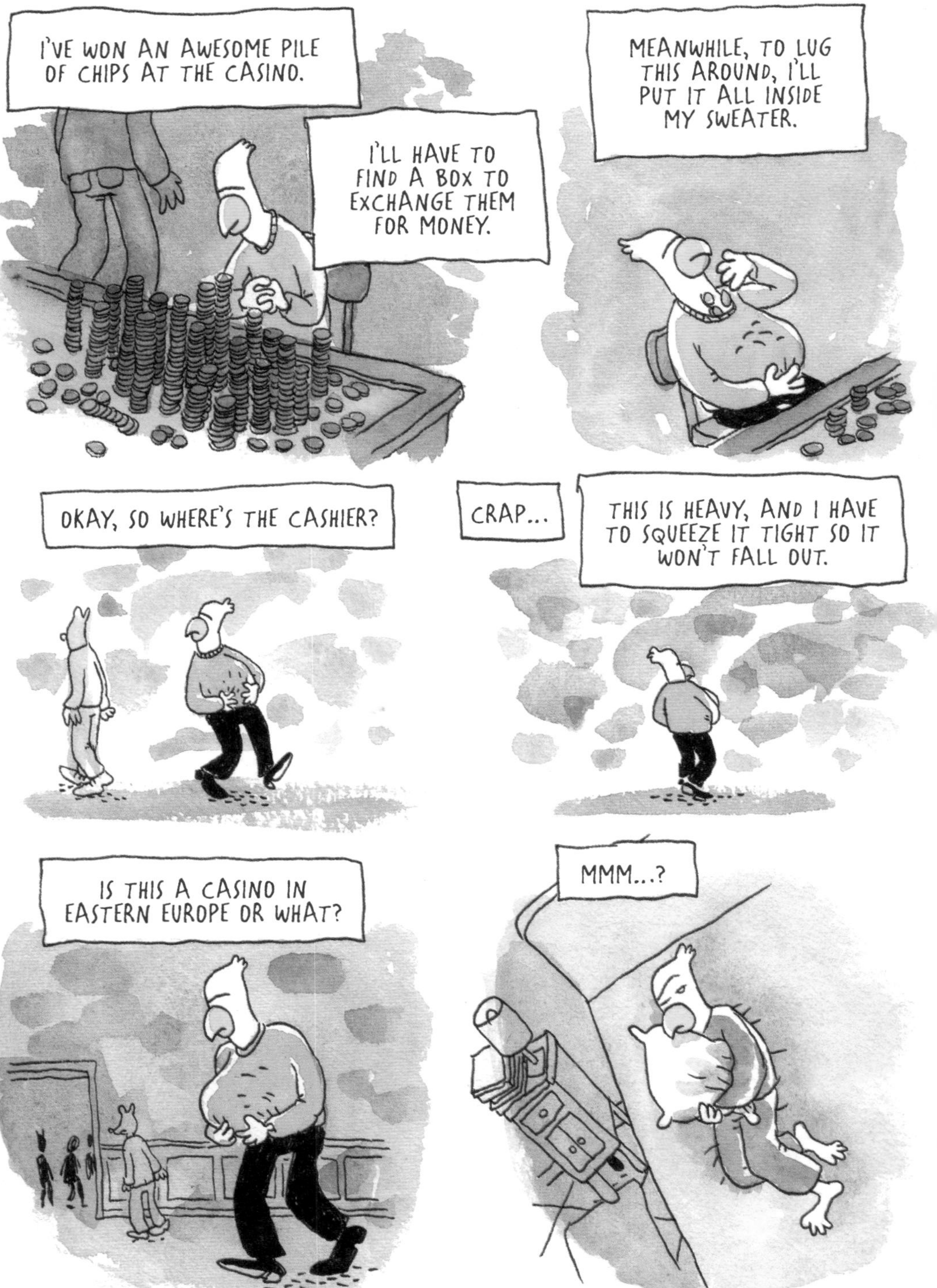
I'VE WON AN AWESOME PILE OF CHIPS AT THE CASINO.
I'LL HAVE TO FIND A BOX TO EXCHANGE THEM FOR MONEY.
MEANWHILE, TO LUG THIS AROUND, I'LL PUT IT ALL INSIDE MY SWEATER.
OKAY, SO WHERE'S THE CASHIER?
CRAP...
THIS IS HEAVY, AND I HAVE TO SQUEEZE IT TIGHT SO IT WON'T FALL OUT.
IS THIS A CASINO IN EASTERN EUROPE OR WHAT?
MMM...?

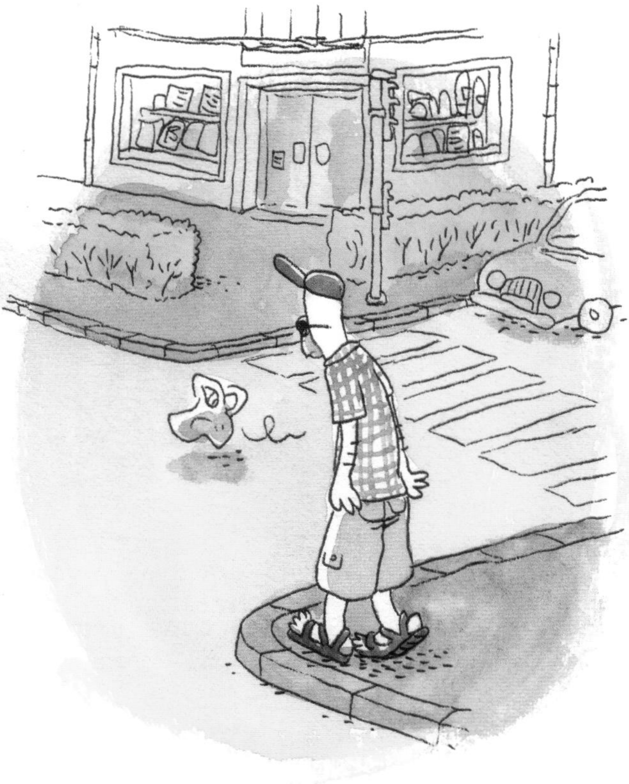

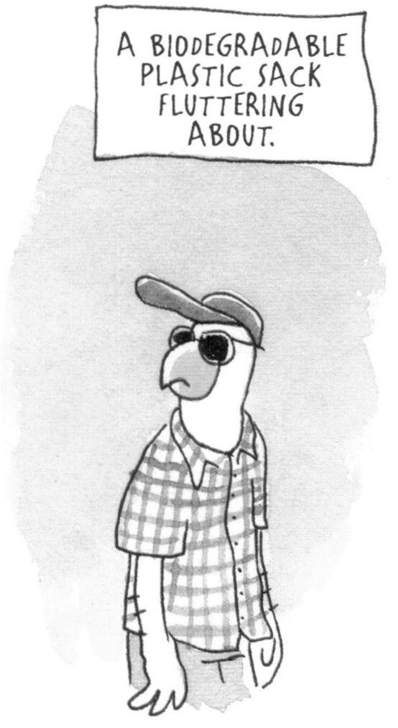
A BIODEGRADABLE PLASTIC SACK FLUTTERING ABOUT.

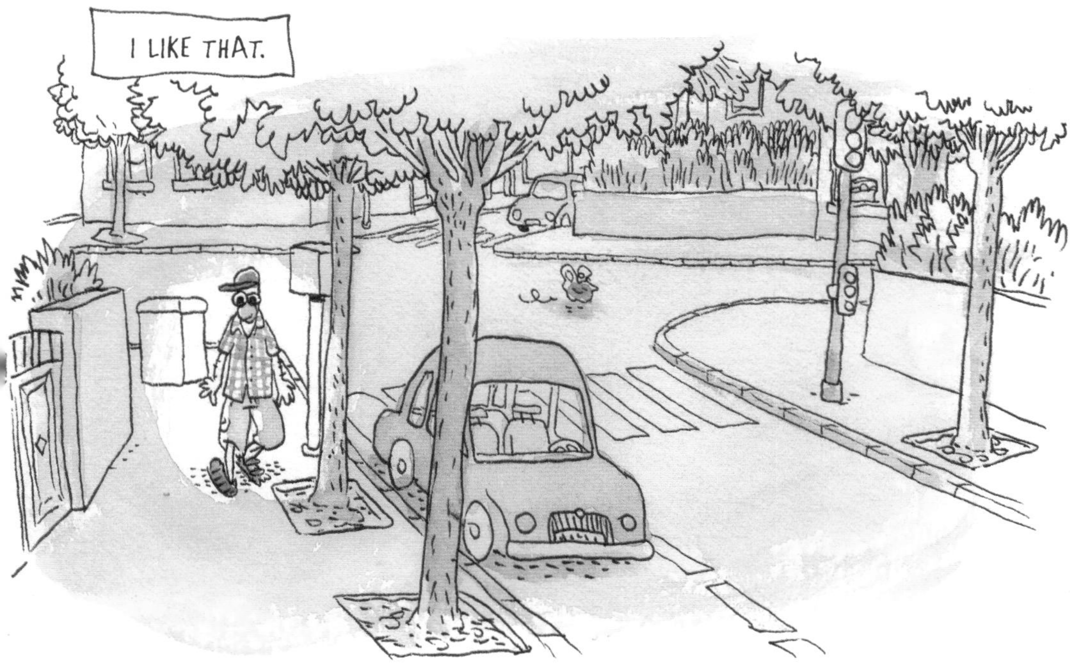
I LIKE THAT.

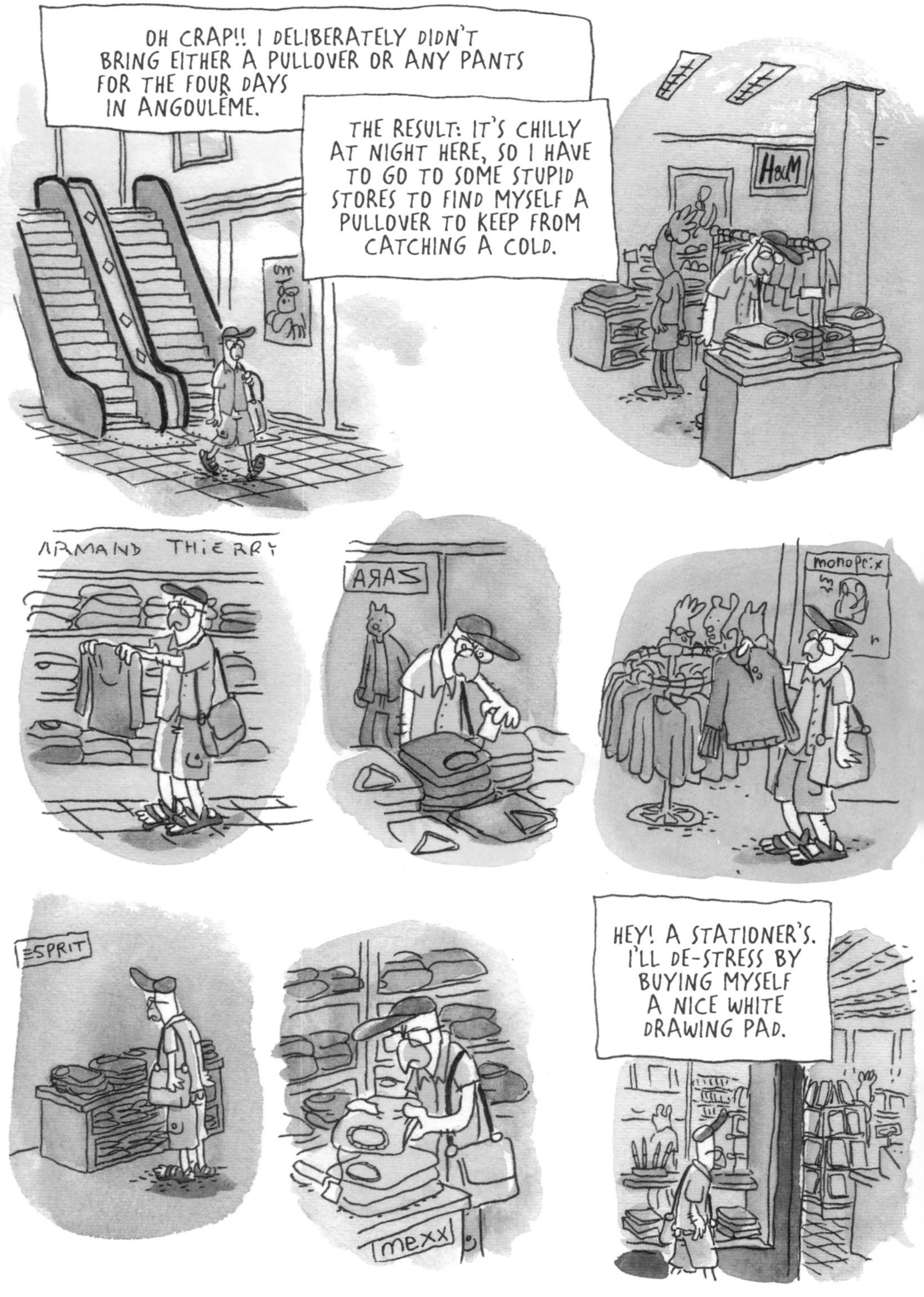
OH CRAP!! I DELIBERATELY DIDN'T BRING EITHER A PULLOVER OR ANY PANTS FOR THE FOUR DAYS IN ANGOULÊME.
THE RESULT: IT'S CHILLY AT NIGHT HERE, SO I HAVE TO GO TO SOME STUPID STORES TO FIND MYSELF A PULLOVER TO KEEP FROM CATCHING A COLD.
H&M
ARMAND THIERRY
ZARA
monoprix
ESPRIT
mexx
HEY! A STATIONER'S. I'LL DE-STRESS BY BUYING MYSELF A NICE WHITE DRAWING PAD.

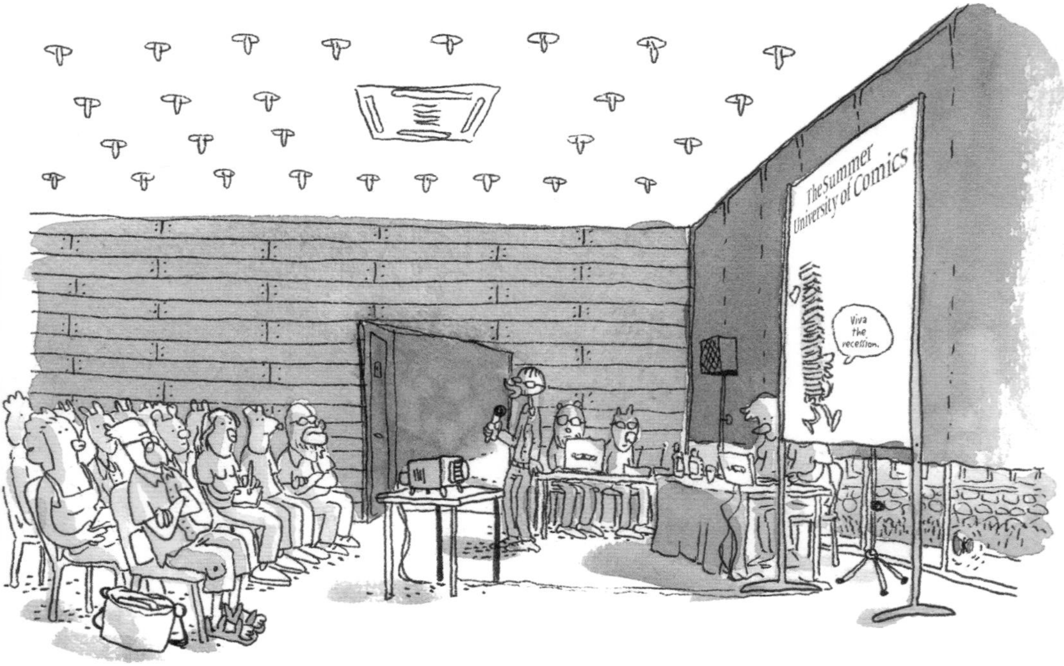
The Summer
University of Comics
Viva the recession.

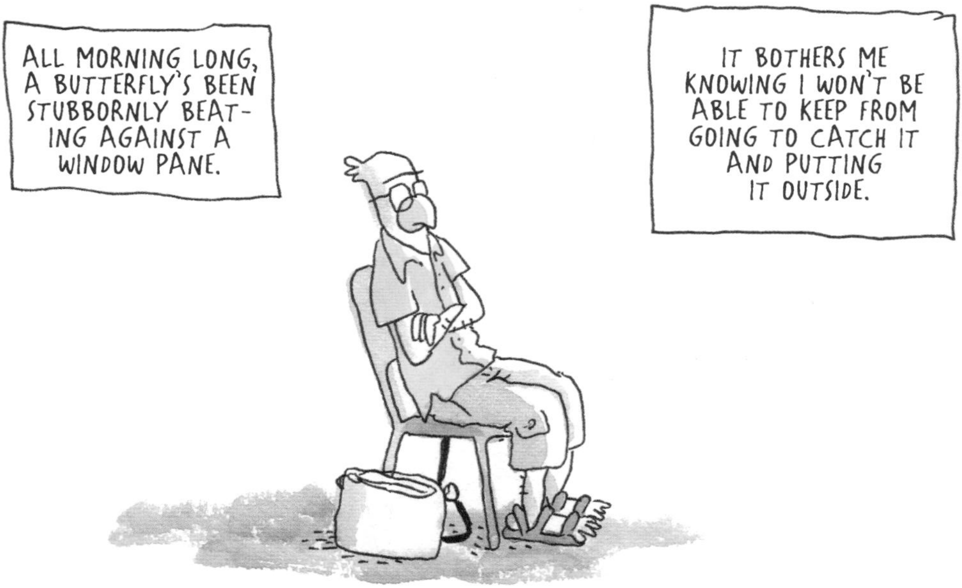
ALL MORNING LONG, A BUTTERFLY'S BEEN STUBBORNLY BEAT-ING AGAINST A WINDOW PANE.
IT BOTHERS ME KNOWING I WON'T BE ABLE TO KEEP FROM GOING TO CATCH IT AND PUTTING IT OUTSIDE.

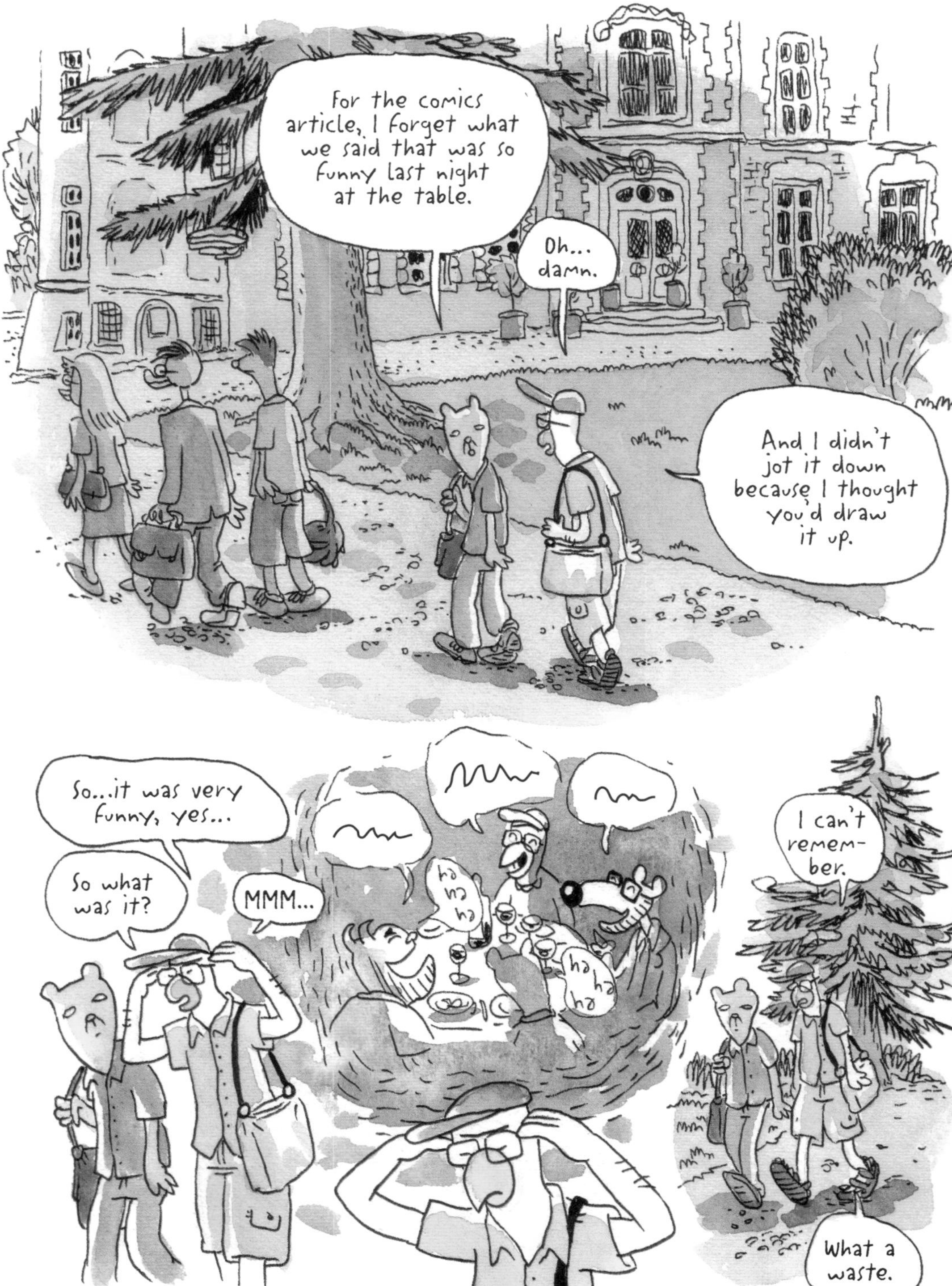
For the comics article, I forget what we said that was so funny last night at the table.
Oh... damn.
And I didn't jot it down because I thought you'd draw it up.
So...it was very funny, yes...
So what was it?
MMM...
I can't remember.
What a waste.

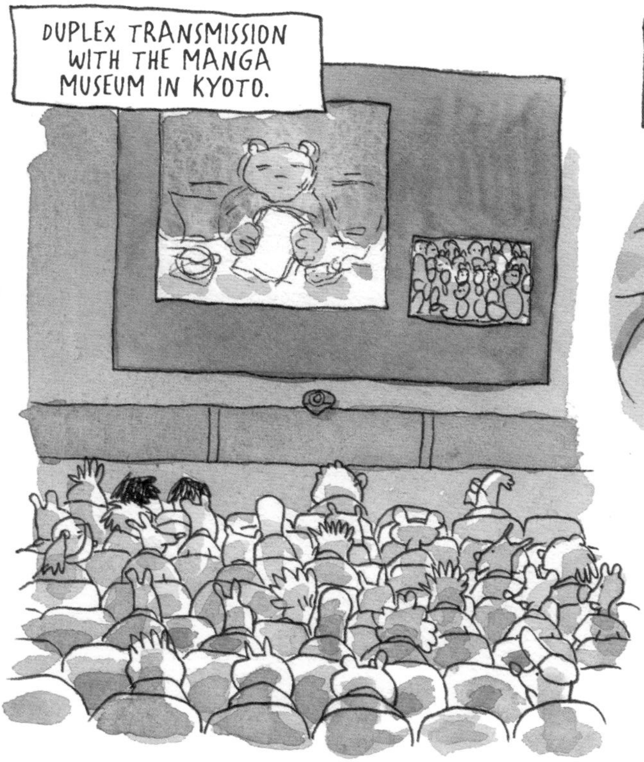
DUPLEX TRANSMISSION
WITH THE MANGA
MUSEUM IN KYOTO.

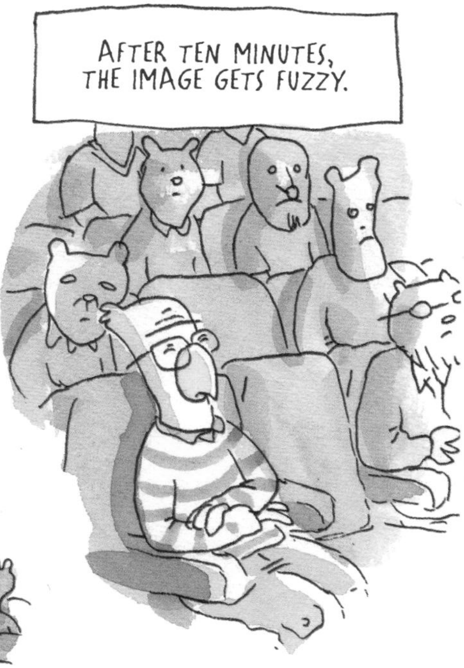
AFTER TEN MINUTES,
THE IMAGE GETS FUZZY.

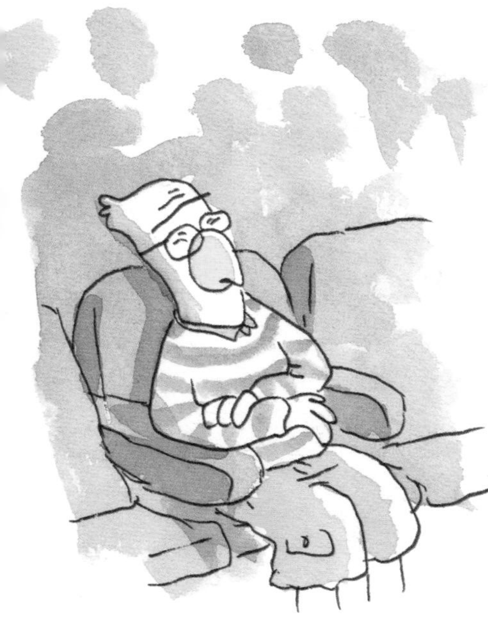

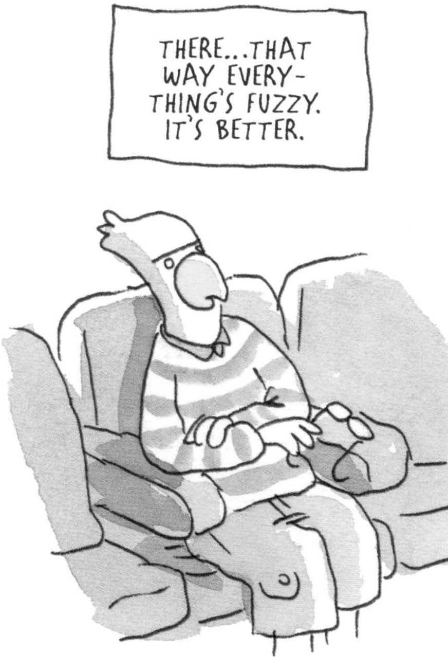
THERE...THAT
WAY EVERY-
THING'S FUZZY.
IT'S BETTER.

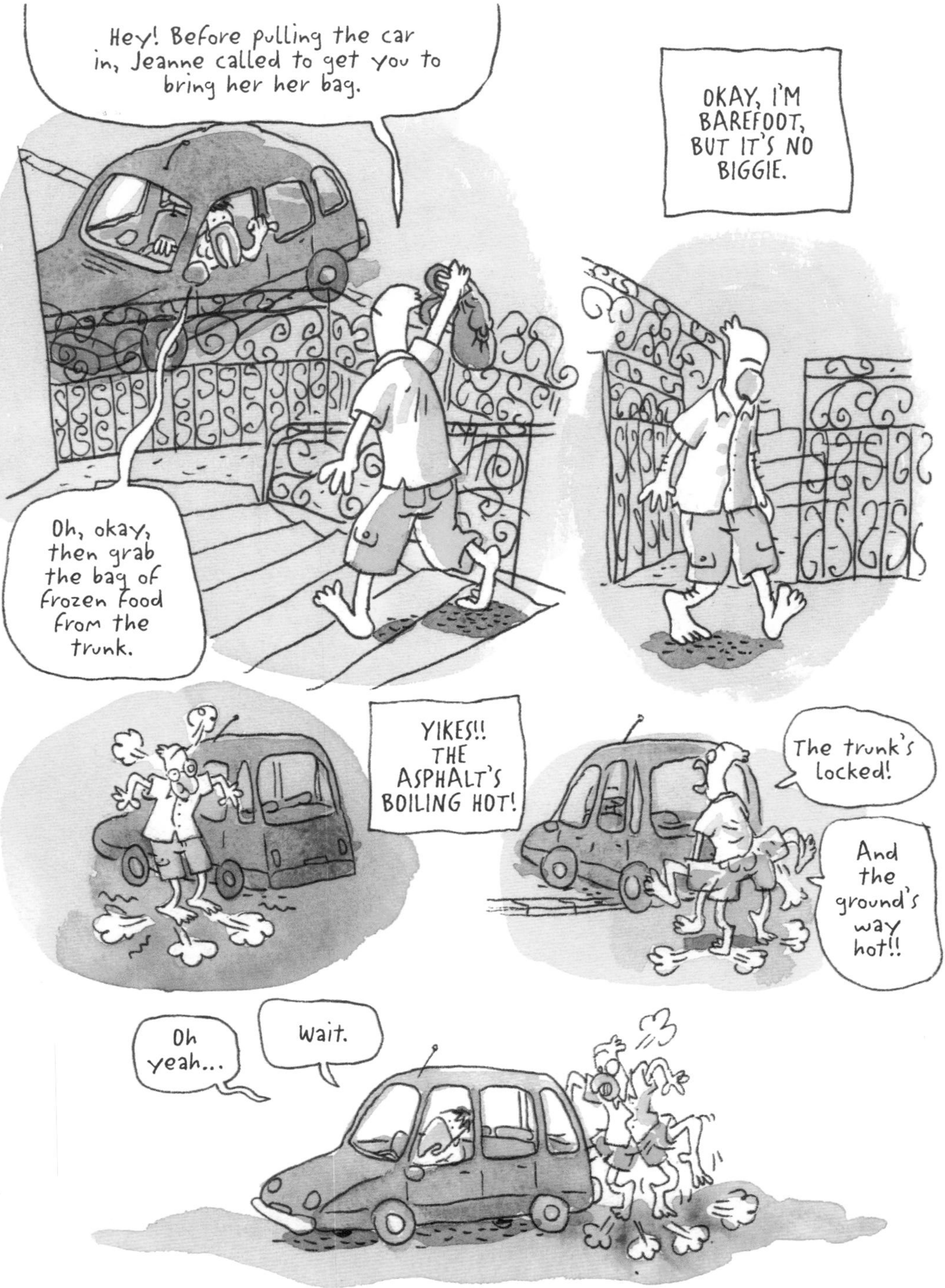
Hey! Before pulling the car in, Jeanne called to get you to bring her her bag.
Oh, okay, then grab the bag of frozen food from the trunk.
OKAY, I'M BAREFOOT, BUT IT'S NO BIGGIE.
YIKES!! THE ASPHALT'S BOILING HOT!
The trunk's locked!
And the ground's way hot!!
Oh yeah...
Wait.

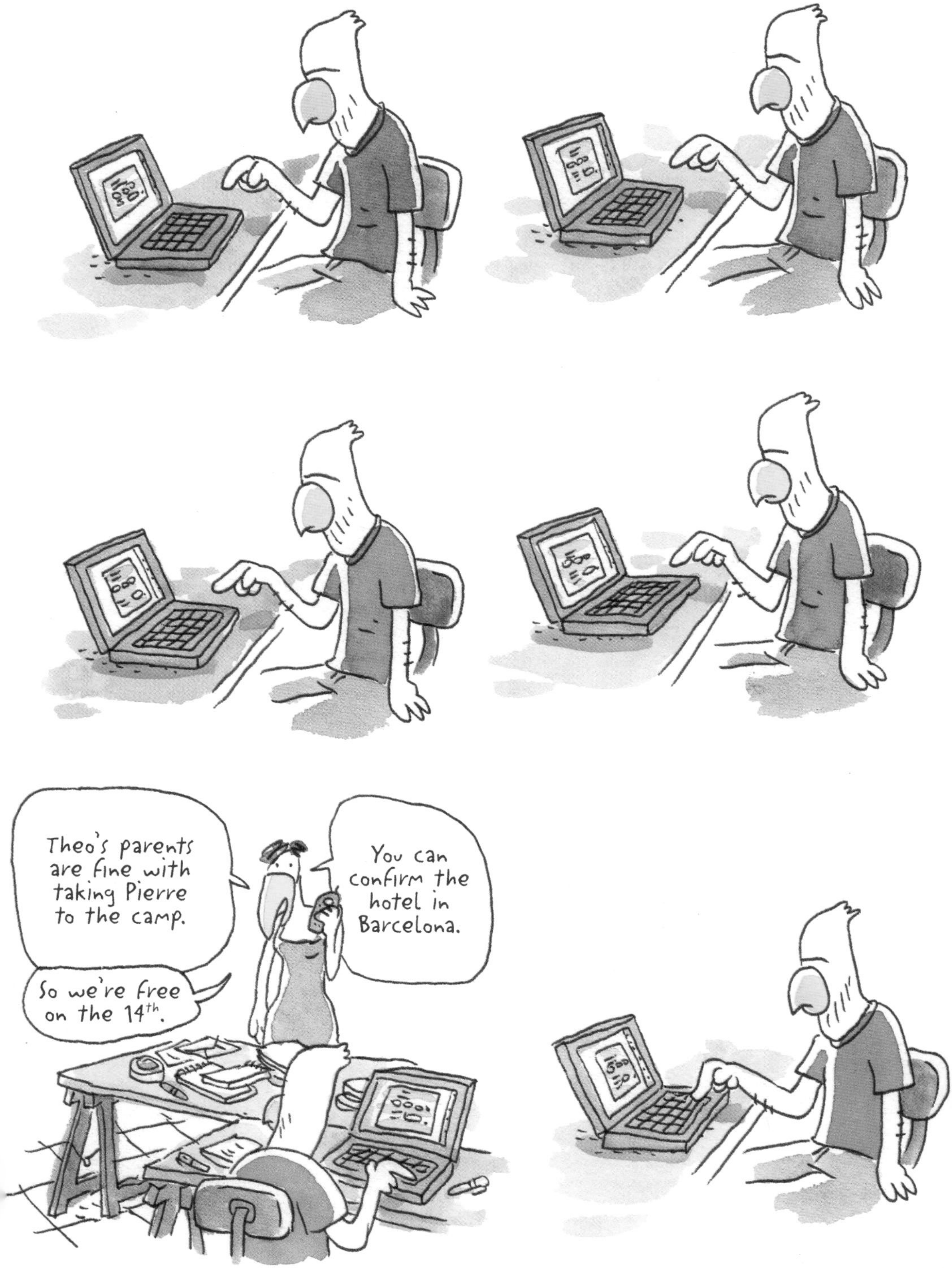
Theo's parents are fine with taking Pierre to the camp.
So we're free on the 14th.
You can confirm the hotel in Barcelona.

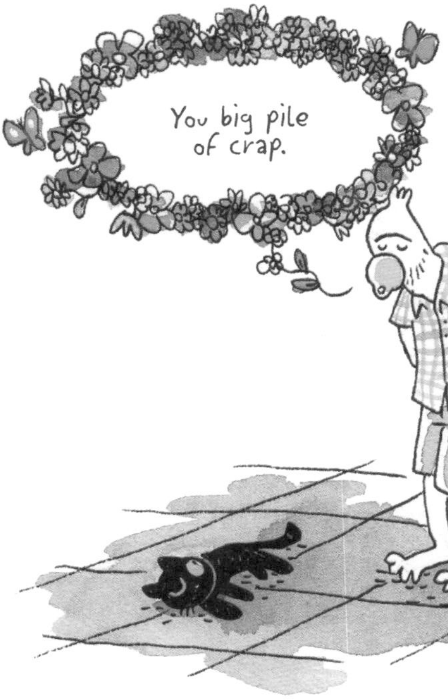
You big pile of crap.

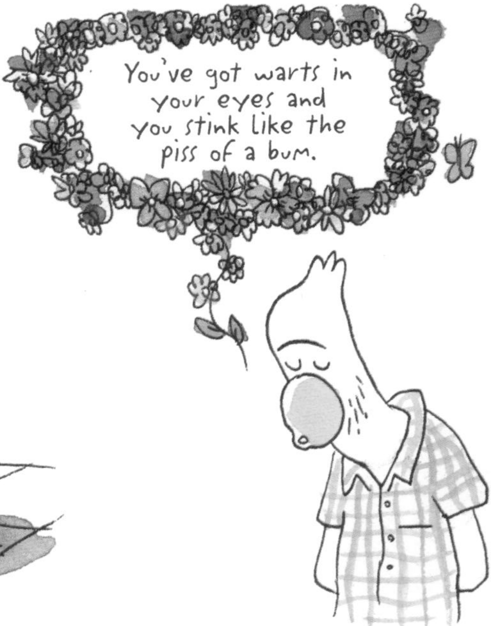
You've got warts in your eyes and you stink like the piss of a bum.

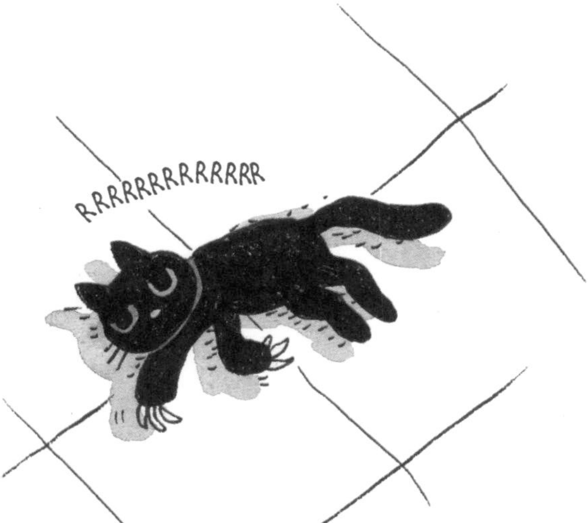
RRRRRRRRRRRR

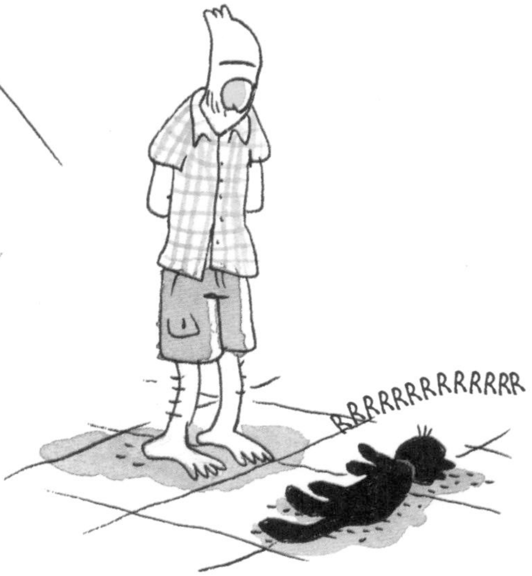
RRRRRRRRRRRRR

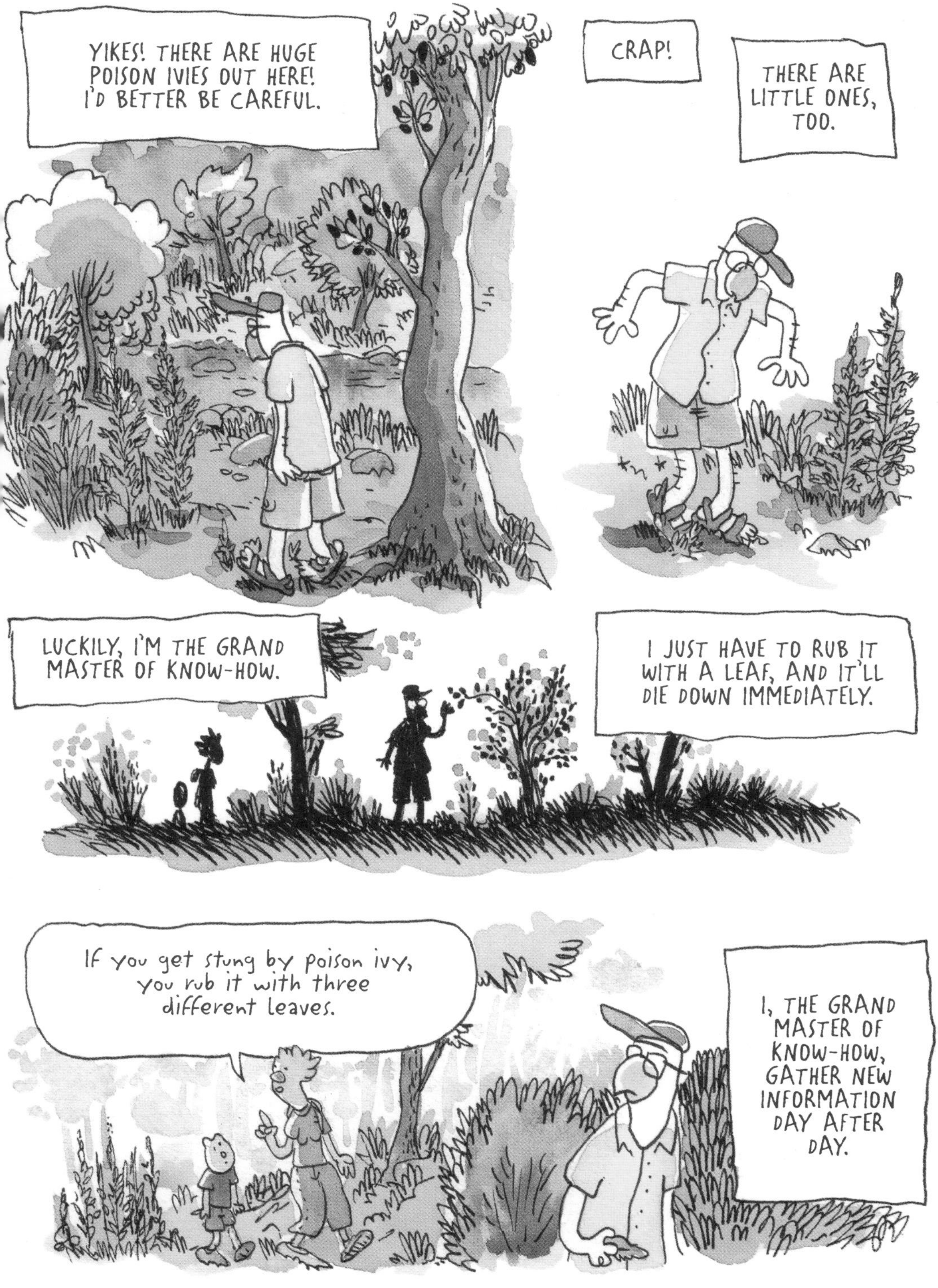

YIKES! THERE ARE HUGE POISON IVIES OUT HERE! I'D BETTER BE CAREFUL.
CRAP!
THERE ARE LITTLE ONES, TOO.
LUCKILY, I'M THE GRAND MASTER OF KNOW-HOW.
I JUST HAVE TO RUB IT WITH A LEAF, AND IT'LL DIE DOWN IMMEDIATELY.
If you get stung by poison ivy, you rub it with three different leaves.
I, THE GRAND MASTER OF KNOW-HOW, GATHER NEW INFORMATION DAY AFTER DAY.

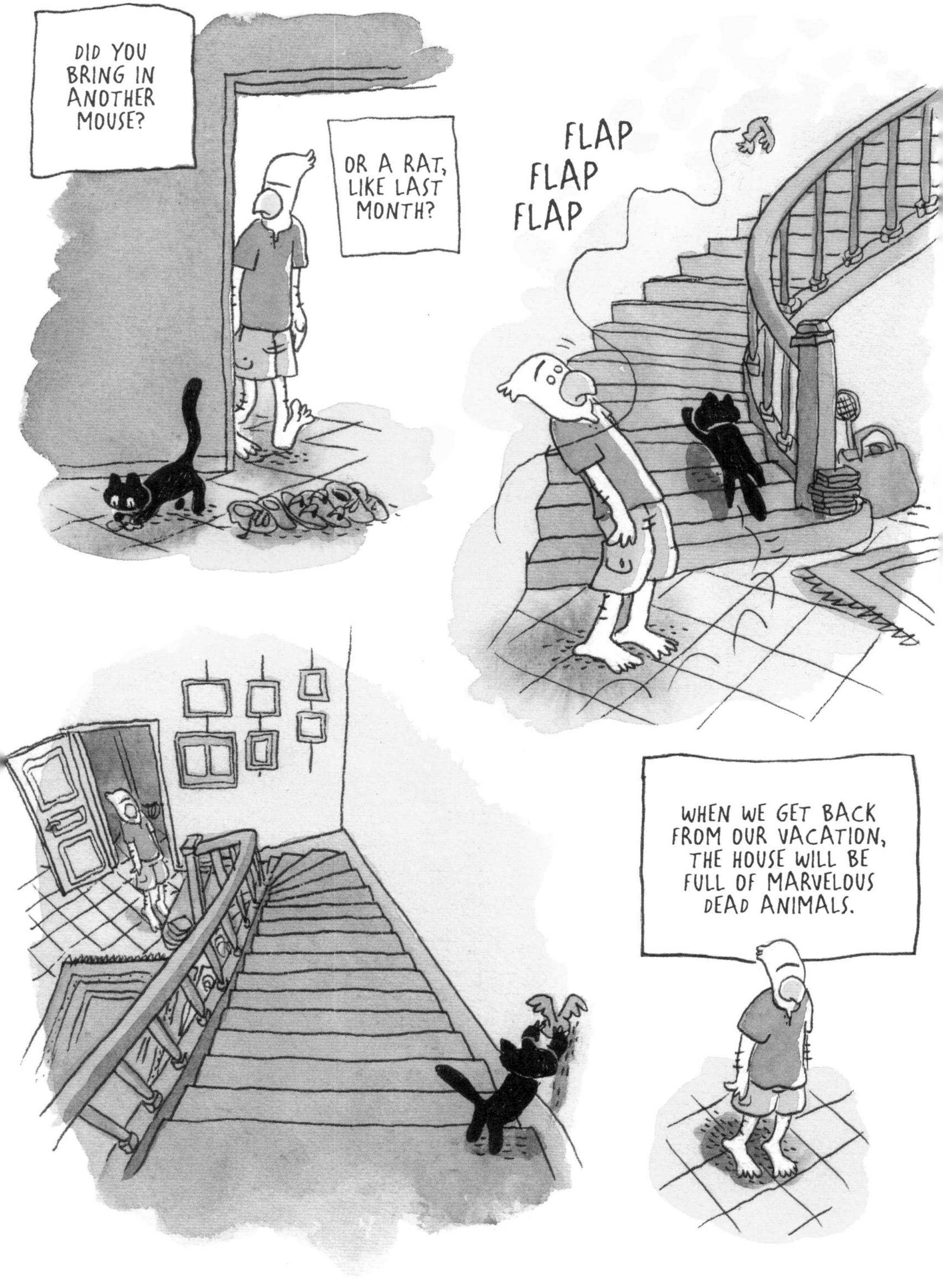
DID YOU BRING IN ANOTHER MOUSE?
OR A RAT, LIKE LAST MONTH?
FLAP
FLAP
FLAP
WHEN WE GET BACK FROM OUR VACATION, THE HOUSE WILL BE FULL OF MARVELOUS DEAD ANIMALS.

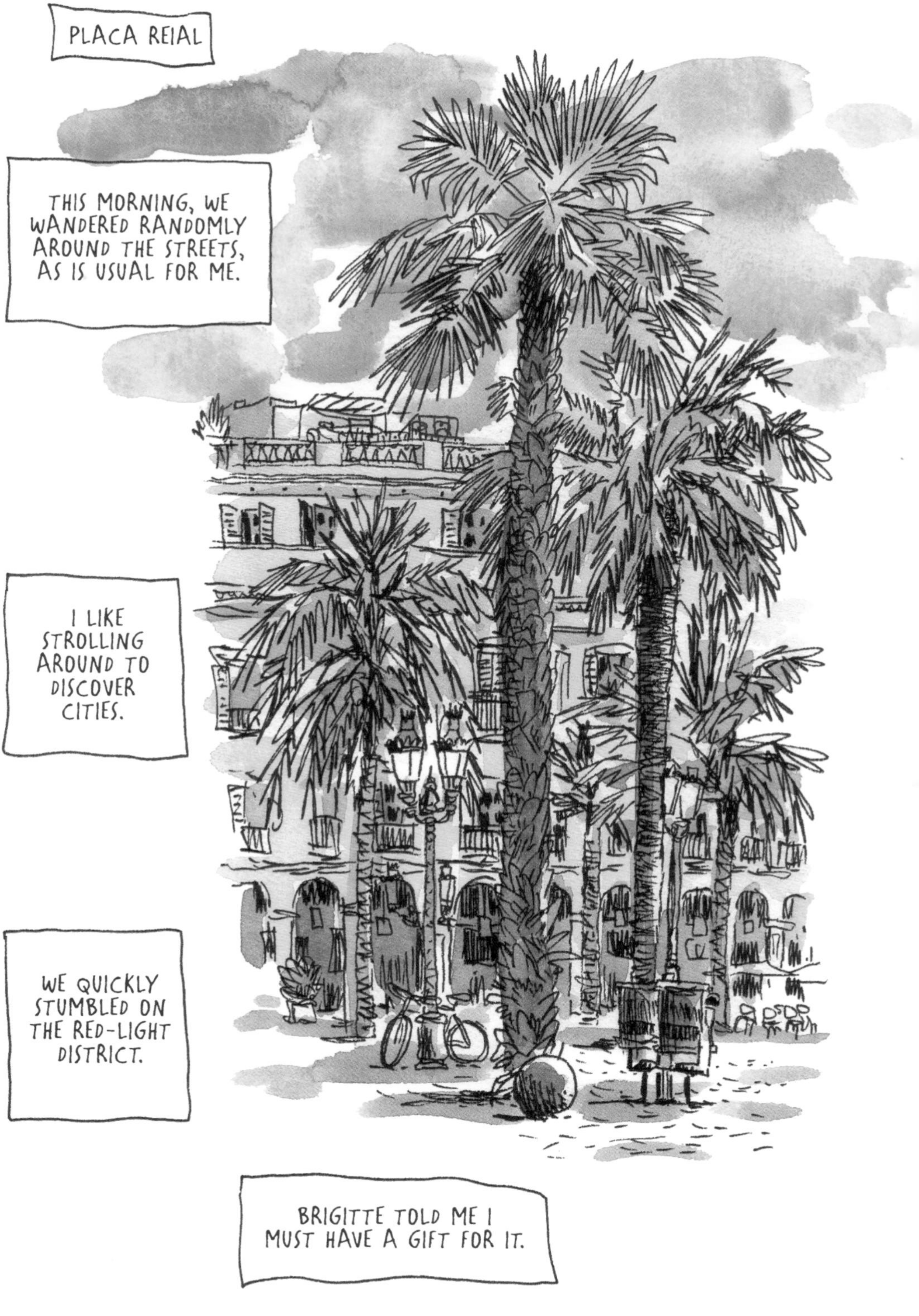
PLACA REIAL
THIS MORNING, WE WANDERED RANDOMLY AROUND THE STREETS, AS IS USUAL FOR ME.
I LIKE STROLLING AROUND TO DISCOVER CITIES.
WE QUICKLY STUMBLED ON THE RED-LIGHT DISTRICT.
BRIGITTE TOLD ME I MUST HAVE A GIFT FOR IT.

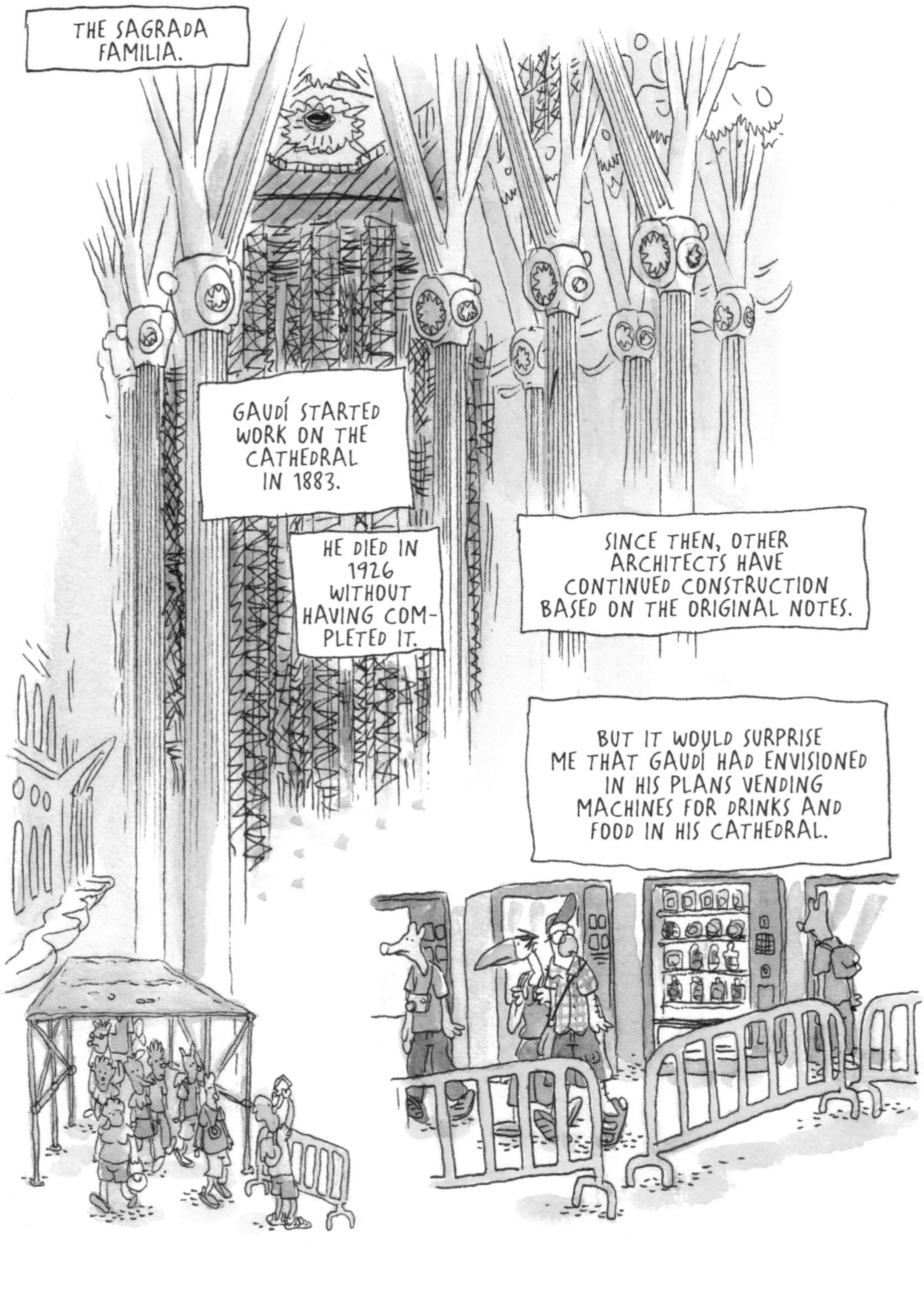
THE SAGRADA FAMILIA.
GAUDÍ STARTED WORK ON THE CATHEDRAL IN 1883.
HE DIED IN 1926 WITHOUT HAVING COMPLETED IT.
SINCE THEN, OTHER ARCHITECTS HAVE CONTINUED CONSTRUCTION BASED ON THE ORIGINAL NOTES.
BUT IT WOULD SURPRISE ME THAT GAUDÍ HAD ENVISIONED IN HIS PLANS VENDING MACHINES FOR DRINKS AND FOOD IN HIS CATHEDRAL.

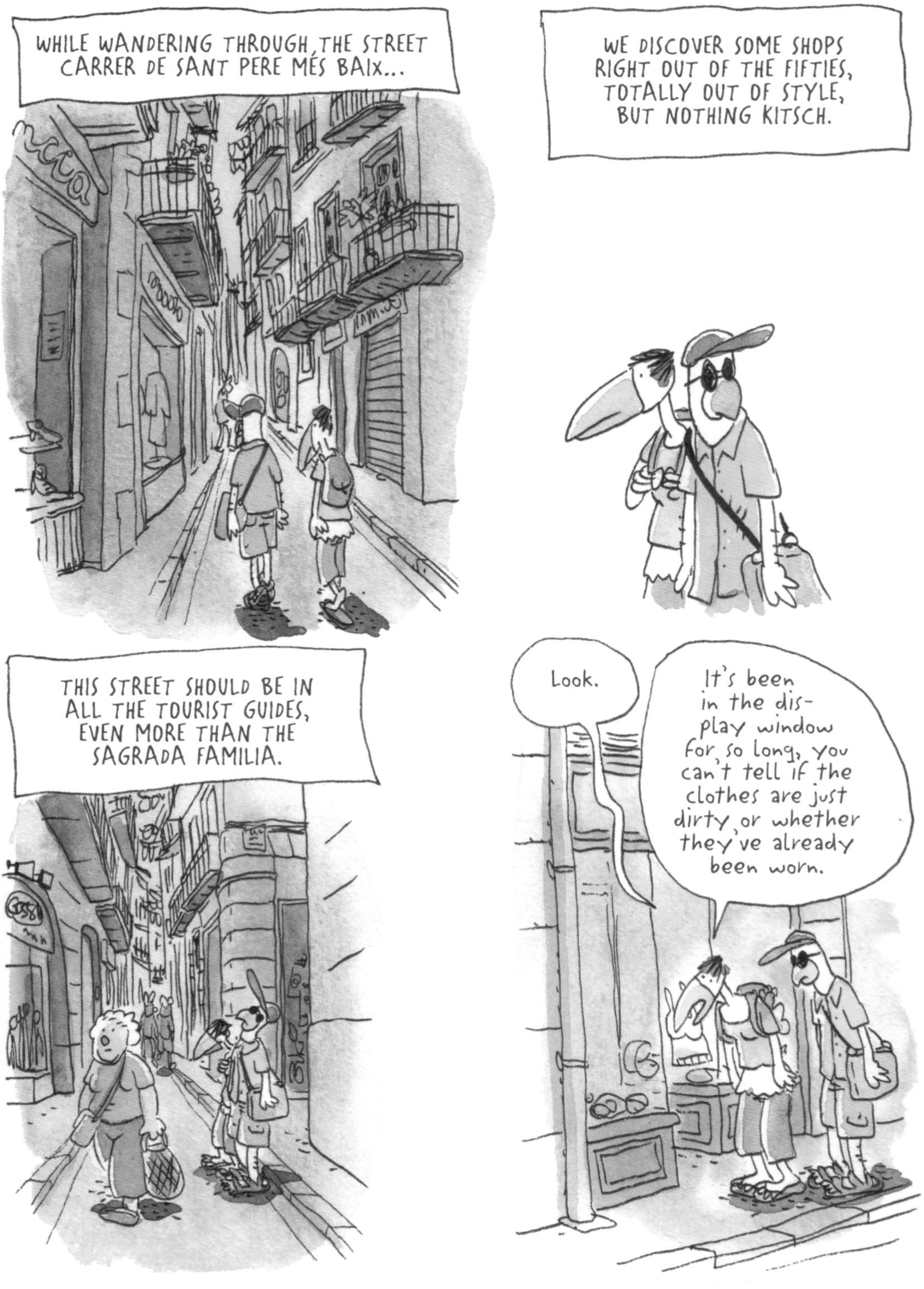
WHILE WANDERING THROUGH THE STREET CARRER DE SANT PERE MÉS BAIX...
WE DISCOVER SOME SHOPS RIGHT OUT OF THE FIFTIES, TOTALLY OUT OF STYLE, BUT NOTHING KITSCH.
THIS STREET SHOULD BE IN ALL THE TOURIST GUIDES, EVEN MORE THAN THE SAGRADA FAMILIA.
Look.
It's been in the display window for so long, you can't tell if the clothes are just dirty or whether they've already been worn.

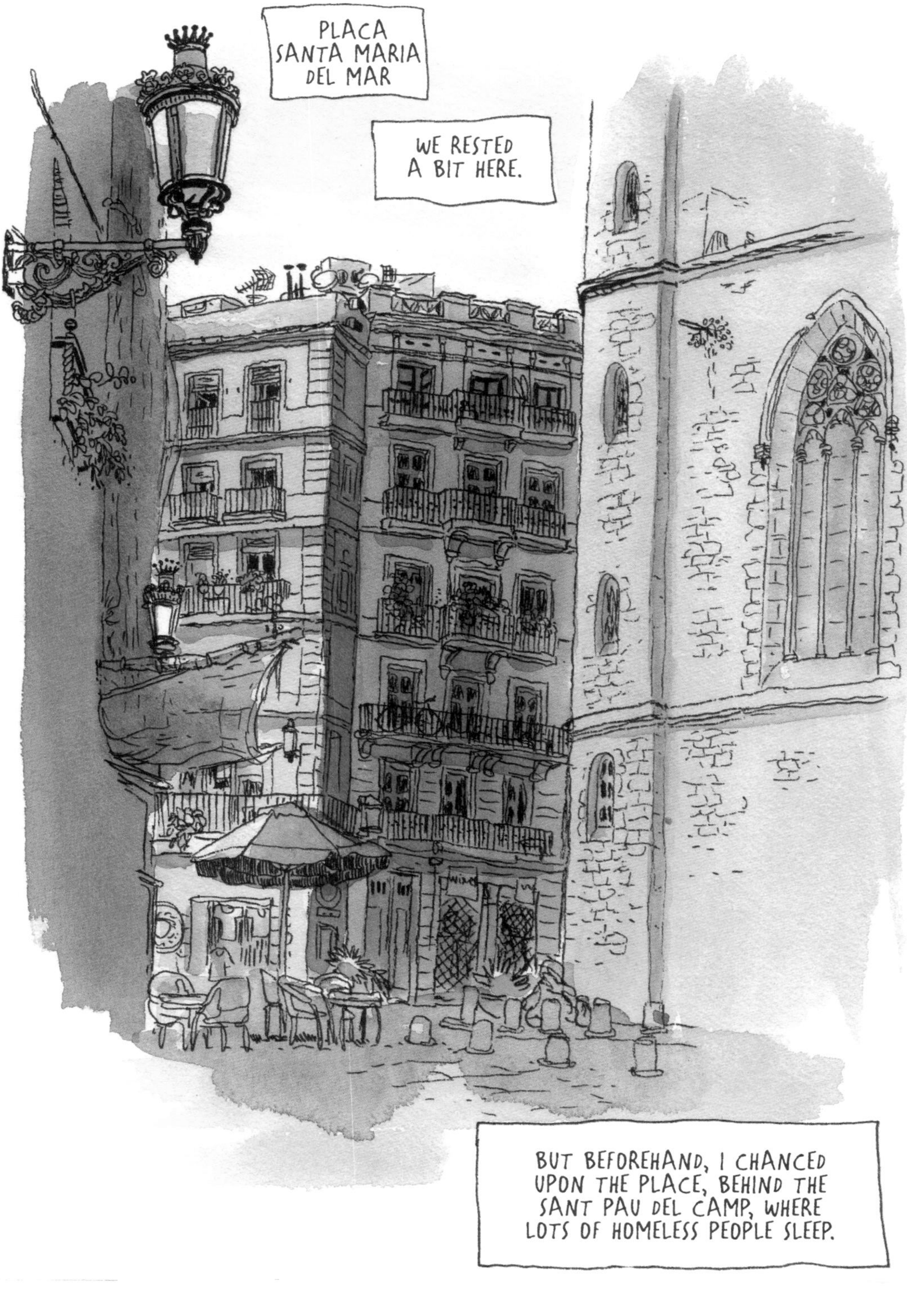
PLACA SANTA MARIA DEL MAR
WE RESTED A BIT HERE.
BUT BEFOREHAND, I CHANCED UPON THE PLACE, BEHIND THE SANT PAU DEL CAMP, WHERE LOTS OF HOMELESS PEOPLE SLEEP.

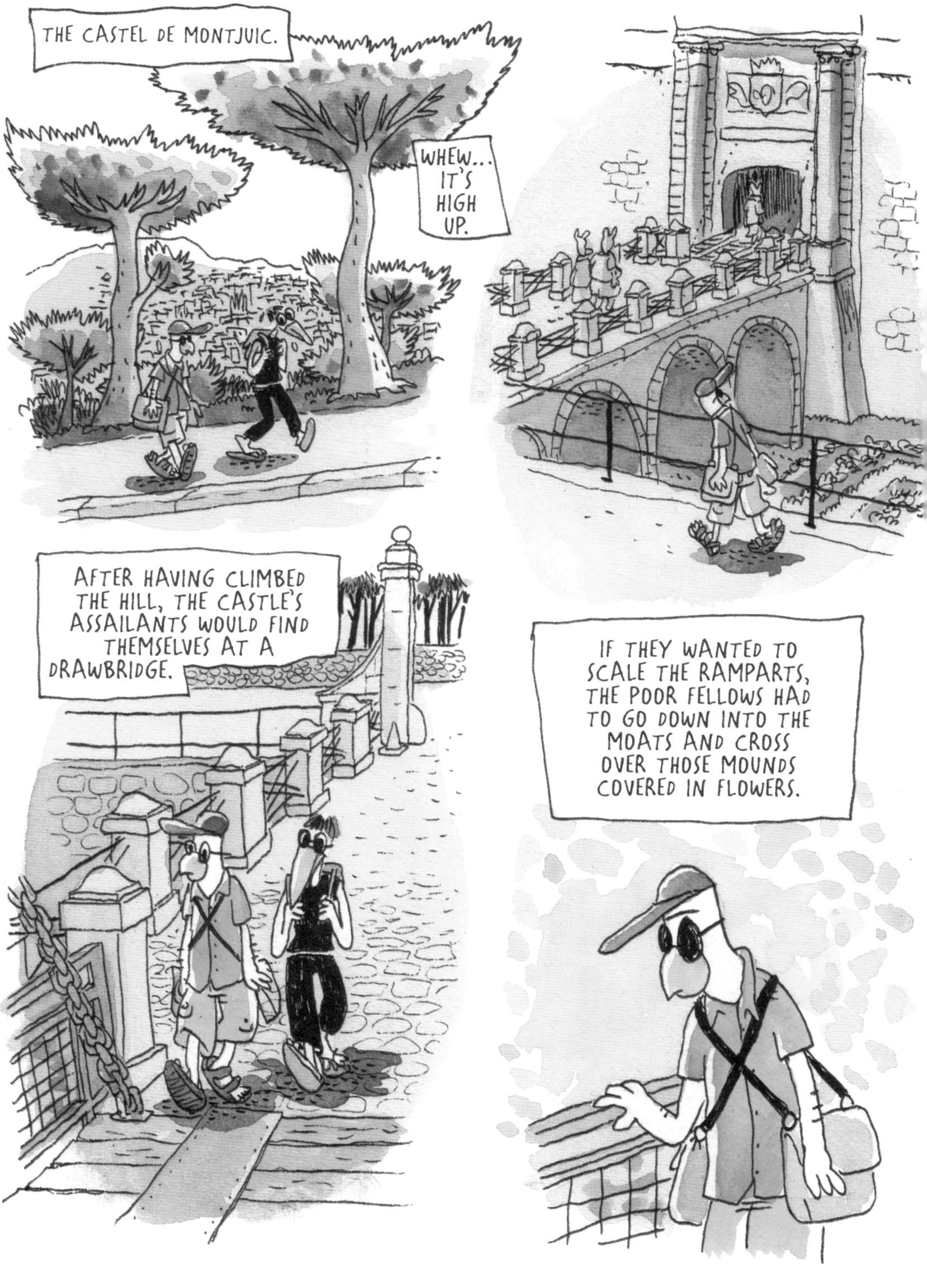
THE CASTEL DE MONTJUIC.
WHEW... IT'S HIGH UP.
AFTER HAVING CLIMBED THE HILL, THE CASTLE'S ASSAILANTS WOULD FIND THEMSELVES AT A DRAWBRIDGE.
IF THEY WANTED TO SCALE THE RAMPARTS, THE POOR FELLOWS HAD TO GO DOWN INTO THE MOATS AND CROSS OVER THOSE MOUNDS COVERED IN FLOWERS.

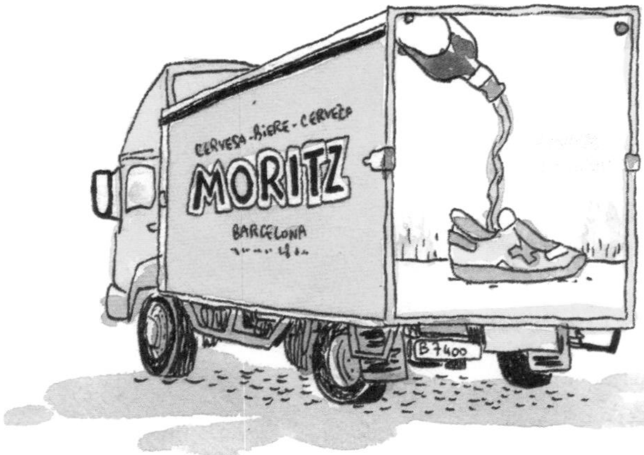
CERVESA - BIERE - CERVEZA
MORITZ
BARCELONA
B 7400

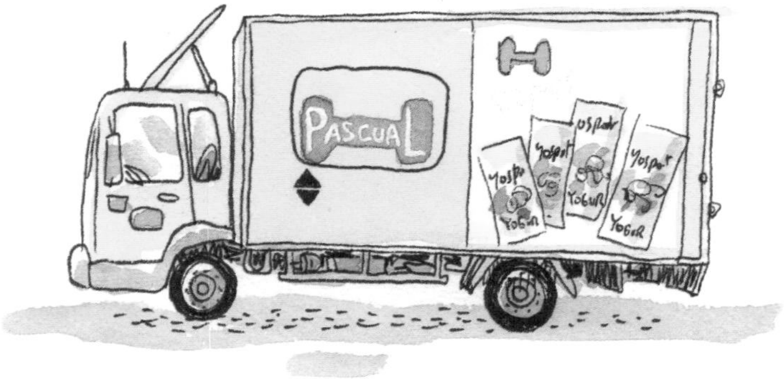
PASCUAL

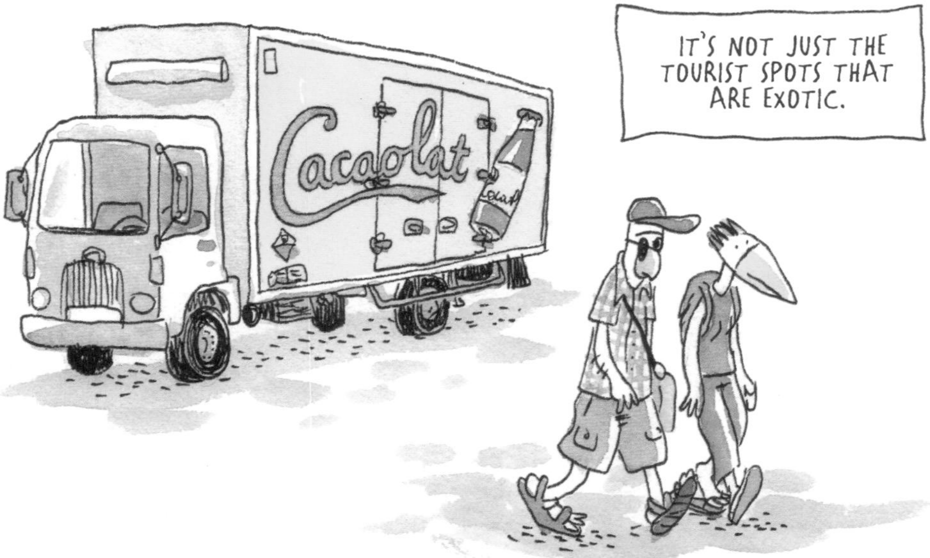
IT'S NOT JUST THE TOURIST SPOTS THAT ARE EXOTIC.
Cacaolat

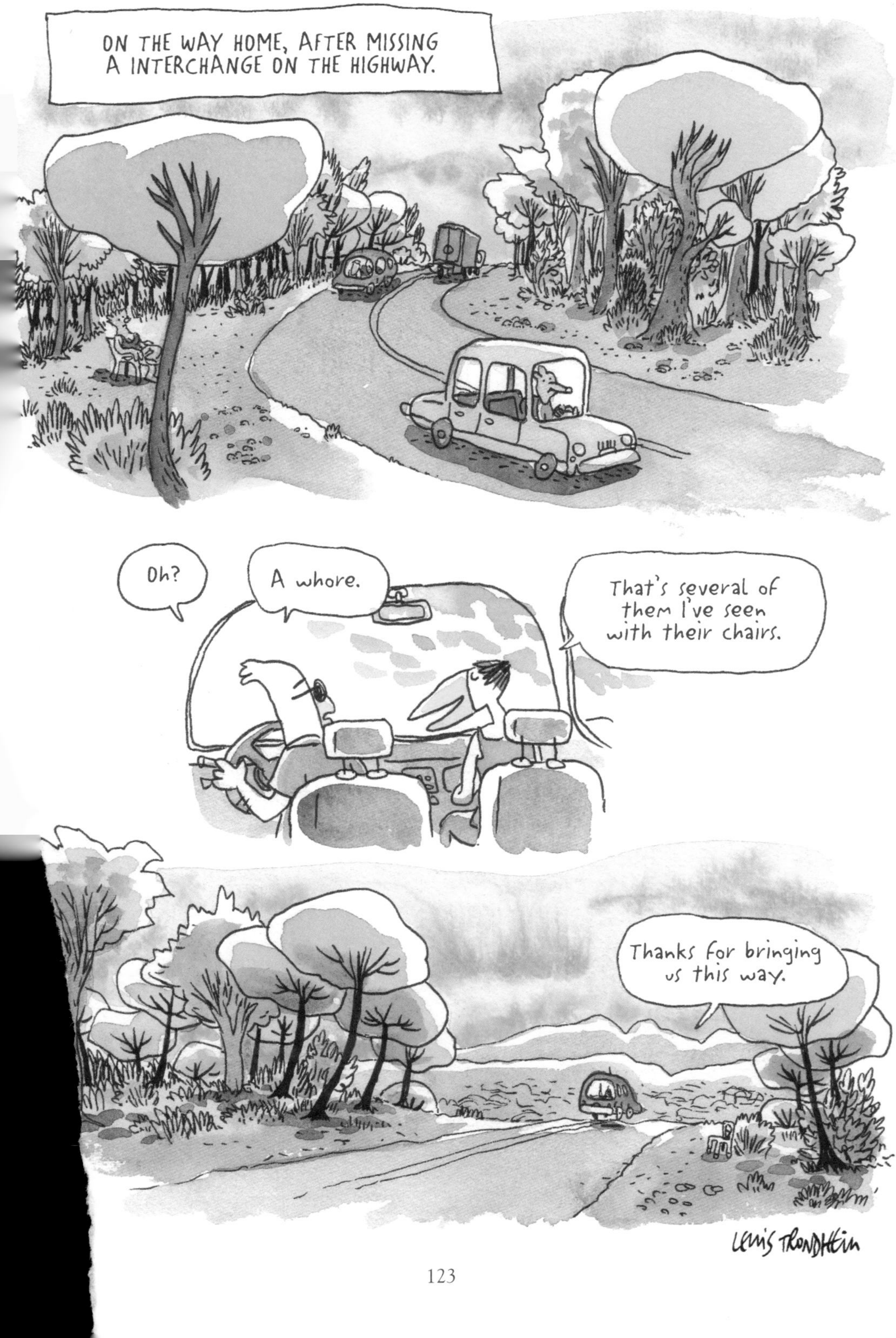
ON THE WAY HOME, AFTER MISSING A INTERCHANGE ON THE HIGHWAY.
Oh?
A whore.
That's several of them I've seen with their chairs.
Thanks for bringing us this way.
Lewis Trondheim

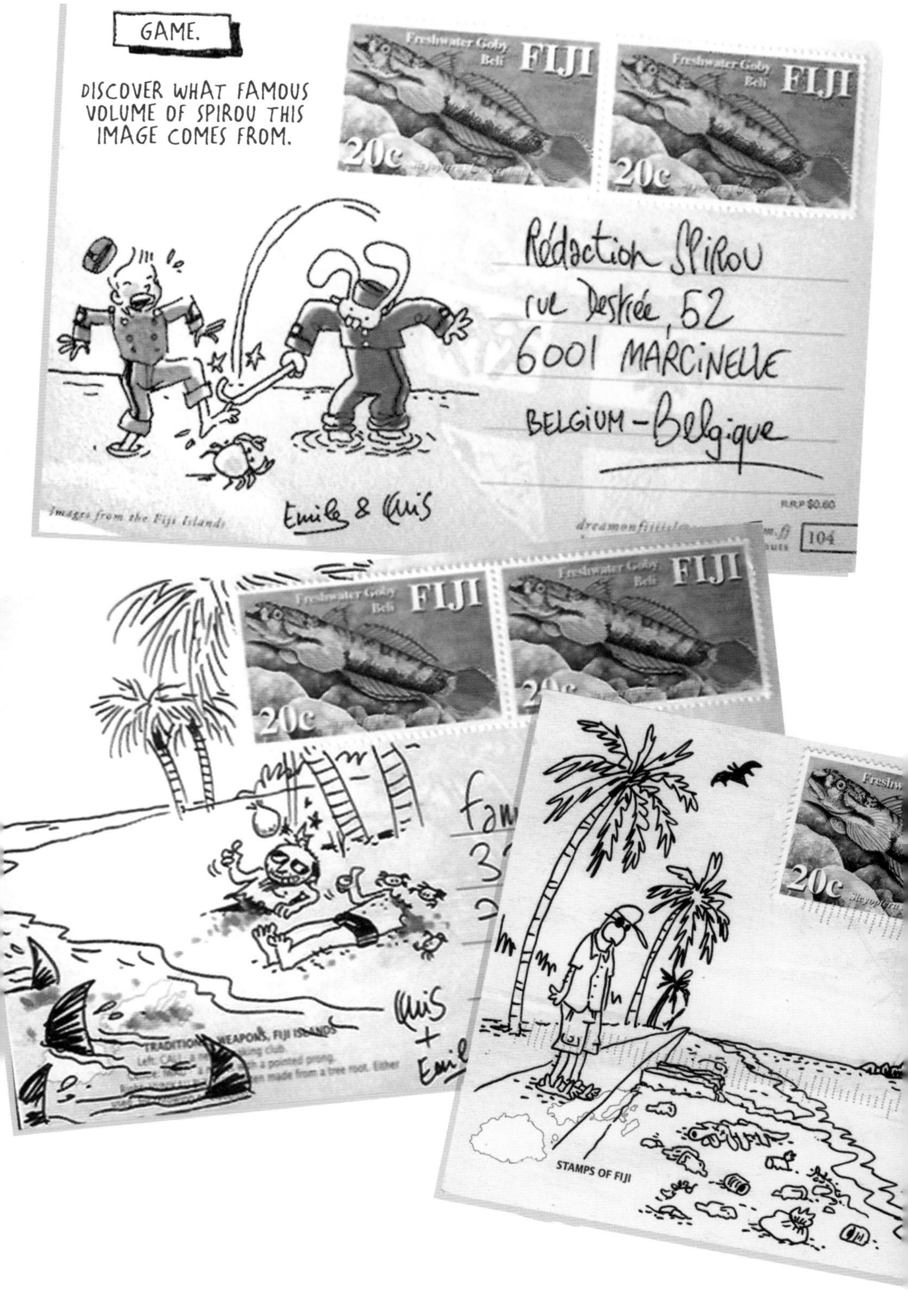
GAME.
DISCOVER WHAT FAMOUS VOLUME OF SPIROU THIS IMAGE COMES FROM.
Freshwater Goby Beli FIJI 20c
Rédaction Spirou
rue Destrée, 52
6001 MARCINELLE
BELGIUM - Belgique
Images from the Fiji Islands
Emile & Quis
R.R.P $0.60
104
TRADITIONAL WEAPONS, FIJI ISLANDS
Quis + Emile
STAMPS OF FIJI

Other books by Trondheim from NBM:
Little Nothings, vols. 1, 2, $14.95 each
Mr. I, $13.95
with Joann Sfar:
Dungeon, Zenith, vols. 1, 2, $14.95 each, 3, $12.95
Dungeon Early Years, vols. 1, 2 $12.95 each
Dungeon, Twilight, vols. 1, $12.95, 2, $14.95 each
Dungeon, Parade, vols. 1, 2, $9.95 each
Dungeon, Monstres, vols. 1, 2, $12.95 each
with Thierry Robin:
Li'l Santa, $14.95
Happy Halloween, Li'l Santa, $14.95

Add $4 P&H first item $1 each additional.

Write for our complete catalog
of over 200 graphic novels:
NBM
40 Exchange Pl., Suite 1308
New York, NY 10005
www.nbmpublishing.com

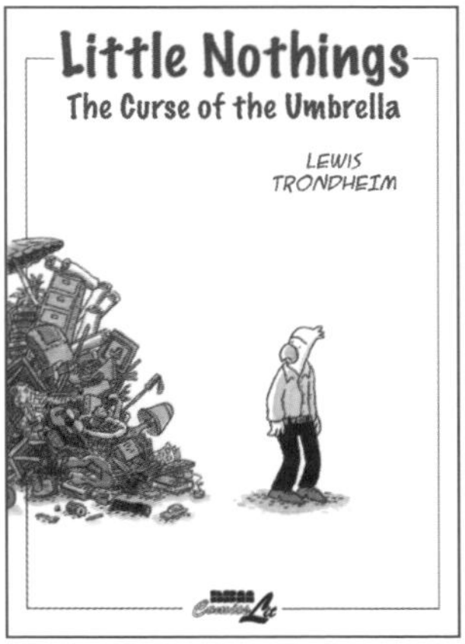
Little Nothings
The Curse of the Umbrella
LEWIS TRONDHEIM

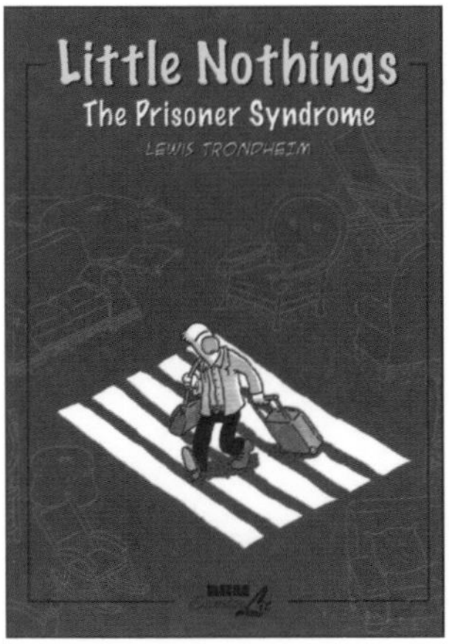
Little Nothings
The Prisoner Syndrome
LEWIS TRONDHEIM

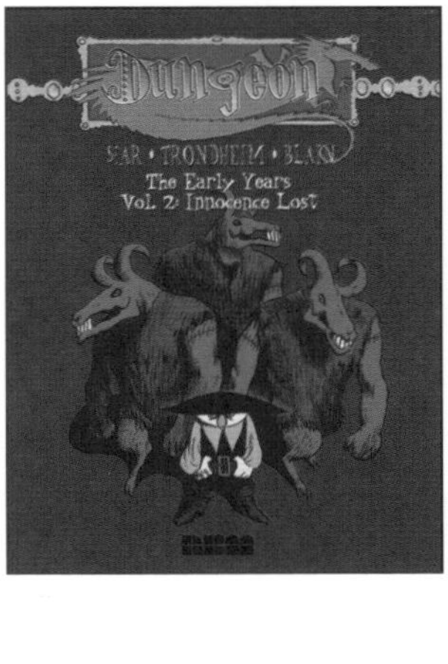
Dungeon
SFAR • TRONDHEIM • BLAIN
The Early Years
Vol. 2: Innocence Lost

X